INSIDE AutoCAD®

The Complete AutoCAD Guide

Sixth Edition by Rusty Gesner
With Assistance From Jim Boyce

Original Authors D. Raker and H. Rice

New Riders Publishing, Gresham, Oregon

INSIDE AutoCAD®
The Complete AutoCAD Guide

Sixth Edition by Rusty Gesner
With Assistance From Jim Boyce

Original Authors Daniel Raker and Harbert Rice

Published by:
New Riders Publishing
1025 E. Powell, #202
Gresham, OR 97030 USA

Printed in the United States of America
1 2 3 4 5 6 7 8 9 0

Library of Congress Cataloging-in-Publication Data

Gesner, Rusty.
INSIDE AutoCAD: The Complete AutoCAD Guide -- 6th ed. / by Rusty
 Gesner with assistance from Jim Boyce.
        p.   cm.
Rev. ed. of : Inside AutoCAD / Daniel Raker and Harbert Rice. 5th ed.
1989.
 Includes index.
 ISBN 0-934035-55-5 : $34.95
  1. AutoCAD (Computer program)   I. Boyce, Jim, 1958- .
  II. Raker, Daniel. Inside AutoCAD.   III. Title.
T385.G467   1990
620'.0042'02855369--dc20   90-21993
                                                               CIP

Warning and Disclaimer

This book is designed to provide tutorial information about the AutoCAD and AutoShade computer programs. Every effort has been made to make this book as complete and as accurate as possible, but no warranty or fitness is implied.

The information is provided on an "as is" basis. The authors and New Riders Publishing shall have neither liability nor responsibility to any person or entity with respect to any loss or damages arising from the information contained in this book or from the use of the disks and programs that may accompany it.

Acknowledgments

The authors wish to thank Patrick Haessly for reworking much of the old exercise material and for developing new material and graphics techniques for the fifth edition of this book.

Extreme thanks are due to Christine Steel for editing, Margaret Berson for production and page layout, Ken Billing for technical editing, Kevin Coleman for producing graphics and testing exercises, and Nancy Trotic for proofreading.

The authors offer profuse thanks to numerous friends and colleagues at Autodesk for encouragement and support over these seven years.

The authors of the sixth edition owe their gratitude to Harbert Rice for his input into this edition and for making it all possible. Thanks are also due to Mark Pierce for preliminary testing and illustration work.

Trademarks

AutoCAD, AutoLISP, and AutoShade are registered trademarks of Autodesk, Inc. IBM/PC/XT/AT, IBM PS/2 and PC DOS are registered trademarks of the International Business Machines Corporation. MS-DOS and OS/2 are trademarks of the Microsoft Corporation. Unix is a registered trademark of the AT&T Company.

The publisher has attempted to identify other known trademarks or service marks by printing them with the capitalization and punctuation used by the trademark holders. New Riders Publishing attests that it has used these designations without intent to infringe on the trademarks and to the benefit of the trademark holders. However, the publisher disclaims any responsibility for specifying which marks are owned by which companies or organizations.

About the Authors

Rusty Gesner

B. Rustin Gesner is publishing director and managing editor of New Riders Publishing in Gresham, Oregon. Prior to joining New Riders, Mr. Gesner was founder and president of CAD Northwest, Inc., in Portland, Oregon. CAD Northwest was an industry leading dealer and authorized training center in the early days of AutoCAD.

Mr. Gesner is a registered architect and formerly practiced the profession in Oregon and Washington after attending Antioch College and the College of Design, Art and Architecture at the University of Cincinnati. He has used AutoCAD since Version 1.1 and writes about AutoCAD from the viewpoint of a professional user and customizer of the program. Mr. Gesner is co-author of the New Riders books *CUSTOMIZING AutoCAD* and *INSIDE AutoLISP*.

Jim Boyce

Jim Boyce is a senior instructor in the Drafting and Design Technology department of Texas State Technical Institute in Harlingen, Texas. He teaches courses in using, customizing, and programming AutoCAD and mechanical engineering software. Mr. Boyce is also a freelance writer and a full Press member of the Computer Press Association. His work appears regularly in CAD and computer magazines, including *PC Magazine*, *CADalyst*, and *CADENCE*.

Prior to joining the faculty of T.S.T.I., Mr. Boyce was with Marathon LeTourneau, a world leader in the design and manufacture of offshore oil exploration platforms. His work there included production planning, steel structure design, and CAD system administration, development, programming, and operator training. Over the past ten years, Mr. Boyce has worked with a wide variety of systems, including AutoCAD, Accugraph ACD-800, Computervision, and Autotrol.

Daniel Raker

Daniel Raker is president of Design & Systems Research, Inc., a Cambridge, Massachusetts-based management consulting firm specializing in computer graphics applications and market research. He is founder of the MicroCAD Institute™, a leading training organization serving professional users of computer-aided design systems. Mr. Raker earned his Bachelor of Arts degree from Harvard College.

Harbert Rice

Originally trained as a plant biochemist, Mr. Rice earned his Ph.D. from Harvard University. While at Harvard, he became interested in using computers to model non-linear systems. Mr. Rice gained computer software experience at ERT, an engineering consulting subsidiary of COMSAT Corp., and the Raytheon Company in Burlington, Mass., where he held research and development positions. Mr. Rice was founder and president of New Riders Publishing, the first and foremost publisher of books on AutoCAD.

Table of Contents

CHAPTER 5   Graphic Entities

CHAPTER 6   Introduction to Editing

IF AT FIRST YOU DON'T SUCCEED, TRY EDITING

CHAPTER 7   Advanced Editing

PUTTING DRAWINGS TOGETHER — CAD STYLE

CHAPTER 8   Drawing Construction Techniques

QUICK WAYS TO BUILD WHOLE DRAWINGS

CHAPTER 9   Grouping Entities Into Blocks

DRAWING WITH PARTS AND SYMBOLS

CHAPTER 10   Sheet Composition, Scaling, and Plotting

COMPOSING AND PLOTTING A FINISHED DRAWING

CHAPTER 13   Attributes and Data Extraction

ADDING INFORMATION TO BLOCKS
AND GETTING IT OUT AGAIN

PART TWO   AutoCAD and 3D Drawing

CHAPTER 16   Dynamic 3D Displays

CONTROLLING YOUR 3D IMAGES

CHAPTER 17   Inside AutoShade

ENHANCING 3D WITH SHADED RENDERINGS

CHAPTER 18   Inside Solid Modeling

ADDING SUBSTANCE TO YOUR 3D MODELS

PART THREE   Customizing AutoCAD

INCREASING YOUR PRODUCTIVITY

CHAPTER 19   Customizing Macros and Menus

AutoCAD YOUR WAY

CHAPTER 20   Using AutoLISP for Drawing Automation

Introduction

AutoCAD, the most popular computer-aided drafting program in the known universe, is a complex piece of work. But don't let its size and complexity intimidate you. Whether you are a beginner looking for an introduction to AutoCAD's basic commands, an intermediate user who needs a tutorial on a specific command sequence, or an advanced user who needs a lasting reference that covers every nuance, *INSIDE AutoCAD* belongs on your bookshelf.

INSIDE AutoCAD is three things: an introduction to the world of AutoCAD-aided drafting and drawing; an easy-going tutorial that will help you unlock AutoCAD's power to do your design and drafting work quickly and easily; and a lasting reference to keep near your computer as you work. Using the general index or the listing of commands in Appendix A, you can quickly find information and examples for everything you always wanted to know about AutoCAD but didn't know who to ask. You will see how every command in AutoCAD works and how your work can benefit from AutoCAD.

How INSIDE AutoCAD Is Organized

INSIDE AutoCAD is organized for both the beginner and the experienced AutoCAD user. The book starts out easy, with the basics of 2D CAD drafting, continues through advanced techniques, and ends with customizing AutoCAD. You do not need any prior knowledge of CAD and the book does not require you to do any programming.

INSIDE AutoCAD is divided into three sections:

Part One shows you how to create and display two-dimensional (2D) drawings. It demonstrates how to communicate with AutoCAD through the keyboard, pointer (mouse or digitizer), and menus. Part One takes you sequentially from setting up AutoCAD through building and editing 2D drawings.

Part Two shows you how to create and edit 3D drawings, how to use 3D surface meshes and solids modeling, and how to pass an AutoCAD 3D drawing to AutoShade for rendering.

Part Three shows you how to take control of AutoCAD and make it into your *own* drawing system. Starting with creating menus and macros, it demonstrates how to customize AutoCAD for your application and how to use AutoLISP to create new commands and automate your drawings.

INSIDE AutoCAD has three helpful appendixes. Appendix A provides a complete listing, both alphabetically and by chapter, of all the AutoCAD commands covered in the book. Appendix B provides additional help setting up AutoCAD, improving performance, and dealing with problems and errors. Appendix C covers the setup and use of AutoCAD's tablet menu, and offers a quick-reference chart of AutoCAD's system variables.

How to Use the Tutorials

Chapters are divided into a series of exercises, each teaching one or more AutoCAD commands. If you just read the text and exercises and look at the illustrations, you will learn a great deal about AutoCAD. But to make your knowledge of AutoCAD concrete, you need to sit down at an AutoCAD-equipped computer and work through the exercises. Explanatory text accompanies each exercise, putting commands and techniques into context, explaining their behavior, and explaining how to use their different options.

We suggest that you work through each part of the book in sequence. Where possible, we've organized it so you can pick and choose topics to explore. The optional *INSIDE AutoCAD* Disk (IA DISK) makes it possible to jump in at several points in each chapter. If you are in a hurry to get started, the following Quick Start Guide provides suggestions for getting started with key topics and techniques. The primary chapters which cover the topics are shown in bold type.

Quick Start Guide	
If You Want to:	**Turn to This Chapter:**
Set Up to Use the Book and IA DISK	Chapter **1**
Set Up AutoCAD	Chapters **1**, 2 and Appendixes **B** and C
Set Up Drawings	Chapters **2**, 3, 4 and **10**
Use Menus and Dialogue Boxes	Chapters 1 and **2**
Use Various Forms of Input	Chapters 1, 2 and **3**
Use the User Coordinate System (UCS) in 2D	Chapters **3**, 8, 9 and 10

Quick Start Guide	
Use the User Coordinate System (UCS) in 3D	Chapters **14, 15,16** and **18**
Use Multiple Views (Viewports) in 2D	Chapters **4** and **10**
Use Multiple Views (Viewports) in 3D	Chapters **14, 15**, 16 and 18
Use Paper Space Viewports in 2D	Chapters **4** and **10**
Use Paper Space Viewports in 3D	Chapters **14**, 15, 16 and **18**
Learn 2D Drawing Commands	Chapters **5**, 7, 8 and 9
Use 2D Drawing Commands to Create 3D	Chapter **14**
Learn 3D Drawing Commands	Chapters **14, 15** and **18**
Learn 3D Solids Modeling	Chapter **18**
Edit 2D Drawings	Chapters **6, 7** and 8
Edit 3D Drawings	Chapters **14, 15** and 18
Create 2D Drawings From 3D	Chapters **14**, 15 and **18**
Plot 2D and 3D Drawings	Chapters **10** and 16
Compose Paper Space Drawing Sheets to Plot	Chapter **10**
Use Blocks (Symbols and Parts) in Drawings	Chapters **9** and 13
Externally Reference One Drawing From Another	Chapter **9**
Add Attribute Information to Drawings	Chapter **13**
Dimension Drawings	Chapter **12**
Use Associative Dimensions and Dimstyles	Chapter **12**
Control 3D Views and Perspectives	Chapter **16**
Render 3D Drawings With AutoShade	Chapter **17**
Customize AutoCAD Menus and Macros	Chapter **19**
Use AutoLISP to Automate Drawing	Chapter **20**
Look Up AutoCAD Commands	Appendix **A**
Look Up System Variables	Appendix **A**

➡ *NOTE: Wherever you start, you should first do the setup (and optional IA DISK installation) exercises in Chapter 1 so that your system setup will correspond with the directions in our exercises.*

The Optional IA DISK

To help you save time and effort, and allow you to pick and choose topics, *INSIDE AutoCAD* has an optional diskette, the IA DISK. The IA DISK will save you from doing repetitive drawing setup sequences. It contains starting and intermediate drawing files for most of the chapter exercises, as well as menu macros and AutoLISP routines used in the customization chapters in Part Three.

You don't need the disk to work through the book. We've designed all the example exercises so that you can do them from scratch, but the disk makes it easier to get to the heart of the topic at hand. Using drawings from the IA DISK insures accuracy and lets you concentrate on learning what you need to know about AutoCAD when you want to know it.

You'll find an order form for the *INSIDE AutoCAD* drawing disk (IA DISK) inside the back of the book. See the instructions in Chapter 1 for backing up and installing the disk.

Note to Instructors

If you are using *INSIDE AutoCAD* for classroom instruction, you will want to know what AutoCAD commands and techniques each chapter covers. Early in each chapter, we specify what tools, techniques, and groups of commands will be covered. For your convenience in lesson planning, Appendix A provides chapter-by-chapter and alphabetical lists of all AutoCAD commands, and directs you to where they are used in the book.

Read This — It's Important

AutoCAD has grown to become a complex program, but we've made *INSIDE AutoCAD* as easy to use and follow as possible. To avoid errors and misunderstandings, please read the following sections before jumping into the book. And be sure to do the setup exercises in Chapter 1 before doing the other exercises.

Chapter 1 explains how to set up your hard disk directories for use with *INSIDE AutoCAD*. We've designed the book's setup and exercises so that they won't interfere with any AutoCAD settings or other work that you may already be doing with AutoCAD. Chapter 1 also shows you how to install the drawing and support files on the IA DISK, if you have it.

How the Exercises Look and Work

The following is a typical exercise. Don't try to work through this exercise; it's only a sample to show you what to expect. Each exercise is illustrated to show you what you should see on your screen when you do the exercise. In our exercise format, AutoCAD's screen display text and your input are in computer-style type on the left of the exercise. Comments and instructions are given on the right.

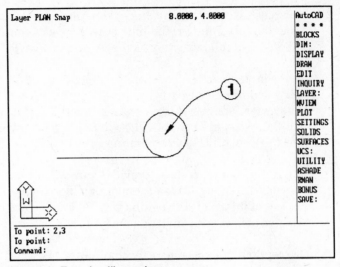

Example Exercise Illustration

Example Exercise Format

`Command: <Snap on>`	Toggle snap on with the <F9> key.
Pull down **[Draw]** *Select* **[Circle >]**	Select CIRCLE command.
`CIRCLE 3P/2P/TTR/<Center point>:`	Pick point ① in the upper right of screen.
`Diameter/<Radius>:`	Drag a radius of 1 inch and pick a point.

Set the PLAN layer current and set color to red.

`Command:` **LINE**	Draw a line.
`From point:` **@0,-1**	Enter point one unit below last point.
`To point:` **2,3**	Enter point at specified coordinates.
`To point:` **<RETURN>**	Exit LINE command.

When you see *Pull down*, you select the indicated pull-down menu. *Select* means to pick the menu item shown. The bracketed items are menu items, labels, or boxes. In the example above, you select [Draw] from the pull-down menu bar at the top of the screen and then select [CIRCLE >] to use the CIRCLE command. To select an item, you highlight its label and press your mouse or digitizer pointer pick button. You can also execute commands by typing them at the keyboard and pressing <RETURN> (also known as the <ENTER> key). LINE (in the example above) is a typed command.

Each exercise shows all necessary commands, prompts, and input at the left-hand side of the page. (In later exercises, we abbreviate or drop repetitive prompts.) The input you need to enter as you work through the exercises is shown in boldface type. The <RETURN> is shown only when it is the sole input on the line; otherwise you should automatically press <RETURN> following any boldface input shown.

Type input exactly as shown (followed by <RETURN>), watching carefully for the difference between the number 0 and the letter O. The @ is the @ character, above the 2 on your keyboard. Keyboard keys are shown in angle brackets, like <RETURN>. <F9> is a function key and <^C> stands for the Control-C key combination.

The right-hand section provides our *in-line* comments in the book's normal text font. These comments will give you instructions and extra pieces of information to guide you. We sometimes use this font at the left to give abbreviated instructions for familiar commands.

Except for exercises in early chapters which specifically show the use of the menus, we just show commands as you would type them. However, you may use any form of selection you like, as long as you end up with the right command! (Caution: some pull-down menu commands are modified and act differently from typed commands.)

We don't expect that you will work through an entire chapter's exercises in a single sitting. Wherever an exercise sequence ends in a SAVE command, you may safely end the drawing and reload it later.

Exercises and Your Graphics Display

Our illustrations were developed on an EGA (Enhanced Graphics Adaptor) display with 640 x 350 resolution. If you are using a different display, particularly a CGA (Color Graphics Adaptor) display, you may need to do more zooms to get better views of your screen display when you work through the exercises. You may also need to adjust your aperture size when using osnap if your screen resolution is very high or very low. If a couple of these terms don't make sense to you, bear with us. You'll understand them soon as you begin to work through this book.

Because different displays vary in the horizontal/vertical display area ratio, you may need to zoom slightly to get the views illustrated when loading drawings from the IA DISK. If your display is configured for a white background, the color that AutoCAD calls white will appear black on your screen.

➥ *NOTE: For clarity, we omit the AutoCAD grid from most of our illustrations, but you should keep your grid on.*

Exercises and the IA DISK

In the exercises that reference the IA DISK, we've marked certain instructions with special symbols. These show you what to do if you have the disk.

Disk Symbols

 Do this if you have the IA DISK.

Do this if you don't have the IA DISK.

What You Need for the Book

To work with *INSIDE AutoCAD*, you need a system that can run AutoCAD Release 10, 11, or a later release. You should have about 1Mb of free disk space (2Mb if you are using the IA DISK). See Appendix B for more information on system requirements.

We assume that you:

- Can use the basic features and utility commands of your operating system.

- Have a copy of AutoCAD Release 10 or 11 installed and configured.

- That you have a graphics display and a mouse or digitizer tablet, all configured for AutoCAD.

Release 10 vs. Release 11

This sixth edition of *INSIDE AutoCAD* has been substantially rewritten for AutoCAD Release 11. If you are using Release 10, don't be alarmed. We give alternative instructions at all critical points. Everything possible in this edition of *INSIDE AutoCAD* is perfectly usable with Release 10 and exceptions are identified. However, some of your menus, dialogue boxes, and a few command prompts will differ slightly from those shown in the exercise sequences and illustrations.

The fifth edition of *INSIDE AutoCAD*, which specifically supports Release 10, is also available from New Riders Publishing — see the order form in the back of the book. An international version, *INSIDE AutoCAD-Metric Edition*, is also available.

We assume that you are using AutoCAD fresh out of the box, but it is a highly adaptable and malleable program. If someone has installed AutoCAD on your system and altered its command or menu structure, your prompts, screen menus, and tablet menu may be slightly different from those represented in the book. If so, get a copy of the original ACAD.MNU file from the SOURCE directory or from the original AutoCAD disks and use the MENU command to load it into the ACAD drawing we create in Chapter 1.

DOS vs. Other Operating Systems

You may see minor differences in AutoCAD's screen display, but all of AutoCAD's files (and our IA DISK files) are usable on any system that runs AutoCAD. To use the IA DISK on non-DOS systems, you may need to install the files on a DOS system and then use a network or alternative disk format to transfer them to your system. (You can use a DOS window to install the IA DISK on OS/2 systems.) If you're using Unix, use lower-case letters to enter all filenames shown in the book's exercises.

Should Problems Occur

- Try again, and go back to the previous exercises to see if you made an error that did not immediately show up.

- Check defaults such as snap, osnaps, aperture, layer, and visibility.

- See Appendix B.

- Check your *AutoCAD Reference Manual.*

- Call your AutoCAD dealer. If you have no current dealer, Autodesk can find you one.

- Try the ADESK forum on CompuServe, the world's largest CAD user group and most knowledgeable source of support.

- If you have the IA DISK, see the UPDATE.TXT file for any possible updated information.

- If there is a specific problem in the book, particularly with an exercise, you can call New Riders Publishing at (503) 661-5745. Have a specific *INSIDE AutoCAD* page reference ready — we cannot give general AutoCAD support.

- If you have a problem installing the IA DISK and if the instructions packaged with the disk do not help, call us.

Now, let's get started.

Working in 2D With AutoCAD

HOW TO GET ACCURATE, PROFESSIONAL DRAWINGS

Basic Drawing Tools

Two-dimensional (2D) drawings are the workhorses of drafting and design. To get good 2D drawings from AutoCAD, you need to know the basics about setting up drawings, creating and editing objects, inserting drawing symbols, dimensioning, and preparing drawings for plotting and presentation. We've designed Part One of *INSIDE AutoCAD* to teach you the basics for producing accurate, professional-looking 2D drawings. You will find all the commands, drawing and editing techniques, tips, and tricks you need for the high quality drawings you want and expect from AutoCAD.

How Part One Is Organized

Part One has thirteen chapters that will take you from starting your program, through two-dimensional drawing and editing, to dimensioning and adding attribute tags to your drawings. These chapters fall into five categories:

- Setup and display controls

- Drawing and editing

- Blocks (symbols) and reference files

- Presentation and plotting

- Dimensioning and attributes

Why Setup and Display Controls Are Important

Whether you work in 2D or 3D, an efficient working environment will help you learn AutoCAD and cut down on drawing time. The first four chapters take you from setting up your files through controlling your display.

Chapter 1 teaches the basics of setting up your system for the book's exercises, and creating and saving drawing files. It teaches you how to communicate with AutoCAD and use menus. By the chapter's end, you will be able to create an AutoCAD drawing file on disk, add lines and text to the drawing, correct errors, and save the drawing for future use.

Chapter 2 explains how to prepare a drawing by specifying a drawing scale and sheet size, and setting up electronic layers with colors and linetypes. You'll also learn to use dialogue boxes for input. Chapter 3 shows how to make precise drawings using AutoCAD's object snaps and other electronic aids. You'll learn to control where you are in your drawing file and how to create your own coordinate system (UCS).

Knowing how to control your display will save you countless hours and frustration when you work with more complex drawings. Chapter 4 shows you how to work with single and multiple viewport displays and to control what you display on the screen with zooms and pans. The chapter demystifies paper space — the bridge between your computer and the paper. By the chapter's end, you will be able to create lines, polylines, circles, and text, and display your work in multiple viewports. You will know how to save both your drawing views and your viewports for future use.

Drawing and Editing

In Chapters 5, 6, 7, and 8, you will learn how to create and edit two-dimensional drawings. Chapter 5 shows how to use *every* 2D drawing command. Chapters 6 and 7 teach you how to edit your drawings. Chapter 6 contains the basics for moving, copying, rotating, arraying, and mirroring entities in your drawings. Chapter 7 covers more exotic editing commands for extending, stretching, trimming, scaling, and offsetting objects. Chapter 7 also explains how to edit polylines to get continuous drawing lines. This is a prelude to 3D editing. If you want a quick look at creating a 3D drawing, take a look at Chapter 7's 2D polyline editing section.

All the drawing and editing chapters have tips and tricks. Chapter 8 is a pure techniques chapter; it shows how to combine construction lines, electronic point filters, and editing commands to quickly build accurate drawings. It also shows how to place editing marks and controls in your editing sequences so that you can try different edits without wasting time. As you apply AutoCAD's drawing and editing commands to your drawings, you will begin to recognize patterns in your own command usage. The trick to improving your productivity is to learn the drawing and editing commands that let you build fast, accurate drawings, then incorporate these editing sequences and techniques in your everyday use. If you are looking for some advanced editing techniques, you will have them by the time you work through the chapters on editing.

Using Symbols and Reference Files

AutoCAD calls symbols blocks. Learning how to use blocks in your drawings saves drawing time and file space. Chapter 9 will show you how to use blocks, and how to update your drawings quickly and easily by redefining blocks.

You will also learn how to create drawings that reference the contents of other drawing files. Reference files coordinate the cooperative editing of a master drawing by letting several people simultaneously work on parts of it. They make drawings smaller by allowing those parts to exist in their own drawing files, yet the master file is automatically updated.

Getting Presentable

Chapter 10 shows how to get plotted output just the way you want it. You will learn how and when to use paper space to compose drawings and to make multi-view plotting a cinch. You'll also discover dozens of plotting tips. Chapter 11 contains techniques for hatching, linetypes, and freehand sketching. This chapter winds up with AutoCAD's inquiry commands that tell you what, where, and when you're drawing.

Dimensioning and Attributes

In Chapters 12 and 13, you will learn how to add dimensions and other nongraphic information to your drawings. Chapter 12 will guide you through AutoCAD's dimensioning settings and commands. It covers associative dimensions and how to use dimensioning styles to control and standardize dimensioning. Chapter 13 describes how to add text data to your drawings, and how to extract this information in a report. You can use these techniques to create bills of materials, specifications, schedules, and other data lists.

Getting From 2D to 3D

We've all heard about the importance of learning the basics. Part One will give you the 2D basics that you need for 3D, which is covered in Part Two. Among other things, you need to know how to control your own coordinate system (UCS) and how to control multiple viewports (VPORTS) to work in 3D. All the basic 2D drawing and editing commands that you learn in Part One can be used in Part Two.

Instead of talking about it, let's see AutoCAD in action. Turn to Chapter 1 to get started *INSIDE AutoCAD*.

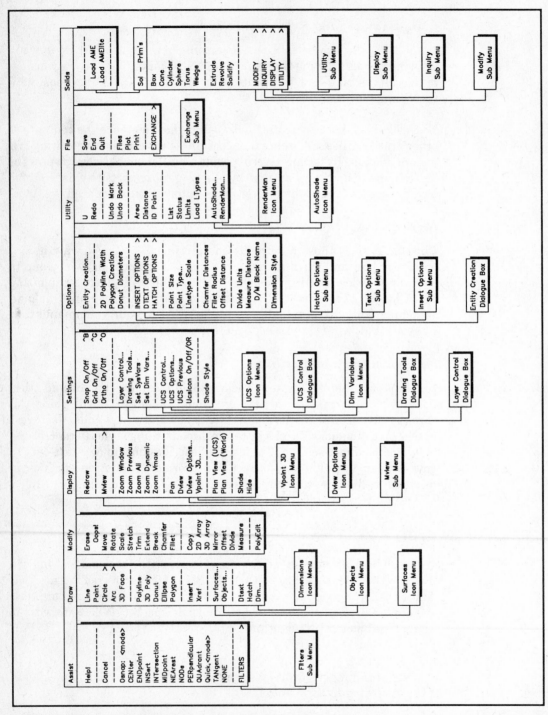

AutoCAD Release 11 Pull-Down Menu, Courtesy of Autodesk, Inc.

Getting Started

GETTING TO KNOW HOW AutoCAD WORKS

The Lay of the Land

This book is a tutorial about AutoCAD. In this chapter we cover the basics on how to set up the program, how to turn it on, and how to draw. By the end of the chapter you will have created an electronic CAD drawing file, played around by drawing a few lines, typed some text, and saved your drawing.

The Benefits of Learning How AutoCAD Works

The benefits of learning how to set up and store an electronic drawing file are obvious. Your real drawing benefits will come from learning about AutoCAD's command structure and how you can interact with AutoCAD to produce the drawings you want. By learning to communicate with AutoCAD, you will unlock AutoCAD's power and versatility for your own use.

Think about learning AutoCAD in the same way that you learn to navigate your way around a big city. You know where you want to go — you just need to get a few basic routes down pat. Then you can explore the byways at your leisure. And before you start exploring AutoCAD, you need to set up a directory to do your exploring from.

Setting Up AutoCAD for Exercises in This Book

Let's get a few chores out of the way. *INSIDE AutoCAD* comes with an optional disk called the IA DISK. The book and disk are designed for use on your AutoCAD workstation. Setting up for *INSIDE AutoCAD* requires that you set aside space on your hard disk to create a directory called IA-ACAD. Even if you don't have the IA DISK, this setup insures that any AutoCAD settings used for the exercises in the book won't interfere with any other AutoCAD settings or projects that you or your co-workers may have under way.

Directories

We assume that you are using the DOS operating system, running AutoCAD on a hard disk called C:, and that you have a directory structure similar to the one shown in the following exercise.

➤ *NOTE: If your drive letter or subdirectory names vary from those shown, you need to substitute your drive letter and directory names wherever you encounter the C: or the directory names in the book. If you are using an operating system other than DOS, your directory creation and setup will differ slightly from what is shown below.*

Making the IA-ACAD Directory

We also assume that you will work in the IA-ACAD directory. You need to make this directory, then copy your AutoCAD configuration files to this directory. By copying the files, you set up a self-contained AutoCAD environment. You should be in the root directory of your hard disk. Make the IA-ACAD directory.

Making the IA-ACAD Directory

`C:\> MD \IA-ACAD`   Creates the directory.

Take a look at your directory names. Get into the root directory of drive C: and type:

`C:\> DIR *.`

Your computer will respond with:

```
Volume in drive C is DRIVE-C
Directory of  C:\
ACAD     <DIR>  12-01-88   11:27a    AutoCAD program, configuration, and standard
                                     support files.
DOS      <DIR>  12-01-88   11:27a    All of the DOS files.
IA-ACAD  <DIR>  12-01-88   11:27a    INSIDE AutoCAD configuration and support files.
```

Your disk may show other directories, like:

```
123      <DIR>  12-01-88   11:27a    Lotus 123 directory.
DBASE    <DIR>  12-01-88   11:27a    dBASE III files.
5 File(s)  8753472 bytes free        Your list will be different.
```

Setting Up AutoCAD Configuration Files

AutoCAD requires a configuration file (and four overlay files with 640K DOS versions). These files are created when AutoCAD is first run. We assume that AutoCAD's configuration files are in the ACAD directory. By copying these files to the IA-ACAD directory, you establish a separate

AutoCAD configuration for this book. (If you are using an operating system other than DOS or are using the 386 DOS version of AutoCAD, skip the steps for copying the .OVL files in the following exercise.)

Copying AutoCAD Files to the IA-ACAD Directory

```
C:\> CD \ACAD <RETURN>                        Change to the ACAD directory.
C:\ACAD> COPY ACADP?.OVL \IA-ACAD\*.*         Do this for 640K DOS version only.
ACADPL.OVL                                    Plotter overlay file.
ACADPP.OVL                                    Printer/plotter overlay file.
2 File(s) copied

C:\ACAD> COPY ACADD?.OVL \IA-ACAD\*.*         Do this for 640K DOS version only.
ACADDS.OVL                                    Display (video) overlay file.
ACADDG.OVL                                    Digitizer (or mouse) overlay file.
2 File(s) copied

C:\ACAD> COPY ACAD.CFG \IA-ACAD\*.*           General AutoCAD configuration file.
1 File(s) copied
```

➡ *NOTE: If your AutoCAD directory is not named ACAD, you will have to make sure that you can find the AutoCAD support files and copy them to the IA-ACAD directory.*

See Appendix B for more help on setting up AutoCAD's system environment and configuring AutoCAD.

Installing the IA DISK

Now you are ready to install the IA DISK files. If you have the optional disk, install it. If you don't have the disk yet, see the order form in the back of the book on how to get a copy. Besides saving you typing and drawing setup time, the disk provides starting drawings for many of our exercises, letting you skip material you already know. For example, if you want to learn about dimensioning, but don't want to first create a drawing to dimension, you can jump right into dimensioning a preset drawing from the disk.

Installing the IA DISK

Put the IA DISK in your disk drive A: Change directories, and type A:IA-LOAD.

```
C:\> CD \IA-ACAD
C:\IA-ACAD> A:IA-LOAD
```

For more complete instructions on installing the IA DISK, or if you have any problems, see the instruction sheet packaged with the disk.

All that's left to do is create a simple batch file that will start AutoCAD without conflicting with your current AutoCAD setup and will keep your drawing exercise files in one place. The batch file calls AutoCAD directly from your ACAD directory to avoid conflict with any possible ACAD.BAT batch file that you might have. It does this by using AutoCAD's environment variables. These are labels that you can tell DOS to equate with a directory. AutoCAD checks with DOS when it starts, to see if these variables have been set. Two of AutoCAD's environment variables are named ACAD and ACADCFG. The easiest way to set environment variables so that they are correct every time you start AutoCAD is in a batch file. Let's make a batch file named IA.BAT to use environment variables with the directory you've created for the IA DISK.

Starting AutoCAD

After you create the IA.BAT batch file, you can start AutoCAD from any directory by typing \IA. The batch file will make sure the ACAD and ACADCFG settings are cleared, automatically change to the IA-ACAD directory, start AutoCAD, and then return you to the root directory when you exit AutoCAD. The simplest form of the IA.BAT file requires only four lines:

```
SET ACADCFG=
SET ACAD=
\acad\ACAD %1 %2
CD \
```

However, if you are using any AutoCAD ADI device drivers (perhaps for your video board or digitizer), you need to add the command to execute the device driver(s) to your IA.BAT file just before the \acad\ACAD line. Similarly, if you already have AutoCAD set up with a startup batch file that makes any memory or swap disk configuration settings, you need to add them to your IA.BAT file also. But don't add any additional lines beginning with SET ACAD= or SET ACADCFG=. Examples of typical device driver and configuration lines are:

```
DS800R11 -I -X
CFIG386 ACAD.EXE -MAXVCPI 3072000
SET ACADFREERAM=24
```

The %1 and %2 in the third line of IA.BAT are known as replaceable parameters. They are used in batch files as place holders for any optional parameters that a program might take. Since AutoCAD can take two optional parameters (which you'll learn about later), we've included two place holders. See the *AutoCAD Installation and Performance Guide* (the IPG) for more information.

➡ *NOTE: If your AutoCAD program files are not in a directory named* acad, *then substitute your directory name for* acad *where shown in lower-case letters in the listing above and the exercise below. If you are using an operating system other than DOS, you can create a similar shell file instead of the batch file. See the AutoCAD IPG.*

The best way to create your batch file is to use a word processor or text editor in ASCII text mode; however, you can use the copy technique shown below if you need to. Add any ADI or configuration lines you need.

Creating the IA.BAT Batch File

Return to the root directory.

`C:\> COPY CON IA.BAT`	To create a file from keyboard input.
`CD \IA-ACAD`	To change directory to IA-ACAD.
`SET ACADCFG=`	
`\acad\ACAD %1 %2`	To call the AutoCAD program.
`CD \`	To return to the root directory after exiting AutoCAD.
`^Z`	Hold down the control key while you type a Z, then <RETURN> to end the IA.BAT file.
`1 File(s) copied`	The IA.BAT file is written to disk.

Now, you can start an *INSIDE AutoCAD* session from anywhere in your hard drive simply by typing \IA. For more information on settings in the startup batch file, see Appendix B.

With these file-handling chores out of the way, it is time to start up AutoCAD.

Starting AutoCAD

`C:\> \IA`

As soon as you type \IA from the operating system, the batch file takes control of your computer. It changes the directory to IA-ACAD, and the AutoCAD program displays the main menu for you. The main menu gives you the choice of creating or editing drawings, plotting drawings, installing (configuring) AutoCAD, and a whole list of special utilities.

If you are like most CAD enthusiasts, you face the first screen with anticipation. The first time around, we all really want to get at drawing.

There is that nagging urge to get in the drawing editor, thinking, "Can I get away with entering a few commands just to see what happens?" Before you satisfy that urge, you need to insure that your *INSIDE AutoCAD* sessions are set to the default settings.

When you begin a new drawing, AutoCAD looks for a drawing called ACAD.DWG. AutoCAD uses this drawing as a *prototype* to establish the default settings for each new drawing. For the purposes of this book, we assume your prototype drawing is the same as when you took AutoCAD out of the box. In order to make sure this is true, you need to create a new prototype drawing (ACAD.DWG) in your IA-ACAD directory. The following exercise creates the new prototype drawing. The equal sign following the drawing name tells AutoCAD to make the ACAD.DWG with its original default settings. You will learn more about the settings in the ACAD.DWG prototype in the next chapter.

```
          A U T O C A D (R)
Copyright (c) 1982-90  Autodesk, Inc.  All Rights Reserved.
Release 11 (10/18/90) 386 DOS Extender
Serial Number:  000-00000000
Licensed to:    New Riders Publishing
Obtained from:  Autodesk, Inc.

Main Menu

   0.  Exit AutoCAD
   1.  Begin a NEW drawing
   2.  Edit an EXISTING drawing
   3.  Plot a drawing
   4.  Printer Plot a drawing

   5.  Configure AutoCAD
   6.  File Utilities
   7.  Compile shape/font description file
   8.  Convert old drawing file
   9.  Recover damaged drawing

Enter selection: 1

Enter NAME of drawing: ACAD=
```

Main Menu With Option 1 Selected

Creating a Prototype Drawing

```
Enter selection: 1                    From main menu.
Enter NAME of drawing: ACAD=
```

The AutoCAD drawing screen appears.

```
Command: END                          Saves the drawing and exits the drawing editor.
```

The Drawing Editor

We can come back later and explore the main menu options; for now let's jump right back into the drawing editor. You get into the drawing editor by selecting option 1 from the main menu. Begin a new drawing file by giving it the name CHAPTER1. AutoCAD will set up a new drawing file called CHAPTER1 in the IA-ACAD directory on drive C:. Then AutoCAD puts you into the drawing editor, clears the screen of text, and sets you up for drawing.

Loading a New Drawing File

```
Enter selection: 1                 Begin a NEW drawing.
Enter NAME of drawing: CHAPTER1    The drawing screen and menu appear.
```

➡ *NOTE: For your drawing names, you can use characters, numbers, and most symbols, but no spaces. AutoCAD adds a filename extension of .DWG when it stores the drawing on disk, creating drawing names like CHAPTER1.DWG. AutoCAD takes care of the .DWG extension (.DWG) so you should not enter it.*

Getting Familiar With the Screen Menus

AutoCAD's first drawing screen displays a graphics drawing area and its screen menu down the right side of the screen. The first screen menu is called the root menu. It has "AutoCAD" at the top of the menu. If you look at the bottom of the AutoCAD screen, you'll see one to three command prompt lines. This is AutoCAD's communication channel. You will learn to keep an eye on the command prompt line to see your input and to read messages from AutoCAD. If you have a dual screen system, you may have a single command line, or no command line, and you'll have to watch your text screen for your input or messages.

As you move your pointing device across the desk top, pad, or tablet, the crosshairs on the screen move too. Make your pointer move the crosshairs towards the items listed in the root menu. When the crosshairs pass into the menu area, a menu item lights up. Now move the pointer up and down to highlight different menu items.

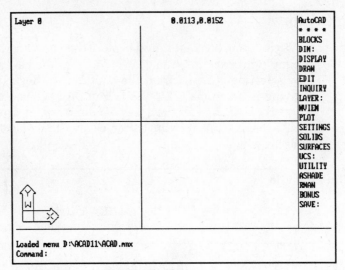

Layer 0   0.0113,0.0152   AutoCAD
                                                                 * * * *
                                                                 BLOCKS
                                                                 DIM:
                                                                 DISPLAY
                                                                 DRAW
                                                                 EDIT
                                                                 INQUIRY
                                                                 LAYER:
                                                                 MVIEW
                                                                 PLOT
                                                                 SETTINGS
                                                                 SOLIDS
                                                                 SURFACES
                                                                 UCS:
                                                                 UTILITY
                                                                 ASHADE
                                                                 RMAN
                                                                 BONUS
                                                                 SAVE:

Loaded menu D:\ACAD11\ACAD.mnx
Command:

AutoCAD Screen With Crosshairs

Using the [DRAW] and [LINE:] Menus

You can select a menu item from the screen by pressing your pointer's pick
button. Select [DRAW]. As soon as you do, you get a new menu. Now select
[LINE:]. When you do this, both the screen menu and the prompt line
change. Move your pointer to the center of the screen's drawing area and
pick a point by clicking your pointer's button. The prompt line will change
again. Play around and draw a few lines, using the following exercise
sequence as a guide.

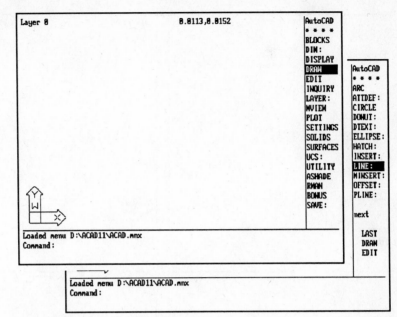

[DRAW] to [LINE:] Screen Menus

Drawing Your First Line

Select **[DRAW]**   [DRAW] screen menu appears.
Select **[LINE:]**   Select from screen menu.

The LINE command starts and prompts for the first point.

Command: LINE From point: Pick the first point at ①.

Move the crosshairs and see the beginning of a line trailing behind them.

To point: Pick a second point at ②.
To point: **<RETURN>**   End the LINE command.

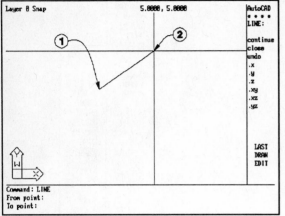

Beginning a Line

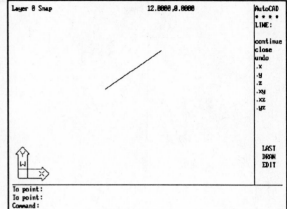

The Completed Line

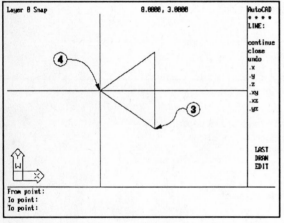

Continuing the Line

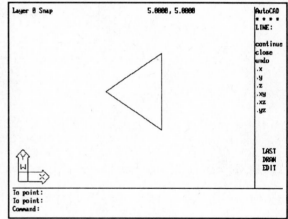

The Completed Continuing Line

Continue your line by repeating the LINE command with a <RETURN>.

Continuing the LINE Command

```
Command: <RETURN>
```
<RETURN> repeats the previous command.

Draw a second set of connecting lines.

```
LINE From point: <RETURN>
To point:
To point:
To point: <RETURN>
```
<RETURN> starts line at last point of first line.
Pick a point at ③.
Pick a point at ④.
End the LINE command.

Rubber Band Cursor

You've seen that AutoCAD's LINE command is simple and straightforward. Issuing the LINE command to AutoCAD begins the process of recording the two endpoints of a line segment. Once a line is created from two endpoints, AutoCAD assumes that you want to continue drawing lines. Not only that, AutoCAD assumes that you want to continue drawing lines from the last endpoint of the previous line.

You can keep on drawing segments every time you see a To point prompt. AutoCAD helps you visualize where the next segment will be located by *rubber-banding* or trailing a segment between your last point and the cursor.

➤   *TIP: A CANCEL or <^C>, a <RETURN>, or a <SPACE> (pressing the space bar) ends the LINE command and returns the command prompt.*

AutoCAD's Pull-Down Menus

At the top of the screen, AutoCAD has a set of pull-down menus in addition to the screen menus found on the right side of the screen. These pull-down menus are quite similar to the screen menus. If your video hardware supports pull-down menus, you will see a menu bar when you move your pointing device to the top of the graphics screen. The menu bar presents a list of titles indicating the selections available in each pull-down menu.

```
Assist  Draw  Modify  Display  Settings  Options  Utility  File  Solids
        Line                                                     * * * *
        Point                                                    BLOCKS
        Circle    >                                              DIM:
        Arc       >                                              DISPLAY
        3D Face                                                  DRAW
                                                                 EDIT
        Polyline                                                 INQUIRY
        3D Poly                                                  LAYER:
        Donut                                                    MVIEW
        Ellipse                                                  PLOT
        Polygon                                                  SETTINGS
                                                                 SOLIDS
        Insert                                                   SURFACES
        Xref                                                     UCS:
                                                                 UTILITY
        Surfaces...                                              ASHADE
        Objects...                                               RMAN
                                                                 BONUS
        Dtext                                                    SAVE:
        Hatch
        Dim...
Command:
Command:
Command:
```

The [Draw] Pull-Down Menu

Pull-down menus require a video board which supports the AUI (Advanced User Interface). If you are uncertain about whether your workstation supports pull-down menus, try the following test by typing the word shown in bold.

Testing for Support of Pull-Down Menus

```
Command: SETVAR                          Access the system variables.
Variable name or ?: POPUPS

POPUPS = 1 (read only)
```

If you got a 1, you can use AutoCAD's pull-down and icon menus. If you got a 0, you need a new video driver from your board manufacturer, or you need a new video board and driver that support the pull-down menus. If you got *Unknown variable name,* you have an earlier version of AutoCAD that doesn't support pull-down menus. If you can't use pull-down menus, you can follow the exercises by using similarly named screen menus, or by typing the commands.

Using Pull-Down Menus

To open a pull-down menu, you *highlight* the menu bar title and press the pick button on your pointing device. Then you are presented with a list of items that you highlight and pick to select. When you make a selection, the pull-down menu closes and the selection executes exactly like the screen menu items.

In the following exercise, try selecting from the pull-down menus as we type in some text and zoom in closer to see it. Enter the text and coordinate values shown in bold and complete the entry with <RETURN>s. If your workstation does not support pull-down menus, you can select the same menu items from the screen menu.

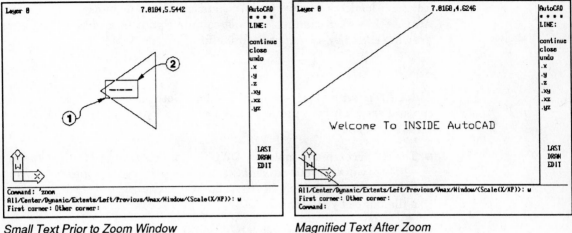

Small Text Prior to Zoom Window   Magnified Text After Zoom

Using the [Draw] Pull-Down Menu

```
Pull down [Draw] Select [Dtext]                 Select from pull-down menu.
Align/Fit/Center/Middle/Right/TL/TC/TR/ML/MC/MR/BL/BC/BR: C    Center text.
DTEXT Justify/Style/<Start Point>: C
Center Point: 7.25,4.5                          Enter coordinates.
Height <0.2000>: .05                            Set the text height.
Rotation angle <0>: <RETURN>
Text: Welcome To INSIDE AutoCAD                 <RETURN> twice to finish the DTEXT command.
```

So where is the welcome? Let's zoom in to see it.

```
Pull down [Display] Select [Zoom Window]        Select from pull-down menu.
Command: 'zoom                                  Magnify an area to read text.
All/Center/Dynamic/Extents/Left/Previous/Vmax/Window/<Scale(X/XP)>: w
First corner:                                   Pick a point at ①.
Other corner:                                   Pick a point at ② and you see it.

Command: <RETURN>                               Repeat the ZOOM command.
ZOOM
All/Center/Dynamic/Extents/Left/Previous/Vmax/Window/<Scale(X/XP)>: ALL
Regenerating drawing.                           Returns to the full magnification.
```

➡ *TIP: When you select menu items from the screen, it is a good idea to glance at the command prompt line at the bottom of your screen to make sure that you and AutoCAD are communicating. Then watch the center of the graphics screen for the action.*

You have loaded a new drawing file and created some lines and text using AutoCAD's screen menus. Why not complete your first pass through the drawing editor by saving your first effort?

Saving a File

AutoCAD provides two saving commands. Both save your work to a .DWG file and secure it by renaming your previous drawing file on disk with a .BAK extension.

■ The SAVE command makes a .DWG file and returns you to the drawing editor to work on your current file. Saving gives you the option of saving your current drawing editor session under the current name or under a filename of your choice.

■ The END command makes a backup file from your previous (last) file, stores the up-to-date copy of your file, and exits the drawing editor. The END command assumes the current drawing filename.

When you use any command that prompts for a filename, such as the SAVE command, AutoCAD presents you with a filename dialogue box (unless you have Release 10). Dialogue boxes are discussed later in this chapter — for now just press <RETURN> to save the drawing with its original name.

Using SAVE to Save Your File

Command: **SAVE**   Type or select from screen menu.
                               The dialogue box appears (or the Release 10 prompt
                               File name <CHAPTER1>:).

Press <RETURN> to save the drawing with its original name.

As we promised, you have just navigated the most basic route with AutoCAD. You have started a new drawing file, done some drawing, and saved it. Now let's take a more leisurely look at AutoCAD's drawing screen.

How AutoCAD Communicates With You (and Vice Versa)

Why is it so easy to draw in AutoCAD? You boot the program, get into the drawing editor, and start entering points. It doesn't matter whether you enter points by picking them with your pointer or by entering them at the keyboard (as you did to center your "Welcome" text). The reason, of course, is that AutoCAD knows its geometry and has a default Cartesian coordinate system set up and ready for your use.

World Coordinate System

When you enter the drawing editor, you enter a coordinate system called the world coordinate system. When AutoCAD asks you to enter a point, you either locate the point with your pointing device or enter the point's coordinates from the keyboard. The system's coordinates consist of a horizontal X displacement and a vertical Y displacement (and a positive Z displacement for 3D). These are called absolute coordinates. Although it is conventional to specify absolute coordinate points with parentheses (3,4), when you type coordinates for AutoCAD at the keyboard you separate the X and Y values with a comma and omit the parentheses: 3,4. Both the X and Y are measured from a zero base point that is initially set at the lower left corner of your screen. This base point's coordinates are 0,0.

The UCS — User Coordinate System

If you look at the lower left corner of your screen, you will see that there is an icon at point 0,0. This is the UCS (User Coordinate System) icon. UCS means that you can establish your own coordinate system and shift your base point in your drawing by changing the position of the coordinate system. You will make extensive use of the UCS when you work in 3D, but for now we will leave it at the default position.

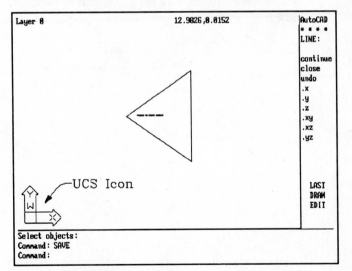

Screen With UCS Icon

The default X axis is horizontal, left to right, and the Y axis is vertical, down to up. If you look closely at the UCS icon, you will see that the X arrow points to the right on the X axis, and the Y arrow points up the Y axis. The "W" on the Y arrow means that you are currently in the default world coordinate system. The UCS icon displays other information about where you are in 3D. For example, the UCS icon displays a "+" when it is shown at the UCS origin (0,0). And the box in the corner indicates the Z axis direction which we will cover in the 3D section. If you find the UCS distracting when you are working in 2D, you can always turn it off. Here is how you turn it off and on.

Turning the UCS Icon Off and On

Command: **UCSICON**	Turn icon off.
ON/OFF/All/Noorigin/ORigin <ON>: **OFF**	
Command: **UCSICON**	Turn it on again.
ON/OFF/All/Noorigin/ORigin <OFF>: **ON**	

The Status Line

If you look at the top of your graphics screen, you will see a line of text. This line is called the status line. Here you'll find information about how AutoCAD is set up, and how it will react when you issue certain commands. Think of the status line as a medical monitor that gives you AutoCAD's vital signs. The illustration called Status Line shows the layer name and other types of settings that you see on the status line. We won't go into detail now for all the signs, but we will have you check a few to see how they work.

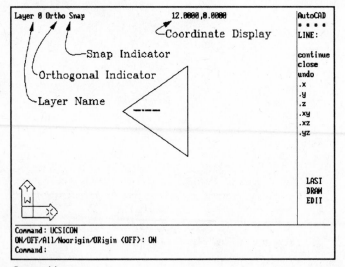

Status Line

If you look at the status line area, you will see several numbers to the right. These numbers represent the latest crosshairs coordinate position.

When you move the pointer around, these numbers don't change. They're stuck at the last point you officially entered as part of a command.

Using the Coords Toggle for Cursor Digital Readout

To make the status line coordinates readout follow your cursor's position, press <^D> (pronounced Control-D — the control key and D pressed at the same time). The <F6> function key does the same thing on most systems. This turns on the continuous update and display of the cursor's position on the coordinates readout. We refer to it as the coords toggle.

Now move your cursor around the screen. The coordinates readout will keep up with you and always let you know where you are. Move the cursor's position to the lower left corner and you will see the coordinates approach 0,0. You can disable the continuous coordinates display by pressing <^D> (or <F6>) again.

The Command Line — Keeping Track of AutoCAD

As you work with the AutoCAD program, you'll come to know what it expects from you and how it reacts when you do something. Many AutoCAD commands set up new drawing environments to receive additional commands. As we said a little earlier, AutoCAD uses the bottom part of the screen to tell you what it's doing. This communication channel is called the *command line*. The command line is usually three lines, depending on your video hardware, and shows you AutoCAD's prompts and your responses or input. It keeps track of your latest communication with AutoCAD.

AutoCAD has a flexible command and menu structure. You can issue an AutoCAD command by typing the command name at the keyboard in response to the command prompt. You have already executed several system commands at the keyboard in this fashion, turning the UCS icon off and on, and testing whether your system supports pull-down menus.

As you type, the letters appear following the command prompt. In order to execute any typed command, you must press the <RETURN> key on your keyboard to let AutoCAD know that you're finished typing. On some systems this is the <ENTER> key, on others it is a broken arrow <↲>. If AutoCAD doesn't understand what you've typed, it will let you know after you press <RETURN>.

Command Line Exercise

```
Command: LI
Unknown command.  Type ? for list of commands.

Command: LINE               Execute the LINE command.
From point:                 Pick any point.
To point:                   Pick any point.
To point: <RETURN>          End LINE command.
```

➡ *NOTE: In the exercise above and throughout the rest of the book, we show the <RETURN> only when it is the only input on a line. However, you must press <RETURN> or <ENTER> to enter your input, such as the LINE command, above. Unless AutoCAD is expecting a text string, such as for the TEXT command, you can use the <SPACE> or <TAB> keys in place of <RETURN>.*

The Flip Screen

In addition to the command line, AutoCAD can display a full screen of text to show you more information. On a single-screen system, use the Flip Screen function to display the text screen instead of the graphics screen. It is usually the <F1> key, or occasionally the <HOME> key. Press the key and the graphics drawing area goes away (along with the screen menu) and a text page appears. On a two-screen system, this text is shown on your second monitor, so using the <F1> key is unnecessary. However, if you accidentally press the <F1> key on a two-screen system, you may need to press it again to return command line response to the graphics screen.

```
All/Center/Dynamic/Extents/Left/Previous/Vmax/Window/<Scale(X/XP)>: W

First corner: Other corner:
Command:
ZOOM
All/Center/Dynamic/Extents/Left/Previous/Vmax/Window/<Scale(X/XP)>: ALL
Regenerating drawing.

Command: UCSICON

ON/OFF/All/Noorigin/ORigin <ON>: OFF

Command: UCSICON

ON/OFF/All/Noorigin/ORigin <OFF>: ON

Command: LI
Unknown command.  Type ? for list of commands.

Command: LINE
From point:
To point:
To point:

Command:
```

Flipped to Text Screen

Flip Screen Exercise

Command: **<F1>**   Use your Flip Screen key.

The graphics screen goes away and a page of text appears.

Command: **<F1>**   Flip back to graphics.

If you look closely at the text, you will see the last sequence of commands you typed (or picked from the screen menu). Using this text screen, you can look back through a set of command lines to see where you've been. If you get interrupted with a phone conversation, using the Flip Screen is an easy way to pick up your place. Some commands (like HELP) automatically flip you to the text screen.

What to Do About Errors and How to Get HELP!

AutoCAD is very forgiving. The worst thing that can happen when you mis-type a command name is that AutoCAD warns you that it does not understand what you want to do. It gives you another chance or prompts you to get help.

What if you catch a typing error before you hit <RETURN>? Using the <BS> (backspace) key on the keyboard erases the characters. Pressing <^X> displays *Delete*, ignores all previous characters on the line, and gives you a blank new line to enter what you intended. What if you start the wrong command and it is already showing on the command line? Press

<^C> one or more times to cancel any command and return you to the command prompt.

Using the ERASE Command

What do you do if you draw something that you don't want, or put an object in the wrong place?

You can remove it using the ERASE command, and try again. When you use ERASE, the crosshairs change to a *pick box*. You move the pick box until it touches the entity that you want to remove. Select the entity by clicking on it with your pointing device's pick button. There are other ways to select entities and other ways to salvage errors without erasing. We will explore them in later chapters. For now, ERASE is enough to get you out of a jam if you get stuck with a screen full of lines that you don't want. Try erasing the "Welcome..." text on your screen, or draw something new to erase. You will find ERASE on the [EDIT] screen menu and on the [Modify] pull-down menu.

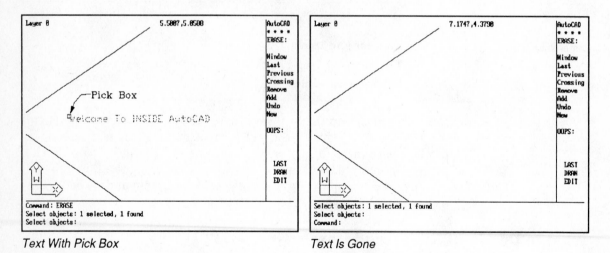

Text With Pick Box   Text Is Gone

Using ERASE to Erase an Entity

```
Command: ZOOM                                Use a window to zoom in on the text.
All/Center/Dynamic/Extents/Left/Previous/Vmax/Window/<Scale(X/XP)>: W
First corner:                                Pick first corner point.
Other corner:                                Pick second corner point.

Select [AutoCAD]                             Return to the root menu.
Select [EDIT]                                Displays [EDIT] menu.
Select [ERASE:]                              Starts the ERASE command.
```

```
Command: ERASE                          Move cursor into drawing area.
                                        The crosshairs turn into a pick box.
Select objects:                         Click to pick the text.
1 selected, 1 found.
Select objects: <RETURN>                The text is gone.
```

Using the U Command to Undo

Sometimes, you will discover you have executed a lot of commands and
that your drawing isn't turning out quite right. It's like the proverbial fork
in the road. If you had turned left back at some command instead of right,
things would have turned out okay. Well, you can use AutoCAD's U (undo)
command to step back one command at a time. Using undo can be more
helpful than just erasing, because the command undoes not only entities,
but zooms and screen settings that you may have changed along the way.

Error Handling With Undo

```
Command: U                              Undoes the erased text from previous exercise.
                                        Undo shows what command was undone.
GROUP                                   Menu items are grouped.
Command: U                              You can keep undoing steps.
ZOOM                                    Undoes the Zoom.
Command: REDO                           Undoes the undo. The zoom is restored.
Command: REDO
Previous command did not undo things    But you only can redo one step.

Command: LINE                           Try canceling a command.
From point:                             Pick any point.
To point: *Cancel*                      Press <^C> to cancel line and return to the command prompt.
Command:
```

If you get lost, what do you do?

Type ? or HELP. AutoCAD always gives you more information.

Help!

Help is almost always available in AutoCAD. You can get a complete
listing of available commands or more information about a specific
command.

If you are at the command prompt, you can either type HELP or ? to invoke
AutoCAD's friendly help. AutoCAD will prompt you for what you want
help with. Enter a <RETURN> for a list of all the available commands as
well as point input information. Or you can enter a command name to get

detailed information about a specific command. When HELP has shown you all it knows, it returns you to the command prompt.

You can usually type '? or 'HELP while you are in the middle of another command to receive help about the command. This type of help is called *transparent* help. With Release 11, transparent help usually gives help for the specific prompt of the current command — this is called *context-sensitive* help. With Release 10, transparent help gives the same information as regular help.

Try getting some help by looking at the COPY command.

```
   AutoCAD Command List  (' = transparent command)

APERTURE    CHANGE      DONUT       FILES       LAYER
ARC         CHPROP      DOUGHNUT    FILL        LIMITS
AREA        CIRCLE      DRAGMODE    FILLET      LINE
ARRAY       COLOR       DTEXT       FILMROLL    LINETYPE
ATTDEF      COPY        DVIEW       'GRAPHSCR   LIST
ATTDISP     DBLIST      DXBIN       GRID        LOAD
ATTEDIT     DDATTE      DXFIN       HANDLES     LTSCALE
ATTEXT      'DDEMODES   DXFOUT      HATCH       MEASURE
AUDIT       'DDLMODES   EDGESURF    'HELP / '?  MENU
AXIS        'DDRMODES   ELEV        HIDE        MINSERT
BASE        DDUCS       ELLIPSE     ID          MIRROR
BLIPMODE    DELAY       END         IGESIN      MOVE
BLOCK       DIM/DIM1    ERASE       IGESOUT     MSLIDE
BREAK       DIST        EXPLODE     INSERT      MSPACE
CHAMFER     DIVIDE      EXTEND      ISOPLANE    MULTIPLE

Press RETURN for further help.
```

Help Screen

```
Select one or more objects for the current command:

   (point)  = One object
   Multiple = Multiple objects selected by pointing
   Last     = Last object
   Previous = All objects in the Previous selection-set
   Window   = Objects within Window
   Crossing = Objects within or Crossing window
   BOX      = Automatic Crossing (to the left) or Window (to the right)
   AUto     = Automatic BOX (if pick in empty area) or single object pick
   SIngle   = One selection (any type)
   Add      = Add mode: adds following objects to selection-set
   Remove   = Remove mode: removes following objects from selection-set
   Undo     = Undoes/removes last

When you are satisfied with the selection-set as it stands, enter RETURN
(except for Single mode, which does not require an extra RETURN).

See also:   chapter 2 of the AutoCAD Reference Manual.

>>Do you want more help for the COPY command? <N>
```

COPY Help Screen

Using HELP to Get Help

```
Command: HELP                              Or enter a ?
Command name (RETURN for list):            You can enter a command name for help
                                           on a specific command, or...
```

```
Command name (RETURN for list): <RETURN>  <RETURN> for general help.
```

A help text screen appears with an alphabetical listing of commands.

```
Press RETURN for further help. <RETURN>
```

Another screen of help appears...and more <RETURN>s display several more screens.

```
Command: COPY                              Start the COPY command.
Select objects: '?                         Enter apostrophe and ? for transparent help.
```

A help screen for object selection is displayed. (Or general COPY help in Release 10.)

```
>>Do you want more help for the COPY command? <N> Y    Ask for more help.
```

More help on COPY appears.

```
Press RETURN to resume COPY command. <RETURN>
```

```
Resuming COPY command.
Select objects: *Cancel*             Cancel the COPY command.
Command: <F1>                        Press the Flip Screen key to get back to the graphics screen.
```

Quitting the Drawing Editor

Of course there are those occasions when you may get hopelessly muddled up in a drawing. In that case, you can make a dignified retreat by quitting your drawing. Unlike the SAVE command, if you quit your drawing using the QUIT command, AutoCAD does not update your drawing (.DWG) file. After you confirm that you really want to quit, AutoCAD discards your drawing and returns you to the main menu.

Follow the prompts below to clear the screen and leave the drawing editor. AutoCAD will diplomatically ask if you want to discard all your changes to your drawing.

Using QUIT to Quit a Drawing

```
Command: QUIT
Really want to discard all changes to drawing? Y      Returns to the main menu.
```

If you have saved your drawing before quitting, the saved copy remains on disk even after you quit.

Comparing AutoCAD's Menus

Where are we? Where are we going? Let's take that second look at AutoCAD's main menu, then get an overview of how AutoCAD's menu systems work.

The Main Menu

The main menu header gives information ranging from your AutoCAD version and serial number to your current default drawing name. It also tells who owns your program's license and what dealer it was obtained from — this is the dealer who is required to provide you with support.

```
          A U T O C A D (R)
Copyright (c) 1982-90  Autodesk, Inc.  All Rights Reserved.
Release 11  (10/18/90) 386 DOS Extender
Serial Number:  000-00000000
Licensed to:    New Riders Publishing
Obtained from:  Autodesk, Inc.
Current drawing:  CHAPTER1

Main Menu

    0.   Exit AutoCAD
    1.   Begin a NEW drawing
    2.   Edit an EXISTING drawing
    3.   Plot a drawing
    4.   Printer Plot a drawing

    5.   Configure AutoCAD
    6.   File Utilities
    7.   Compile shape/font description file
    8.   Convert old drawing file
    9.   Recover damaged drawing

Enter selection:
```

AutoCAD's Main Menu

Here's a listing of what each main menu selection does.

Main Menu Options

Option 0 (Exit AutoCAD) gets you back to the operating system. You will use this option every time you finish an AutoCAD session. Typing \IA <RETURN> at the DOS prompt starts the batch file that gets you in, option 0 gets you out.

Options 1 (Begin a NEW drawing) and 2 (Edit an EXISTING drawing) are where you create, edit, and store your drawings in AutoCAD. You will spend the majority of your AutoCAD hours inside the drawing editor. The drawing editor is the AutoCAD equivalent of your drafting board — the interactive part of the program that lets you create and modify drawings.

There are two ways to get into the drawing editor. If you are starting a new drawing file, type 1 <RETURN> in response to the main menu selection prompt. AutoCAD will prompt you for the name of a NEW drawing file. If you want to edit a drawing that already exists, type 2 <RETURN>, and AutoCAD will prompt you for the name of the existing disk file you want to work with.

Options 3 (Plot a drawing) and 4 (Printer Plot a drawing) are where you can print and plot your drawings.

Option 5 (Configure AutoCAD) steps you through AutoCAD's interactive utility to let the ACAD program know what hardware you are using. You can find more details about this option in Appendix B.

Option 6 (File Utilities) lets you perform disk file maintenance operations just as if you were using the operating system. You can use the AutoCAD file utility to perform housekeeping chores on your files. If you feel more comfortable using the commands directly from the operating system prompt, there is no harm in doing so — they perform the same tasks:

```
AutoCAD File Utility Options      DOS Equivalent
0. Exit file utility menu
1. List drawing files             DIR *.DWG
2. List user specified files      DIR
3. Delete files                   DEL
4. Rename files                   REN
5. Copy file                      COPY
6. Unlock file                    none
```

➡ *NOTE: If you get a* `Waiting for file: ... Locked by ...` *`Press Ctrl-C to cancel.` message, check to be sure no one else is using the file. If you are sure no one else is using it, it may have been left locked accidentally. If so, you can use item six to unlock it. File locking enhances security on networks and is not included in Release 10.*

You also can access the AutoCAD file utility from within the drawing editor by typing FILES at the command prompt.

Options 7 (Compile shape/font description file) and 8 (Convert old drawing file) are special situations and will not be covered in this book. See *CUSTOMIZING AutoCAD* (New Riders Publishing) or the *AutoCAD Reference Manual* for details.

Option 9 (Recover damaged drawing) is for salvaging a drawing file in which AutoCAD detects an error and will not load (not included in Release 10.)

Let's get back into the drawing editor for an overview of AutoCAD's commands and menus. You can reload your previous drawing file from the main menu. (If you exited to the operating system, start up AutoCAD again by typing \IA.)

Loading an Existing Drawing

```
Enter selection: 2
Enter NAME of drawing (default CHAPTER1): <RETURN>
```

AutoCAD's Six Standard Menu Types

AutoCAD has more than 150 commands and numerous subcommands. Most of these commands relate to specific functions such as drawing, editing, or dimensioning. Because many of us are somewhat handicapped when it comes to typing, AutoCAD provides an ACAD.MNU file which contains six alternate ways to enter commands with menus:

- Screen Menu

- Pull-Down Menu

- Dialogue Box

- Icon Menu

- Tablet Menu

- Button Menu

You have already used the screen menu and a pull-down menu. Menus provide a convenient way to organize and group commands into screen *pages* so they can easily be selected and executed. A screen, icon, or pull-down *menu page* is a listing of commands, options, and branches. A *branch* is our name for an item which activates another AutoCAD submenu. The groupings of menu pages are for convenience only and have no effect on AutoCAD's command structure. AutoCAD doesn't care how you tell it what to do.

When you select a menu item, it changes menu pages or sends a command, option, or a series of commands to AutoCAD for execution. This command execution is the same as if you had typed the input.

➥ *NOTE: Most menu items begin with several <^C>s to cancel any previous commands.*

AutoCAD's standard menus give you many different ways to execute some of the same commands. The following illustration shows all the different ways that you can execute the END command to end a drawing.

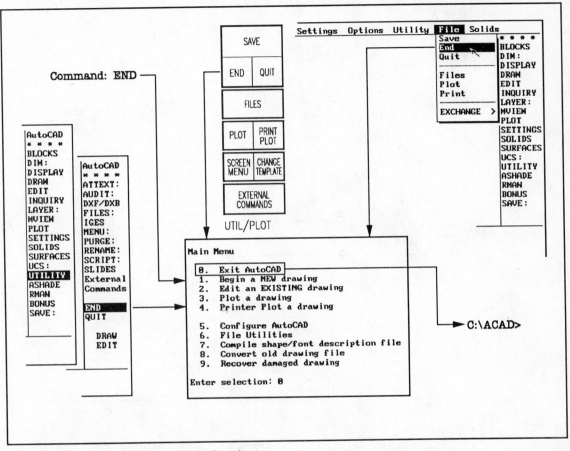

Summary of the Menu Options to End a Drawing

You should try all the types of menus available to you to see which menu method you prefer. Feel free to experiment with the menus as you read on. If you get lost, just select [AutoCAD] at the top of any screen menu. This returns you to the initial screen menu, called the *root menu*, and restores the initial pull-down menu bar. We'll explain menus more fully and give you practice using the various menus in the next chapter. Later in the book, you will learn how to change these standard menus and create your own custom menu selections.

The Screen Menu

The most commonly used menu is the screen menu. You saw the screen menu on the right side of the display screen when you first entered the drawing editor. Recall that you make your screen menu selections by highlighting the item with your pointing device and pressing the pick button.

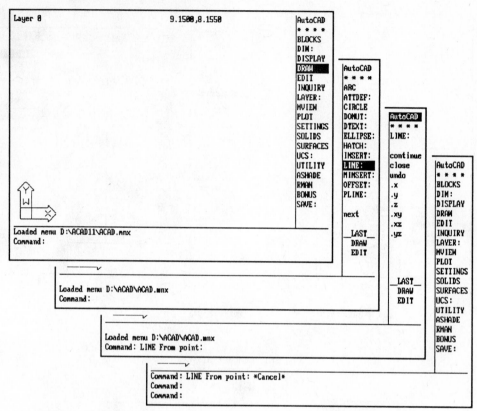

Screen Menu Paging

Keyboard Access to the Screen Menu

You can also access the screen menu from the keyboard. The keyboard offers two methods of screen menu selection. The first method is to press the menu cursor key (usually <INS>) to highlight a menu selection. Use the up and down arrows to move the highlighted bar to the menu item you want and press <INS> again (or <RETURN>) to execute the selection.

The second method is to start typing characters of the menu selection at the command prompt. As you type, the menu label beginning with the characters you type becomes highlighted. Most selections can be highlighted by typing one or two characters, then you press <RETURN> or the <INS> key to execute the selection.

Screen Menu Conventions

As you move through the screen menus, you will notice some selections are followed by colons, [DIM:], [LAYER:], [UCS:] and [SAVE:]. These selections not only branch to a new menu page, but also start the command. Any selection which automatically starts a command has a colon after the menu label. Many commands require subcommands in order to complete their chores. These subcommands are usually listed in lower-case letters. As you flip through menu pages, remember you can always return to the root menu by selecting [AutoCAD] at the top of the menu page. If you get really lost, look at the screen menu map in Appendix C.

At the bottom of most menu pages are shortcut branches that let you return to your [_LAST_] menu page or to the [DRAW] and [EDIT] menu pages. Some menu pages offer more selections than can fit on one page. In such cases, the [next] and [previous] selections flip forward and back through pages to access all the selections available.

Finally, every menu page has [* * * *] below the [AutoCAD] selection. Choosing this selection presents you with a menu page of options called osnaps. These are aids for drawing objects. We will cover the osnap options later in Chapter 3 when we look at drawing basics.

To summarize the screen menu conventions:

- Commands are listed in upper-case letters and are followed by a colon. They usually both begin the AutoCAD command and present a page of subcommand selections.

- Selections without a colon following them are either subcommands or branches to other menu pages.

- Subcommands are usually listed in mixed or lower-case letters.

- Selecting [AutoCAD] at the top of the menu page will always return you to the root menu.

- Selecting [* * * *] will present a selection of osnap options.

- The bottoms of most menu pages have a selection of shortcut branches: [_LAST_], [DRAW], and [EDIT].

- Some menu pages present you with [next] and [previous] selections in order to display all the menu item selections available.

Pull-Down Menus

AutoCAD's pull-down menus are similar to screen menus. You have already tested your video hardware for pull-down support. If you have pull-down menus, you will see a menu bar when you move your pointing device to the top of the graphics screen. (If you do not have a pointing device, you cannot access the pull-down menus.) The menu bar presents a list of titles indicating the selections available in each pull-down menu. You can have up to ten pull-down menus available, but the standard AutoCAD menu bar uses only nine. (Release 10 uses eight.) All nine choices are shown in the Menu Bar illustration.

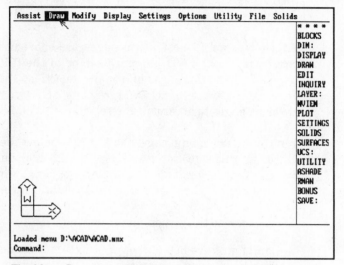

The Menu Bar

Many pull-down menu selections open a screen menu page to help with subcommand selection. Some AutoCAD pull-down menus present dialogue boxes for commands with multiple settings, and groups of related commands. Many people find pull-down menus easier to use than screen menus because each submenu occupies a different spot on the screen. Pull-down menus are also a little quicker than screen menus since you don't have to return to the root menu as often. The complete set of pull-down menus is shown in the facing page illustration at the beginning of the chapter.

Pull-down menus have their own conventions — they don't follow the upper-case, lower-case, and colon convention of screen menus. Most pull-down menu items are capitalized.

■ Pull-down selections followed by three dots, such as [Vpoint 3D...], call a dialogue box, icon menu, or AutoLISP program.

■ Upper-case selections followed by an angle bracket, such as [HATCH OPTIONS >], do not execute commands, but call submenus which replace their menu's position in the pull-down menu bar.

■ Lower-case selections followed by an angle bracket, such as [Circle >], both execute commands and call options submenus which replace their menu's position in the pull-down menu bar.

Many pull-down menu selections, such as the [Line] or [Ellipse] items on the [Draw] menu, both execute a command and call a screen menu page of options for that command.

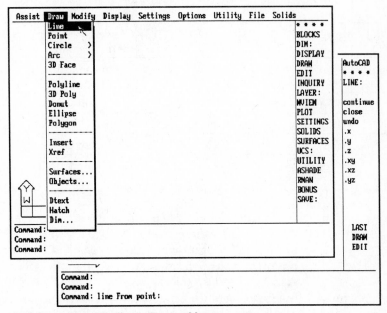

Pull-Down Menu Calling a Screen Menu

➡ *NOTE: Some commands act a little differently depending on whether you type them from the command line, use screen menus, or use pull-down menus. For example, the pull-down menu [Point] and [Erase] items automatically repeat until canceled. If you type them from the command line, they only execute once. Several selections, such as [Insert] and [Dtext] on the [Draw] menu, are AutoLISP-modified commands. These items require you to set defaults on the [Settings] or [Options] menus before using them. Then, these menu items will execute their commands with those defaults and not prompt you for the options you preset.*

Dialogue Boxes

AutoCAD's dialogue boxes offer a unique and convenient way to view and adjust certain AutoCAD settings, to enter and edit text strings, and to enter filenames. Like pull-down menus, dialogue boxes require AUI video support. Although dialogue boxes are actually brought up by commands beginning with DD, such as DDEMODES, you can also access them through menu selections which contain their commands.

AutoCAD Dialogue Boxes		
Command	Pull-down	Purpose
DDEMODES	[Entity Creation...] (DDEntityMODES)	Set layer, color, linetype, and other default properties for new entities.
DDLMODES	[Layer Control...] (DDLayerMODES)	Create layers, set their default properties, and control visibility.
DDRMODES	[Drawing Tools...] (DDdRawingMODES)	Control snap grid axis and isometric settings.
DDATTE	none (DDAttributeEditing)	Easily edit attributes in blocks.
DDUCS	[UCS Control...]	Control User Coordinate Systems.
DDEDIT	none	Easily edit text entities or attribute definitions.
all file commands	various	Display and scroll through lists of filenames.

When a dialogue box pops up on the screen, it shows a list of settings and their current values. Some settings are on/off toggles with a check mark in a box to indicate when they're on. You click on the box with the pick button on your pointer to turn it on or off. Other settings display values such as names, colors, or distances. You change these settings by highlighting and editing them or entering a new value. Some values, such as file or layer names, are presented in lists which may be too long to fit on screen at one time. These have scroll bars at the right side to scroll up and down the lists, as the following illustration shows.

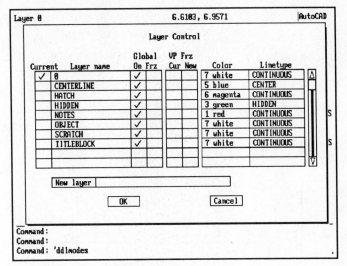

The Layer Control Dialogue Box

Although dialogue boxes duplicate the functions of other commands, they provide clearer and more convenient control over complex commands or groups of commands. We'll more fully explain and practice using dialogue boxes in the next chapter.

The Icon Menu

If your hardware supports pull-down menus, it also supports a third type of screen menu called an icon menu. An icon menu displays menu selections as graphic images. AutoCAD uses slide files to construct these icon menus, displaying four, nine, or sixteen images at one time. After displaying an icon menu, you select a menu item by highlighting the small square to the left of the image and pressing the pick button on your pointing device. AutoCAD executes the corresponding selection like any other menu selection. Icon menus can page through other icon menus the same way screen menus page through other menu pages. AutoCAD has a number of preset icon menus such as for hatch patterns and text styles.

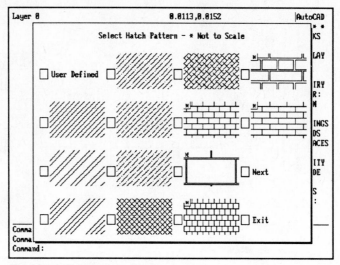

The Hatch Pattern Icon Menu

Menus are a powerful tool within AutoCAD, giving you flexibility in command entry. With a little practice, you will soon find your preferences. Many users prefer to use a tablet menu.

The Tablet Menu

AutoCAD comes with a standard tablet menu that performs many of the same functions as the screen and pull-down menus. The complete tablet menu is shown on the next page. The tablet menu offers a few advantages over the other menu options. It's easy to remember where to find tablet menu selections and they're always available without flipping through menu pages. The tablet menu also includes graphic images to help you identify the selection. Many selections from the tablet menu call the appropriate screen menu pages to help you in your subcommand option selections.

➡ *NOTE: Bringing up AutoCAD's standard tablet menu requires running through a small set of configuration steps. See Appendix C to help you configure the AutoCAD standard tablet menu.*

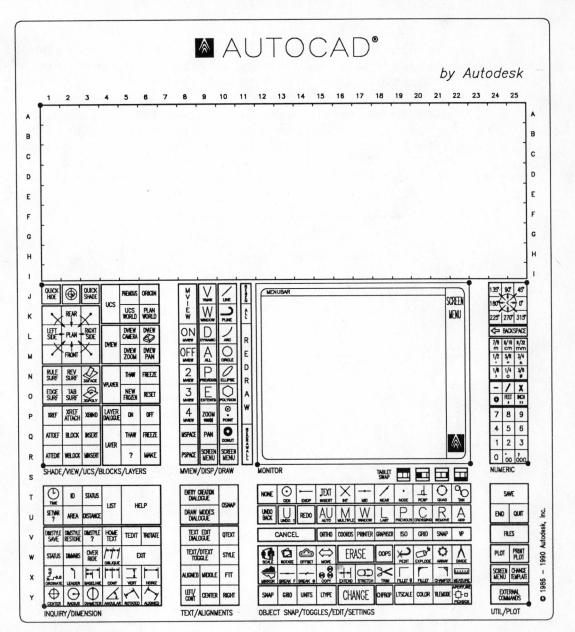

AutoCAD Tablet Menu

The Buttons Menu

We all use some type of pointing device with AutoCAD, usually a tablet puck or a mouse. AutoCAD reserves one button on the puck or mouse for picking points and selecting screen and tablet menu items. This is the button that tells AutoCAD to pick a point or select an object where the cursor or crosshairs are positioned on the screen. A mouse usually has two or three buttons, and a puck can have up to sixteen buttons. The position of the pick button varies with the device. The second button acts like a <RETURN> key. Most of the other buttons are assigned to the same toggles as the function keys and control settings we'll explore in the next chapter.

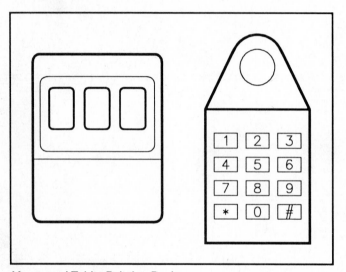

Mouse and Tablet Pointing Devices

You can assign the buttons to execute other menu selections by creating a custom button menu. For details on creating button menus, see *CUSTOMIZING AutoCAD* (New Riders Publishing).

Keyboard Commands vs. Menus

Many users think that keyboard command entry can be just as fast if not faster than using menus. This is particularly true with AutoCAD's *command alias* feature (not available prior to Release 11). A command alias is an abbreviation that you can use instead of typing the entire command name. When you use an alias, AutoCAD replaces it with the full command name and executes the command normally. For example, to execute the CIRCLE command with a menu, you pull down the [Draw] menu or select the [DRAW] screen menu, then select the [Circle] or

[CIRCLE] items. Or, you can merely type a C, press <RETURN> and be done with it. AutoCAD's standard abbreviations are:

Abbrev.	Command	Abbrev.	Command
A	Arc	LA	LAyer
C	Circle	M	Move
CP	CoPy	P	Pan
DV	DView	PL	PolyLine
E	Erase	R	Redraw
L	Line	Z	Zoom

While these abbreviations cover only a few of AutoCAD's many commands, it is quite easy to create your own abbreviations by modifying the ACAD.PGP file. This is explained in Appendix B, and a more comprehensive IA-ACAD.PGP file is included on the optional IA DISK. We recommend you use it, or create your own custom ACAD.PGP file for your most frequently used commands.

AutoCAD offers a similar keyboard shortcut for command options. Instead of flipping through menus for command options, virtually any command option can be abbreviated to the one or two letters that are unique for that option at the current command prompt. For example, recall the ZOOM command prompt:

```
All/Center/Dynamic/Extents/Left/Previous/Vmax/Window/<Scale(X/XP)>:
```

Earlier, the [Zoom Window] menu item you used responded to this prompt with merely a W, not with the entire word WINDOW. You need only type the characters that are shown as upper-case in AutoCAD prompts to execute an option.

When to Use the Keyboard or Menus

In the next chapter, you'll use a lot of menus, but in most of the book we'll just show commands as entered from the keyboard. The purpose of the book is to thoroughly teach you AutoCAD, so we want you to become intimately familiar with its commands. After you learn the commands, you can decide if keyboard entry or menus are better for you.

AutoCAD's standard menus are general purpose, but you may do specific types of drawings for which custom menus would be much more efficient. You can purchase custom menus for many different applications. See the *AutoCAD Sourcebook*, published by Que Corporation, for a listing. Or you can create your own custom menus, as explained later in this book and comprehensively covered in *CUSTOMIZING AutoCAD* from New Riders Publishing.

We recommend using command abbreviations and options from the keyboard for ordinary, commonly used commands, and creating or purchasing a custom menu for using AutoCAD more efficiently with your particular application.

One More Utility — Ending Your Work

You have already seen that AutoCAD provides a quick way out of the drawing editor through QUIT. Quitting is fast, but does not save anything. Save your work now using the END command. Remember, ending makes a backup file from your previously saved file, stores the up-to-date copy, and exits the drawing editor. The END command saves the drawing to the current drawing filename.

Using END to Save a Drawing

Command: **END**   You've completed your first AutoCAD session.

Exit AutoCAD with a 0 from the main menu.

➥ *TIP: At times, you may need your drawing files to be as small as possible for archiving or exchanging with others. You can sometimes reduce the size of an AutoCAD drawing file by ending twice. That is, end your drawing once, reload it, and end it a second time. When you erase objects in a drawing, they aren't actually removed from the drawing database until the drawing is loaded the next time. Double-ending a drawing will completely purge it of deleted entities. This can save disk space, especially after an extensive editing session.*

Summing Up

You've had a chance to set up AutoCAD and play around with the drawing editor by entering a few commands. Surprise! It does not bite, and it does not laugh when you make mistakes. AutoCAD is cooperative. It only takes action when you tell it to do something. AutoCAD lets you know that it's waiting for your input with the command prompt or other prompts on the prompt line. Help is always available to you if you type HELP or ? at the command prompt, or if you type 'HELP or '? when you are in commands. If you get stuck drawing, you can always undo a command, erase your drawing, or quit the drawing and start over.

Now that you know your way in and out of AutoCAD, you can move on to organizing AutoCAD's drawing environment and experimenting with using menus.

CHAPTER 2

Setting Up an Electronic Drawing

PREPARING TO DRAW

Preparing to draw in AutoCAD is much like preparing to draw on a drafting board. In manual drafting, you select your drawing tools to fit your particular drawing — you might select a 1/16" scale for instance. In AutoCAD, you set up parameters to fit your particular drawing — creating, in effect, custom tools. You set up the right units, scale, linetype, sheet size, and text. Then you are ready to begin drawing.

A little advance preparation before you start each drawing makes AutoCAD easier and faster to use in the long run. While it takes a little more time to set up, you can save your settings and use them in your next drawing. Setting up is like the old adage: "Once right is better than twice wrong." You will save time and grief later on.

This chapter will show you how to get set up for drawing, and how to save those settings in a prototype drawing. As we promised in the last chapter, we'll also explore and further explain the use of AutoCAD's various menus.

Organizing Your Drawing Setups

While organizing an electronic drawing is similar to organizing a manual drawing, there are differences. You have to adjust your way of thinking about scale, layers, and drawing entities. Before you prepare an electronic drawing sheet, take a moment to become familiar with the concepts behind scale, layers, and entities.

How Full Scale Electronic Drawings Work

Inside AutoCAD, drawing elements are stored in real-world units. AutoCAD can track your drawing data in meters, millimeters, feet, inches, fractions, decimals, or just about any unit system that you want to use.

When drawing on a drafting board, you usually create the drawing to fit a specific sheet size or scale. The text, symbols, and line widths are generally about the same size from one drawing to another.

In AutoCAD this process is reversed. You always draw the image at actual size (full scale) in real-world units. The only time you need to worry about scale is for plotting. You scale your full-size electronic drawing up or down to fit the plot sheet. You have to plan ahead for this and make settings that adjust the scale of the text, symbols, and line widths so that they plot at an appropriate size.

A bolt which is two inches long may look one foot when it's blown up on the screen, but AutoCAD thinks of it as two inches no matter how you show it or plot it. To help you get comfortable with electronic scale, we will take you through some setups with different units and sheet sizes in a few pages.

How Electronic Layers Work

Even in manual drafting, almost everything you design and draw can be thought of as separated into layers. Printed circuit boards have layers. Buildings are layered by floors. Even schematic diagrams have information layers for annotations. In AutoCAD, unlimited electronic layers give you more flexibility and control in organizing your drawing.

Perhaps you have used overlay drafting to actually separate your drawings into layers. Think of AutoCAD's electronic layers in 2D as sheets of clear acetate laid one over the other. When you are working in 2D, you are looking down through a stack of sheets. You can see your whole drawing built from the superimposed sheets. You can pull a single sheet out to examine or work on, or you can work with all the layers at once.

In 3D, layers become more of an organizational concept and have less physical resemblance to overlays. Any layer may contain any group of objects, which may be superimposed in space to coexist with other objects on other layers. Think of 3D layers as containing classes of objects. You can look at all layer groups together, or you can look at any combination, by specifying the layers you want to see.

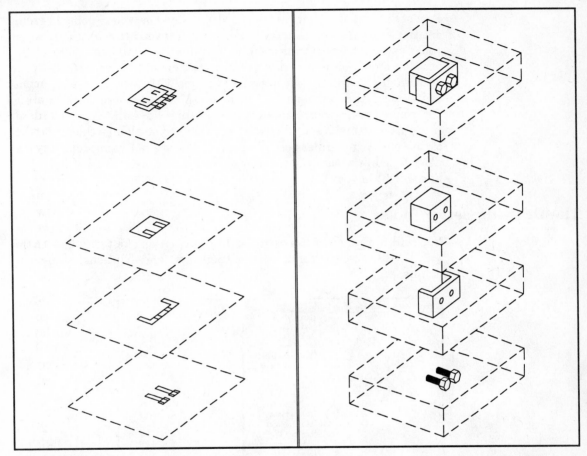

2D and 3D Layer Concepts

Each layer can have any color and linetype associated with it. When you set up your AutoCAD layers, you need to determine what parts of your drawing you are going to place on each layer, and what color and linetype you are going to use on each layer. You can make as many, or as few, layers as you need.

Electronic Entities and Properties

When you use AutoCAD's drawing tools to draw on one of these electronic layers, you create a *drawing entity*. A line segment is an entity, circles and text are entities. Besides its geometric location, each entity has an associated color, layer, linetype, and thickness (for 3D). AutoCAD calls these associations *properties*. Color is commonly used in AutoCAD to control the line weight of entities when they are plotted. You can preset the color and linetype for each layer.

Part of the organization process is to determine how you're going to group entities on layers and what colors and linetypes you are going to use when you construct your drawing entities. The simplest (and in many cases the best) organization is to use your layers to control the properties of your entities. If you are going to draw a red gizmo with dashed lines, then you draw it on the red dashed-line layer. Many of these decisions are determined by drawing standards that you may have already established. If you need to make exceptions, AutoCAD lets you change the properties of any entity, regardless of its layer. (If you are not using color in your plotted and printed output, you may want to consider using it to control line weight in your plots.)

The Drawing Setup Tools

You will find most of the setup tools you need on the two pages of the [SETTINGS] screen menu, or the [Settings] and [Options] pull-down menus.

Settings Screen and Pull-Down Menus

Setting Up a Drawing

When you begin a new drawing, AutoCAD makes several assumptions about drawing setup, including display and input units, scale, and linetype. These pre-established settings are called *defaults*.

ACAD.DWG — AutoCAD's Prototype Drawing

AutoCAD sets up many default settings by reading a prototype drawing stored on your hard disk. AutoCAD's standard prototype drawing, which comes with your AutoCAD software, is called ACAD.DWG. You created a fresh copy of it in your IA-ACAD directory in Chapter 1 (if you didn't, you should before proceeding).

The standard ACAD.DWG assumes you want to draw entities on layer 0. By default, layer 0 has white, continuous lines. (These may *appear* inverted as black lines on a white background on some systems, but AutoCAD still thinks of them as white lines.) ACAD.DWG also assumes a default system of measurement display (called units) that uses decimal units and initial drawing *limits* of 12 units in the X direction and 9 units in the Y direction. The drawing limits define your intended drawing area.

When you set up your drawing, you are actually modifying settings that were passed by AutoCAD from the prototype drawing into your new drawing. As you work through your drawing setups, AutoCAD lets you know what defaults are set by showing you default values in brackets in the command prompt. You can accept the default value that AutoCAD offers by just pressing <RETURN>. You can also tell AutoCAD what prototype drawing to use. You will see how to change a prototype drawing and tailor it for your own use in the book's last part (Part Three) on making AutoCAD more productive.

Determining a Scale Factor and Drawing Limits

How do you work out your scale? First, you establish your system of units. Then, you determine a *scale factor* so you can calculate the AutoCAD settings which will allow you to draw at actual size (full scale) and produce a plot at the size you want. You set your electronic sheet so that you can draw at full scale.

We'll start tailoring AutoCAD settings by taking a case study approach to scale. First, we will take you through setting up an architectural drawing. Second, we will work through an engineering drawing. Then, we will show you how to set up layers using a simple one-to-one scale drawing.

Scale Factor Settings

When you determine a drawing scale factor, it affects several AutoCAD settings. These include:

- Sheet size (limits)
- Line width
- Text height
- Symbol size
- Linetype scale

Sheet size is the most important. AutoCAD's electronic equivalent of sheet size is limits. You set your limits during your initial drawing setup. You set the other drawing effects later.

Determining Scale Factor and Sheet Size

Sheet size is calculated in much the same way as in manual drafting, except you use the resulting scale ratio to scale your sheet size up to fit around the full scale size of what you are drawing instead of scaling the drawing down to fit within the sheet. Then you scale everything back down by the same factor when you plot it.

Take an architectural calculation as your first case. You have a floor plan that is 75 feet x 40 feet, and you want a drawing scale at 1/4 inch = one foot (12 inches). What is your scale factor, and what size electronic sheet are you going to use? The size of your electronic sheet is set by the limits that you choose. These are the X,Y values of the lower left and upper right corners of your electronic sheet.

If you convert your drawing scale to a ratio of 1:n, then n is your scale factor. If you already have selected a drawing scale, it is easy to determine the scale factor. For example, if you had selected a drawing scale of 3/8" = 1'-0", your drawing scale factor would be 32.

```
3/8:12/1 converts to 1:96/3 or 1:32 for a scale factor of 32.
```

You currently are working at 1/4" = 1'-0", so your scale factor is 48.

```
1/4:12/1 converts to 1:48/1 or 1:48 for a scale factor of 48.
```

Calculating a Sheet Size for a Known Scale and Object Size

From your scale factor, you determine your electronic drawing limits by running some test calculations on possible plotting sheet sizes. You set your limits by multiplying the sheet size that you select by your scale factor. Here is a sample set of calculations.

```
Size of floor plan                          75' x 40'
Scale                                       1/4" = 12"
Determine scale factor                      48
```

Test a 17" x 11" sheet:

```
17" x 48 = 816" or 68'
11" x 48 = 528" or 44'
A 17" x 11" sheet equals 68' x 44' at 1/4" to 12" scale.
```

This sheet size is too small. Test a 36" x 24" sheet:

```
36" x 48 = 1728" or 144'
24" x 48 = 1152" or 96'
A 36" x 24" sheet equals 144' x 96' at 1/4" to 12" scale.
```

This should work with plenty of room for dimensions, notes, and a border.

In this example, you determined your limits by the number of units that fit across a standard sheet (D size, 36" x 24", for 144' across 36" at 1/4" = 12"). If you have to fit the drawing to a predetermined sheet size, you start with that size and the size of what you are drawing, and then calculate the scale factor from them.

Setting your limits doesn't actually limit how big your drawing can be. Think of AutoCAD's limits as an *electronic fence* which AutoCAD can use to warn you if you draw outside your boundary. This boundary is an ideal way to represent a sheet size. It gives you a frame of reference for zooming or plotting. If you draw outside your electronic sheet, you can expand the sheet by resetting the limits.

How do you get these settings into AutoCAD? You can set limits explicitly, or you can use an AutoCAD setup routine that will automatically set limits by stepping you through the calculations for your sheet size and scale, based upon your chosen limits. First, we'll use the automatic limits set up on an architectural sheet, then we'll use the UNITS and LIMITS commands to set up an engineering drawing.

Setting Limits Automatically

The [MVSETUP] item on the [BONUS] screen menu (or [Setup] on the Release 10 root screen menu) loads and executes an AutoLISP program that sets up your limits. It also draws a border around the drawing, or inserts a complex title block (title block not available in Release 10). The border is drawn as a reference line that matches your limits, around the perimeter of the sheet. This border is not intended to be plotted, but shows you your sheet edges. [MVSETUP] also includes another option that sets up the drawing in paper space with optional viewports (both topics of Chapter 4), and inserts a complex title block.

To get started, you need to start AutoCAD and create a new drawing with the main menu. Try stepping through the setup sequences in the following exercise.

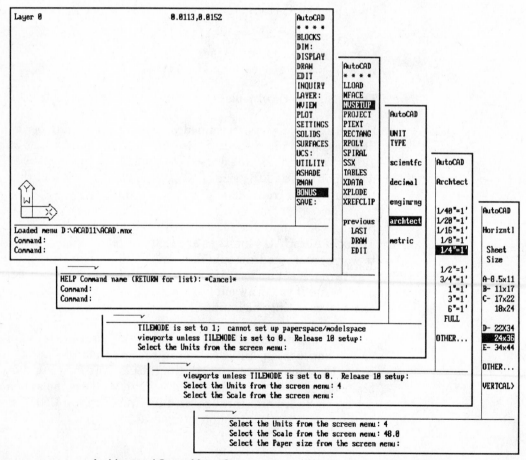

Architectural Setup Menu Sequence

Using [MVSETUP] to Prepare an Architectural 1/4" Scale Drawing

Load AutoCAD with your IA.BAT batch file to get the main menu.

```
Enter selection: 1
Enter NAME of drawing: ARCH
```

Select **[BONUS]**   Displays the [BONUS] menu.
Select **[next]**
Select **[MVSETUP]**   Displays the following prompt.

```
Paperspace/Modelspace is disabled.  The old setup will be
invoked unless it is enabled.  Enable Paper/Modelspace?  <Y>: N
```

With Release 10, you skip all of the above and simply select [Setup] from the root menu.

```
Select the Units from the screen menu: 4          Select [archtect].
Select the Scale from the screen menu: 48.0       Select [1/4"=1'].
Select the Paper size from the screen menu: 36.0 24.0   Select [24X36],
                                                  completing the setup.
```

A border is drawn around the screen and the coordinates at the top of the screen are 1728.0000,1152.0000, which, in inches, is 144' x 96' at 1/4"=1' scale. But the automatic setup didn't set the units to feet and inches.

Setting Units

AutoCAD offers units suitable for nearly any normal drawing practice. If you normally use architectural units, then use AutoCAD's architectural units. Select your system of units with the UNITS command. Setting units does two things for your drawing. First, it sets up the input format for entering distances and angles from the keyboard. Second, it sets up the output format AutoCAD will use when displaying and dimensioning distances and angles.

When you use the UNITS command, your screen flips to text mode and AutoCAD prompts you for units information. For this example, you'll select architectural units: feet and inches with 1/64" as the smallest fraction displayed.

➥ *TIP: Even though you may not need finer fractions than 1/2" at this scale, setting it to 1/64" will ensure precision. If you set it to 1/2", everything drawn will be rounded to 1/2" when displayed, even if not accurate. Individual errors in drawing will be less likely to show up, but may cause cumulative errors. Setting it to 1/64" will make drawing errors more likely to show up — if a coordinate displays as*

49/64" when you know it should be 1", you know it is not drawn correctly.

AutoCAD prompts you through setting angle measurements and angle display, giving examples for each system setting. The default screen setting for zero angle is usually to the right or *east*. The default setting for angle measurement is *counterclockwise*. Use these default settings in your setup. You can type the UNITS command or use the menu selection sequence shown below.

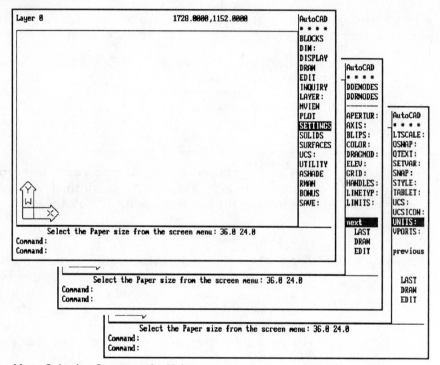

Menu Selection Sequence for Units

Using UNITS to Set Architectural Units for a Drawing

Select **[SETTINGS] [next] [UNITS:]**   AutoCAD flips to text screen.
```
System of units:          (Examples)
1. Scientific             1.55E+01
2. Decimal                15.50
3. Engineering            1'-3.50"
4. Architectural          1'-3 1/2"
5. Fractional             15 1/2
```

With the exception of Engineering and Architectural formats,
these formats can be used with any basic unit of measurement.
For example, Decimal mode is perfect for metric units as well
as decimal English units.

```
Enter choice, 1 to 5 <2>: 4                        Architectural.
Denominator of smallest fraction to display
(1, 2, 4, 8, 16, 32, or 64) <16>: 64               1/64".

System of angle measure:           (Examples)

1. Decimal degrees                  45.0000
2. Degrees/minutes/seconds          45d0'0"
3. Grads                            50.0000g
4. Radians                          0.7854r
5. Surveyor's units                 N 45d0'0" E

Enter choice, 1 to 5 <1>: <RETURN>
Number of fractional places for display of angles (0 to 8) <0>: 2
Direction for angle 0.00:
East     3 o'clock  =  0.00
North   12 o'clock  =  90.00
West     9 o'clock  =  180.00
South    6 o'clock  =  270.00
Enter direction for angle 0.00 <0.00>: <RETURN>

Do you want angles measured clockwise? <N>: <RETURN>

Command: <F1>                       Flip screen to get back to the graphics screen.
Command:                            Pick a point near the top right corner of the border.

Command: END                        Saves the drawing and exits.
```

After you set the units, the coordinates display shows feet, inches, and
fractions. If the format of the current coordinate is too long to fit in the
coordinates display area, it displays in scientific units, like
1.704450E+03,95'-9 51/64". When you pick a point, the coordinates
change to a point near but not exactly at 144'-0",96'-0", verifying that the
limits were set correctly.

We'll see how to precisely control pick points in the next chapter.

Usually, you set units only once for a drawing, but you can change units
in midstream should the need arise.

Fractional units represent inches by default, but the inch marks (") are
not shown. You can use fractional units for units other than inches by
adjusting dimensioning and plot setups.

Entering and Displaying Values in Various Units

No matter what your units are set to, you can enter values in integer, decimal, scientific, or fractional formats (only decimal or scientific in Release 10). When you are using architectural or engineering units, you can input values as feet, inches, or both. AutoCAD assumes the value is in inches unless you use a foot mark (') to indicate feet, so you can omit the inches mark ("). In fact, you do not need to type the inches value at all if it is zero. 2'0" or 2'0 or 2' or 24" are all equivalent in engineering units. No space is allowed between the foot and inch value, just the foot mark, like 1'3". The inch mark (") is optional; you can enter 1'3" or 1'3.

A dash is used to separate fractions, as in 1'3-1/2. Fractions must be entered without spaces, like 1-3/4 instead of 1 3/4, because AutoCAD reads a space as a <RETURN>. The input format and display format differ. You input 1'3-1/2" but it displays as 1'-3 1/2". However, in Release 11, you can force feet and inches, angles, and fractions to display in the same form as entered by setting the UNITMODE system variable to 1. To do so, just type UNITMODE at the command prompt.

Now, let's look at setting limits manually .

Using the LIMITS Command

You have used AutoCAD's automatic limits setup. Try stepping through a setup sequence for the engineering sheet using AutoCAD's individual settings commands for units and limits.

Determining a Scale for a Known Object and Sheet Size

Take an engineering example as a second case for setting limits. Say you want to draw a 24-inch manhole cover on an 8 1/2" x 11" plotting sheet. Okay, this isn't quite a full engineering case, but you get the idea. How do you compute your scale factor and determine your electronic limits? You need to do a little trial and error:

```
Size of manhole cover                        24" diameter
Sheet size                                   11" x 8 1/2"
```

Test 1/2" = 1" scale (1 unit = 2 units) scale factor of 2:

```
    11"    x 2 = 22"
    8 1/2" x 2 = 17"
```

This scale factor gives 22" x 17" limits — too small.

Test 1/4" = 1" scale (1 unit = 4 units) scale factor of 4:

```
11"     x 4 = 44"
8 1/2" x 4 = 34"
```

These 44" x 34" limits should work.

For this example, you'll select engineering units: feet and inches with the inch as the smallest whole unit. Engineering fractions are decimals of an inch. We'll abbreviate the prompts since you've already seen them.

Using UNITS to Set Engineering Units for a Drawing

```
Enter selection: 1                              Begin a NEW drawing.
Enter NAME of drawing: ENGR
Command: UNITS                                  Or select from the [SETTINGS] screen menu.

System of units:                    (Examples)

3. Engineering                      1'-3.50"
Enter choice, 1 to 5 <2>: 3                     Engineering.
Number of digits to right of decimal point (0 to 8) <4>: 2

System of angle measure:            (Examples)

1. Decimal degrees                  45.0000
Enter choice, 1 to 5 <1>: <RETURN>
Number of fractional places for display of angles (0 to 8) <0>: 2

Enter direction for angle 0.00 <0.00>: <RETURN>
Do you want angles measured clockwise? <N>: <RETURN>

Command: <F1>                                   Flip screen to get back to the graphics screen.
```

Setting Limits

Next, you'll set your drawing file sheet boundaries with the LIMITS command. You can type the command or select it from the [SETTINGS] screen menu. AutoCAD shows you <0'-0.00",0'-0.00"> as a default prompt for the lower left-most corner — home base. It is telling you that the lower left-most boundary of your intended drawing area is X = 0,Y = 0. You can enter a new lower left corner by typing new X,Y coordinates or by accepting the default with a <RETURN>. You'll enter your estimated limits of 44",34" for the upper right corner.

Setting Limits for an Engineering Drawing Sheet

```
Select [SETTINGS] [LIMITS:]
Command: LIMITS
Reset Model space limits:
ON/OFF/<Lower left corner ><0'-0.00",0'-0.00">: <RETURN>
Upper right corner <1'-0.00",0'-9.00">: 44",34"
```

Manually setting limits doesn't insert a border, so how can you see where your limits are? One easy way to see your drawing limits is to set a drawing grid, then extend your screen image using the ZOOM command. A grid is also useful for eyeballing coordinate values and distances. You can type GRID or select [GRID:] from the [SETTINGS] menu, and type ZOOM or select [ZOOM:] from the [DISPLAY] menu in the exercise sequence that follows.

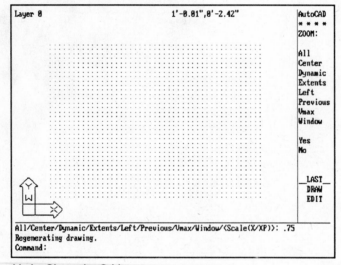

Limits Shown by Grid

Seeing Your Limits With a Grid

```
Select [SETTINGS] [GRID:]          Set grid to 1".
Command: GRID
Grid spacing(X) or ON/OFF/Snap/Aspect <0'-0.00">: 1

Select [DISPLAY] [ZOOM:]           Zoom so the limits and grid cover the screen.
Command: 'ZOOM
All/Center/Dynamic/Extents/Left/Previous/Vmax/Window/<Scale(X/VP)>: A
Regenerating drawing.
Select [DISPLAY] [ZOOM:]           Zoom so limits and grid cover 75 percent of screen.
Command: 'ZOOM
All/Center/Dynamic/Extents/Left/Previous/Vmax/Window/<Scale(X/VP)>: .75
Regenerating drawing.
```

Your screen should look like the Limits Shown by Grid illustration. The area covered by the grid is your defined limits, representing an 11" x 8 1/2" plotting sheet. If you drew outside the grid, you would actually be drawing outside the area that represents your intended plot area.

➡ *TIP: When you set drawing limits to match your plotting sheet size, remember that plotters grip a portion of the sheet's edge during plotting. Make sure your drawing allows enough room at the borders for your plotter. A safe margin varies from 1/4" to 1 1/4", depending on the plotter brand and on which edge it grips.*

Turning the Limits Warning On

You may have noticed the ON/OFF prompt or [ON] and [OFF] menu selections for the limits. When you turn limits checking on, AutoCAD will not allow you to draw outside the limits. Let's try it in the next exercise.

Drawing Full Scale on a Small Sheet

Although your limits represent a plot area of 11" x 8.5", they cover 44" x 34" in real-world units. Try drawing a 24-inch diameter circle to represent the manhole cover and see that it fits within your limits. Type CIRCLE or select it from the [DRAW] screen menu or [Draw] pull-down menu. If you use the pull-down, you can ignore the [CIRCLE] submenu that appears; it will disappear when you enter a point. If you use the screen menu, you need to select the [CEN,RAD:] option from the [CIRCLE] submenu to actually execute the CIRCLE command in its default center point and radius mode.

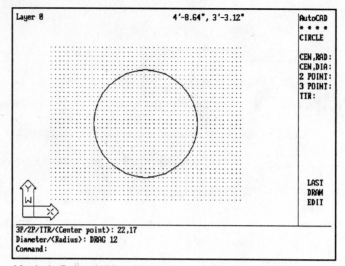

Manhole Drawn With a Circle

Testing Your Drawing Scale Factor and Limits

```
Command: LIMITS
Reset Model space limits:
ON/OFF/<Lower left corner> <0'-0.00",0'-0.00">: ON
```

Select **[DRAW] [CIRCLE] [CEN,RAD:]**   Draw a circle at 22,17 with a 12" radius.

```
CIRCLE 3P/2P/TTR/<Center point>:     Try to pick a point outside the grid.
**Outside limits
```

```
3P/2P/TTR/<Center point>: 22,17     Type it.
Diameter/<Radius>: DRAG 12
```

Your manhole should fit neatly on your drawing, as shown in the Manhole Drawn With a Circle illustration.

Setting Other Drawing Effects

Settings such as text height and symbol scale are a matter of drawing standards. If you have an established standard, you should adjust AutoCAD's settings to your normal standard. Just as you set your electronic sheet size to accommodate the manhole cover, you adjust your text, symbols, and line width in proportion to your sheet size. Once you have a drawing scale factor, this is a simple procedure. You determine the size you want your text, symbols, and other elements to be when the drawing is plotted, then multiply that size by the scale factor.

Here are some examples for the manhole cover.

Plotted Size	x	Scale Factor	=	Electronic Size
0.2" Text height	x	4	=	0.8"
1/2" Bubble	x	4	=	2" diameter
1/16" Line width	x	4	=	1/4"

AutoCAD also provides a variety of linetypes, such as hidden and dashed linetypes. You adjust linetypes by the scale factor, with the LTSCALE command. Like text and symbols, LTSCALE should be set for the plotted appearance, not how it looks on the screen. Linetype scale is largely a matter of personal preference, but setting it to your scale factor is a good starting point. Linetype selection is discussed later in this chapter.

Try applying some of the examples to the manhole drawing, creating the bubble with a circle and the number 1. You will find [LINETYPE] and [LTSCALE] on the [SETTINGS] menu. Use the following illustration as a guide for the exercise.

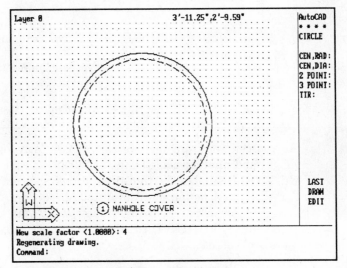

Manhole With Text, Symbol, and a Linetype

Setting Text Height, Symbol Size, and Linetype Scale

```
Command: ZOOM
All/Center/Dynamic/Extents/Left/Previous/Vmax/Window/<Scale(X/VP)>: A
Regenerating drawing.
```

Command: **<F6>**   Or <^D> to toggle continuous coordinate display on.

```
Command: DTEXT
```

```
Justify/Style/<Start point>: M        M is for middle justification. (The Release 10 prompt
                                      is a little different, but you still enter M.)

Middle point: 22,3
Height <0'-0.20">: .8
Rotation angle <0.00>: <RETURN>
Text: MANHOLE COVER
```

Move text cursor by using coordinate display to pick approximate point 1'-3.00", 0'-3.00" with your pointer.

```
Text: 1
Text: <RETURN>                        Ends the command.

Command: CIRCLE                       Draw a circle at 15,3 with a 1" radius.
3P/2P/TTR/<Center point>: 15,3
Diameter/<Radius>: 1

Command: LINETYPE                     Set current linetype to hidden.
?/Create/Load/Set: S                  Set.
New entity linetype (or ?) <BYLAYER>: HIDDEN
?/Create/Load/Set: <RETURN>

Command: CIRCLE                       Draw a circle at 22,17 with an 11" radius.
```

The circle has a hidden linetype, but you need to adjust the linetype scale to see it.

```
Command: LTSCALE
New scale factor <1.0000>: 4          Set linetype scale to scale factor.
```

As you can see from the exercise, it is relatively simple to adjust text height and linetype scale by using a drawing scale factor. The important thing to remember is that this drawing scale factor is *external* to AutoCAD. It is not an internal AutoCAD setting. You apply a scale factor to get your initial drawing limits, then you apply it to individual commands, like DTEXT, to adjust your text proportionately by setting your text height.

➤ *TIP: A linetype scale range of 0.3 to 0.5 times your drawing scale factor yields the best plotted output, but may not be visually distinguishable on screen. You may need to set one linetype scale when drawing and reset it for plotting.*

We'll save this drawing before moving on. When we save, we'll take a closer look at using dialogue boxes, particularly the file selection dialogue box.

Using Dialogue Boxes

The efficiency of dialogue boxes can't be beat for settings where you need to view or change several items at a time, or for filenames where you need to see a list of files (not available in Release 10). We'll examine the file dialogue box — it contains all dialogue features except on/off toggles. On/off toggles are check boxes that appear next to key words of items that can only be on or off. If a check mark appears in the box, it is on; if the box is blank, it is off. You click on the box with your pointer to turn it on or off.

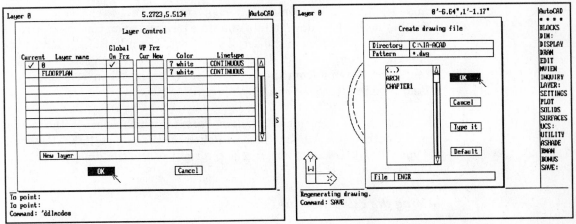

Layer 0 On, Layer Floorplan Off   *The File Dialogue Box for Save*

You use *input buttons* in dialogue boxes to enter text and values such as file, color, or layer names, or distances or scale factors. In the file dialogue box, the long, rectangular boxes immediately to the right of the [Directory], [Pattern], and [File] labels are input buttons. You can highlight an input button by moving your cursor over it. Then, if you start typing, what you type replaces the current value and the input button expands. An input button expands with a [Cancel] button and an [OK] button, which you use to close and cancel or accept the new value. If you want to edit the current value instead of replacing it, you can click on the input button before you start typing. However you enter the value, you can use the left and right arrow cursor keys, backspace, and delete, as well as typing new characters. The <RETURN> key and <^C> are alternatives to the [OK] and [Cancel] buttons (except in Release 10). If AutoCAD won't accept your new value, it is invalid and you'll have to edit it or cancel. If the value is too long to fit into the button, it will scroll to the left or right, using an angle bracket to indicate that it overflows (not available in Release 10). Some input buttons, such as the color buttons in the layer control dialogue box, open into other dialogue boxes, which you use to enter a new value from a list.

➡ *NOTE: If you accidentally press an arrow key when not in edit mode, your cursor may appear to lock up. Press the <END]> key to free it.*

Some lists are too long to see in their entirety. These lists have *scroll bars* at the right for moving up and down through the list (Release 10 has up, down, page up and page down buttons instead). The file list in the file dialogue box is a typical example of a list with a scroll bar. Imagine that your file dialogue list has 50 filenames. The list displays one page full of names at a time. The elevator box, initially near the top of the scroll bar, shows you where in the list the currently displayed page is. You can move up or down a page at a time by clicking on the bar above or below the box. You can move up or down a line at a time by clicking on the boxed arrows at the top and bottom of the scroll bar. Some input buttons, such as the [File] button on the file dialogue box, are associated with scroll bar lists. You select a name from the list by clicking on it. When you do so, the associated input button's value changes.

Dialogue boxes also include *action buttons*, which execute the action indicated by their labels when you click on them. The [OK], [Cancel], [Type it] and [Default] buttons at the right of the file dialogue box are typical action buttons.

Using the File Dialogue Box

The input buttons of the file dialogue box show the current defaults for the directory, wildcard filename filter pattern and filename. These defaults reset themselves each time you enter the file dialogue box; any changes you make are not saved as defaults. When you change the directory or pattern, the file list is redisplayed. The pattern uses a wildcard convention similar to common Unix systems and offers more wildcard characters than the DOS command line does. See Chapter 13 for a complete list.

When you know exactly what filename you want, it may be quicker to type than to find and select it from a long list of names. You could click on [Type it], or you could turn the automatic file dialogue feature off. To turn it off, you set FILEDIA to 0. With the file dialogue box turned off, file commands prompt for the filename on the command line, but you can easily pop up the file dialogue box when you want to use it. To pop it up, you just enter a tilde (~) when prompted for a filename. After we save our drawing, let's turn FILEDIA off, and leave it off for the rest of the book.

Let's save the drawing and try out the file dialogue box at the same time.

Saving an Architectural Sheet With the File Dialogue Box

Command: **SAVE**   The file dialogue box appears.

(In Release 10 you just get the `File name <ENGR>`: prompt. Enter ENGR<RETURN> and skip
to the QUIT at the end of this exercise.)

`Open [Pattern]`   Open it by clicking on the [*.dwg] box to the right.
`Enter *.*`   Change the pattern filter to *.* and click on [OK].
                                       The file list now shows your entire IA-ACAD directory.

`Open [Directory]`   Open it by clicking on the directory box to the right.
                                       Change it to your AutoCAD directory (probably \ACAD) and
                                       <RETURN> for OK.
                                       The file list now shows your entire ACAD directory.

Click on the scroll bar, under the box, to page down the list.
Click on the scroll bar, above the box, to page up the list.
Click on the down arrow box to scroll down one line.
Click on any filename. It appears in the [File] input button.

`Select [Default]`   Restores the ENGR default.
`Select [Type it]`   The dialogue box disappears and you get a filename prompt.

`File name <ENGR>:` **ENGR**   Type ENGR and then enter it with <RETURN>.

Command: **FILEDIA**
`New value for FILEDIA <1>:` **0**   Turns automatic file dialogue boxes off.

Command: **SAVE**   See, no file dialogue box appears.
`File name <ENGR>:` ~   Enter a tilde, and then the dialogue box appears.

`Select [Cancel]`   Cancels it.

Command: **QUIT**   Quit the drawing to start over fresh.

Now, and for the rest of the book, the file dialogue box will only appear
when we call it up with a tilde.

As a quick aside related to the file dialogue box, let's look at file-naming
conventions before we jump back into scaling, units, and limits.

File-Naming Conventions

As you work in AutoCAD, it helps to think ahead about how you are going
to name and organize your drawing files. If you already have a naming
convention, try adapting it to AutoCAD. While you can have up to 254

characters in your drawing names with some operating systems, MS-DOS is still limited to eight characters. Try to anticipate how you are going to sort your files in MS-DOS. PROJ01 and PROJ02 sort in order with PROJ??, but PROJ1 sorts after PROJ02.

As you invest time in your drawings, they become more valuable and you need to save them frequently. Use SAVE to record your work-in-progress. Adopt a temporary naming convention that lets you save as you go, PTEMP01, PTEMP02, etc. Your work isn't secure until it is saved to file on your hard disk (and copied to a backup disk or tape).

Now that we've saved the drawing, let's plot it.

Getting a Quick Printer Plot

If you have a printer configured for plotting in AutoCAD, you can do the following exercise to get a hard copy of the manhole drawing. Don't be too concerned about the sequence of the exercise. We will explain plotting in detail in the plotting chapter. The plotted drawing will show how all the calculations that you made provide a plotted drawing at 1/4-inch scale. If you don't have a printer that can do an AutoCAD printer plot but do have a plotter, you can use it instead. All of the prompts will be quite similar.

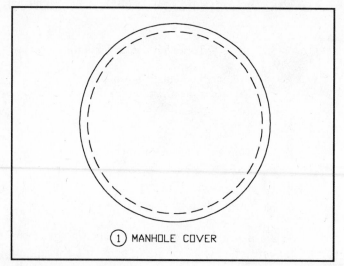

1 MANHOLE COVER

Plotted Manhole Drawing

Making a Quick Printer Plot

```
Command: PRPLOT
What to plot -- Display, Extents, Limits, View, or Window <D>: L
Plot will NOT be written to a selected file
Sizes are in Inches
Plot origin is at (0.00,0.00)
Plotting area is 7.99 wide by 11.00 high (MAX size)
Plot is NOT rotated
Hidden lines will NOT be removed
Scale is 1=1.00

Do you want to change anything? <N> Y
Write the plot to a file? <N> <RETURN>
Size units (Inches or Millimeters) <I>: <RETURN>
Plot origin in Inches <0.00,0.00>: <RETURN>

Standard values for plotting size
Size    Width   Height
MAX     7.99    11.00

Enter the Size or Width,Height (in Inches) <MAX>: <RETURN>
Rotate plot 0/90/180/270 <0>: 90          (Respond Y to the similar Release 10 prompt.)
Remove hidden lines? <N> <RETURN>

Specify scale by entering:
Plotted Inches=Drawing Units or Fit or ? <1=1.00>: 1=4
Effective plotting area:  7.99 wide by 11.00 high
Position paper in printer.
Press RETURN to continue: <RETURN>

Processing vector: nnn               AutoCAD cycles through whole drawing.

                                     Plotting takes place.

Printer plot complete.
Press RETURN to continue: <RETURN>

Command: QUIT                        To start a fresh drawing.
```

You should be able to take a drafting scale to your printout and measure a 24-inch circle at 1/4 scale and 0.2-inch-high text with a 0.25 bubble.

Setting Up Layers, Colors, and Linetypes

Next, we'll set up a new drawing using engineering units and limits for an 8 1/2" x 11" sheet with a drawing scale factor of one (full scale). We will use this setup to create a set of layers and to set colors and linetypes.

Setup Drawing for Layers

```
Enter selection: 1                  Begin a new drawing.
Enter NAME of drawing: CHAPTER2

Command: UNITS                      Set units to engineering with 2 decimal places of accuracy and
                                    2 fractional places for angles. Default all other settings.

Command: LIMITS                     Set your limits for 8.5" x 11".
ON/OFF/<Lower left corner ><0'-0.00",0'-0.00">: <RETURN>
Upper right corner <1'-0.00",0'-9.00">: 11,8.5

Command: ZOOM
All/Center/Dynamic/Extents/Left/Previous/Vmax/Window/<Scale(X/VP)>: A        Zoom all.
```

Layers

Layers help you control your drawing and keep it organized. If your drawing becomes too dense or complicated, you can turn selected layers off. If you neglect to anticipate drawing certain parts, you can create new layers for those parts.

We have compared layers to acetate sheets. In effect, you create your drawing by building it on a family of sheets. Each sheet has a name, a default color, and a linetype. You can work on any layer. Editing commands, such as ERASE, work on any number of layers at once. But you can only *draw* on one layer at a time.

The active layer is called the *current* layer. When you draw an entity, it is attached to the current layer. Your current layer name is displayed on the status line. In the new drawing you just started, your current layer is the default layer 0 from the prototype drawing.

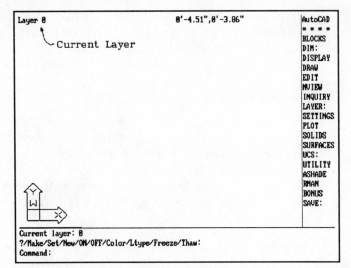

The Status Line Shows the Current Layer

You set up and control your layers using the LAYER command or the layer control dialogue box. You use LAYER to switch from layer to layer, and to turn layer visibility on and off. You can type the LAYER command or select [LAYER:] from the root screen menu.

You can see the properties associated with your layers by having AutoCAD display the layer status with the LAYER command or with the dialogue box. Using the LAYER command, you respond to the first prompt by typing a question mark. The <*> in the default layer name prompt is a *wildcard*, meaning "Tell me about every layer." You can also use question marks or any of the other wildcard pattern matches that AutoCAD supports to select groups of layers. Let's try it.

Displaying Layer Information

```
Command: LAYER                        Type or pick from screen menu.
?/Make/Set/New/ON/OFF/Color/Ltype/Freeze/Thaw: ?
Layer name(s) for listing <*>: <RETURN>
```

AutoCAD responds by flipping to the text screen and displays:

```
Layer name    State    Color          Linetype
----------    -----    -----------    --------------
0             On       7 (white)      CONTINUOUS


Current layer: 0
?/Make/Set/New/ON/OFF/Color/Ltype/Freeze/Thaw:
```

As you might have anticipated, you have AutoCAD's default drawing properties: layer 0 with white, continuous lines. Layer 0 is fine for playing around and has some special properties that you will see later, but for most drawing work, you will want to set up your own layers.

Layering Conventions

Well, how do you go about setting up layers? Like setting other drawing effects, setting up layers is a matter of standard practice and style. The most common-sense approach to layers is to use them to separate different types of objects in your drawing. For example, put drawing components on one layer and their dimensions on another. Try to anticipate the number of types that you want to separate. Here is an example set:

```
Objects on Layer                Layer Names
Components                      OBJ01
Dimensions                      DIM01
Symbols & Annotations           ANN01
Text                            TXT01
Title Sheets                    REF01
```

You can create an unlimited number of layers, but for most applications, 10 to 20 layers is more than enough. When you name your layers, it helps to apply DOS-type naming conventions and use *wildcards* to organize them. Layer names can be up to 31 characters long. However, the status line will only show the first eight characters of the layer name. You can use letters, digits, dollar signs ($), hyphens (-), and underscore (_) characters. AutoCAD converts all layer names to upper case.

There are many different layer-naming schemes in use. Some code the color, linetype, and line weight. Others specify the trade and work location, like ARCH-FLR01 or ELEC-CLG03. One popular convention codes layers with the CSI material code. Whatever scheme you use, there are three important considerations. First, coordinate with those with whom you may be trading drawings, such as consultants and subcontractors. Second, whatever types of information you code in your names, always put the same type of information in the same column (character position) so you can select groups of layers by wildcard. For example, ARCH-FLR01 and ARCH-FLR03 allows you to select all floor plan layers with ????-FLR?? or all architectural layers with ARCH*. But if you name the second floor A-2NDFLR, you can't select it with the same wildcards. Third, make the scheme extensible — capable of growth. Even if you're drawing a three-story building, use two characters for floor numbers so the naming scheme will be compatible with the 33-story building you do next year.

Using the LAYER Command

Think about what having separate layers means operationally. You need a way to let AutoCAD know which layer you want to draw on. The LAYER command lets you tell AutoCAD which layers you want to set current and which layers you want to turn on. Then AutoCAD prompts you for the name(s) of the layers you want this property applied to. You can only operate on one property at a time, but you can apply one property to several layers in one pass with wildcards, or by naming several layers on one line.

The LAYER command sets the following properties:

LAYER Properties

ON — Makes the layer visible.

OFF — Makes the layer invisible.

Color — Defines a single default color so that anything drawn directly on that layer will take on the color unless specifically overridden with an entity color.

Ltype — Defines a single default linetype. Lines (and other drawing elements) drawn on a layer will take on the linetype unless you specifically override it.

Freeze — Makes the layer invisible and all entities are ignored during a regeneration, increasing the performance of AutoCAD searches and screen displays.

Thaw — Unfreezes layers.

The LAYER command also offers these options:

LAYER Options

? — Lists all the layers in your current drawing including their status and default properties.

Make — Creates a new layer and sets it current.

Set — Makes the layer current or active for drawing.

New — Creates a new layer, but doesn't make it current.

Creating New Layers

AutoCAD provides two options for creating layers. The Make option creates one layer and automatically sets it as the current layer. If you want to make more than one layer, use the New option, and then use Set to specify the current layer.

Right now, there is only one layer in the drawing file. We'll put in several more, set them up, and then save them for future use. The target layers are shown in the following table.

```
Layer Name          State           Color           Linetype
0                   On              7 (white)       CONTINUOUS
CIRCLE              On              3 (green)       CONTINUOUS
PARAGRAM            On              5 (blue)        CONTINUOUS
SQUARE              On              2 (yellow)      CONTINUOUS
TEXT                On              4 (cyan)        CONTINUOUS
TRIANGLE            On              1 (red)         CONTINUOUS


Current layer: 0
```

Layer Configuration Table

The following exercise shows how to create the new layers with the LAYER command.

Creating New Layers

Continue with the LAYER command.

```
?/Make/Set/New/ON/OFF/Color/Ltype/Freeze/Thaw: N        Type NEW or just N.
New layer name(s): TRIANGLE,SQUARE,CIRCLE,TEXT,PARAGRAM
?/Make/Set/New/ON/OFF/Color/Ltype/Freeze/Thaw: ?        Displays layer information.
Layer name(s) for listing <*>: <RETURN>                 See the list.
```

Your text screen should look like the following illustration. Notice that AutoCAD presents the layers in alphabetic order (except in Release 10).

```
───────────── ──────── ──────────  ────────────
0                On         7 (white)   CONTINUOUS

Current layer: 0

?/Make/Set/New/ON/OFF/Color/Ltype/Freeze/Thaw: N

New layer name(s): TRIANGLE,SQUARE,CIRCLE,TEXT,PARAGRAM
?/Make/Set/New/ON/OFF/Color/Ltype/Freeze/Thaw: ?

Layer name(s) to list <*>:

   Layer name     State     Color       Linetype
─────────────── ──────── ──────────  ────────────
0                On         7 (white)   CONTINUOUS
CIRCLE           On         7 (white)   CONTINUOUS
PARAGRAM         On         7 (white)   CONTINUOUS
SQUARE           On         7 (white)   CONTINUOUS
TEXT             On         7 (white)   CONTINUOUS

TRIANGLE         On         7 (white)   CONTINUOUS

Current layer: 0

?/Make/Set/New/ON/OFF/Color/Ltype/Freeze/Thaw:
```

Default Properties for New Layers

You can enter as many names as you want on the New layer name(s): line. Separate layer names with commas because a space or <RETURN> ends your input. If you input a space, AutoCAD thinks you are trying to end the input line just like a <RETURN>.

Take a look at the layers information. Since you didn't set any properties for the new layers, AutoCAD automatically set them with the same defaults as layer 0. Each layer is color 7 (white) with a continuous linetype. Next we'll change the layers to the desired properties, starting with color.

Setting Layer Color

A layer has only one color, but several layers can have the same color. Color is assigned to layers by names or numbers (up to 255 different colors — limited by your hardware, not AutoCAD). Colors are commonly used to assign plotting line weights to objects in the drawing. AutoCAD uses the following naming and numbering conventions for seven standard colors:

```
       AutoCAD's Seven Standard Colors
        1 - Red          5 - Blue
        2 - Yellow       6 - Magenta
        3 - Green        7 - White
        4 - Cyan
```

➡ *NOTE: Colors above number seven do not have names and their availability varies depending on your video card and display. You can see them by loading the CHROMA or COLORWH drawings, on the*

*AutoCAD SAMPLE disk and probably in your SAMPLE subdirectory.
CHROMA can also be seen by viewing the slide named ACAD(CHROMA)
and COLORWH can be seen by viewing the slide named COLORWH. The
VSLIDE command is explained later in the book. Be cautious in your
use of colors above number 15 because they all plot the same as color
15. These colors are primarily intended for 3D work.*

When you assign a color to a layer, you can use a color number or a color
name for the standard seven colors. Actually, you need only the first
character of the name, like R for Red. Each color requires a separate
execution of the color subcommand, but you can make several layers the
same color by entering more than one layer name on the prompt line.
AutoCAD prompts you with the current layer name as a default.
Assigning a color automatically turns the specified layers on, but
assigning a negative color, like -7, turns them off.

Setting Layer Color

Continue with the LAYER command.

```
?/Make/Set/New/ON/OFF/Color/Ltype/Freeze/Thaw: C
Color: 1
Layer name(s) for color 1 (red) <0>: TRIANGLE
?/Make/Set/New/ON/OFF/Color/Ltype/Freeze/Thaw: C
Color: YELLOW                                         Or just type Y.
Layer name(s) for color 2 (yellow) <0>: SQUARE
?/Make/Set/New/ON/OFF/Color/Ltype/Freeze/Thaw: C
Color: 3
Layer name(s) for color 3 (green) <0>: CIRCLE
?/Make/Set/New/ON/OFF/Color/Ltype/Freeze/Thaw: C
Color: C                                             Or type CYAN.
Layer name(s) for color 4 (cyan) <0>: TEXT
?/Make/Set/New/ON/OFF/Color/Ltype/Freeze/Thaw: C
Color: 5
Layer name(s) for color 5 (blue) <0>: P*            Abbreviate. It's the only name
                                                     starting with P.

?/Make/Set/New/ON/OFF/Color/Ltype/Freeze/Thaw: ?   Check the colors.
Layer name(s) for listing <*>: <RETURN>             See previous Layer Configuration
                                                     Table.
```

Setting Layer Linetype

The LTYPE subcommand sets your layer linetype. CONTINUOUS is always
offered as a default. When you specify a non-continuous linetype,

AutoCAD first looks in its linetype library (the ACAD.LIN file) to see if it has a linetype definition that matches your request. If it finds your linetype, everything is okay. If not, you have to select another.

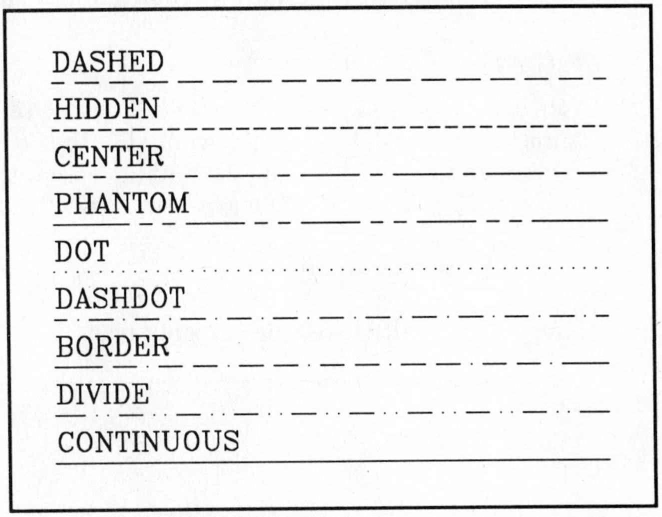

DASHED

HIDDEN

CENTER

PHANTOM

DOT

DASHDOT

BORDER

DIVIDE

CONTINUOUS

Standard AutoCAD Linetypes

In addition, each of the linetypes shown above has corresponding double scale and half scale linetypes, such as DASHED2 for a half scale dashed line and DASHEDX2 for a double scale dashed line. The half scale linetypes all end in 2 and the double scale ones end in X2.

Set the layer linetypes shown in the previous Layer Configuration Table.

Setting Layer Linetype

Continue with the LAYER command.

```
?/Make/Set/New/ON/OFF/Color/Ltype/Freeze/Thaw: L
Linetype (or ?) <CONTINUOUS>: DASHED
Layer name(s) for linetype DASHED <0>: CIRCLE
?/Make/Set/New/ON/OFF/Color/Ltype/Freeze/Thaw: L
Linetype (or ?) <CONTINUOUS>: HIDDEN
Layer name(s) for linetype DASHED <0>: PARAGRAM
?/Make/Set/New/ON/OFF/Color/Ltype/Freeze/Thaw:
```

➡ *NOTE: You can create your own custom linetypes with the LINETYPE command — see Chapter 11 for details.*

You now have a complete set of layers. You can modify their other properties by indicating the layers that you want to modify.

Next we'll look at setting the current layer and modifying layer visibility.

Setting the Current Layer

You can only draw on the current layer. Use the Set option to tell AutoCAD which layer you want as the current layer. The Set subcommand will show the current layer name as the default in the prompt. If you want to leave the current layer alone, just press <RETURN>. Setting a new current layer automatically makes the *old* current layer inactive.

Make the SQUARE layer the current layer.

Setting the Current Layer

Continue with the LAYER command.

```
?/Make/Set/New/ON/OFF/Color/Ltype/Freeze/Thaw: S
New current layer: SQUARE
?/Make/Set/New/ON/OFF/Color/Ltype/Freeze/Thaw: <RETURN>
Regenerating drawing.                              The changes take effect.
```

Look at the layer name on the screen status line to see that SQUARE is the current layer.

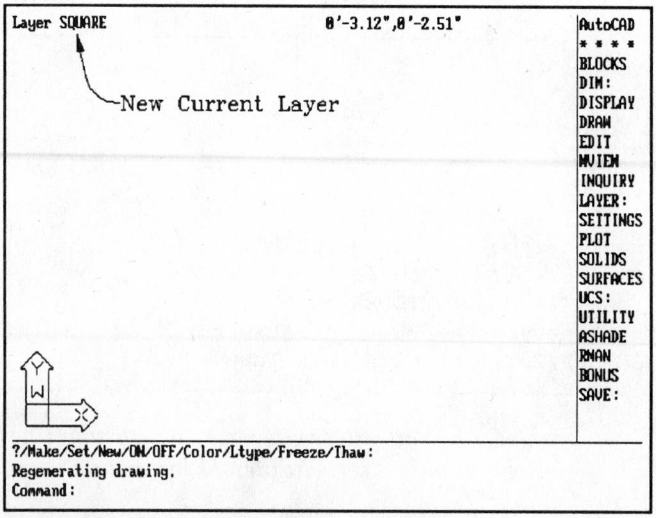

The Status Line Shows the New Current Layer

You can change layer settings at any time while you are in the drawing. If you alter the properties of layers on the screen (like linetype or color), AutoCAD regenerates the screen image to reflect these changes when you exit the LAYER command.

Making Layers Invisible

Try turning a layer on and off. Both work the same way. If you turn the current layer off, AutoCAD will ask if you are sure you want to. Remember you have to see what you are drawing!

Draw a square with lines, then turn the SQUARE layer off, then on again.

Setting Layer Visibility

```
Command: LINE                                         Draw a square with lines.

Command: LAYER
?/Make/Set/New/ON/OFF/Color/Ltype/Freeze/Thaw: OFF
Layer name(s) to turn Off: SQUARE
Really want layer SQUARE (the CURRENT layer) off? <N>  Y
?/Make/Set/New/ON/OFF/Color/Ltype/Freeze/Thaw: <RETURN>    It disappears.

Command: <RETURN>                                     Repeats the command.
LAYER ?/Make/Set/New/ON/OFF/Color/Ltype/Freeze/Thaw: ON
Layer name(s) to turn On: SQUARE
?/Make/Set/New/ON/OFF/Color/Ltype/Freeze/Thaw: <RETURN>
```

Remember you can use a wildcard (* or ?) to turn collections of layer names on or off. However, you can't use wildcards with the Make, Set, or New options.

➡ *TIP: If you are drawing but you can't see anything happening, check to see if you've turned the current layer off.*

Freezing also turns a layer off. When a layer is frozen, the entities on it do not display, regenerate, or print. This means that your screen will refresh more quickly after you invoke a command (like ZOOM) that requires a regeneration. The disadvantage to freezing layers is that layers have to regenerate when you thaw them. Thawing takes a little longer to do, so use it instead of off and on when you know you won't need to display, regenerate, or print a layer (or layers) for a while.

Testing Drawing Layer Properties

During the last few minutes, you have created a working drawing file with real units, limits, and a foundation of layers. It would be nice to know that all these layers really work. You just saw the yellow square on layer SQUARE. Set your CIRCLE layer current, and draw a circle to see how entities adopt other layer settings.

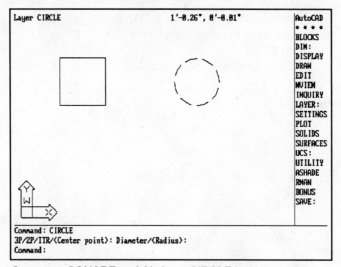

Square on SQUARE and Circle on CIRCLE Layer

Testing Your Drawing Layers

```
Command: LAYER                          Set layer CIRCLE current.
?/Make/Set/New/ON/OFF/Color/Ltype/Freeze/Thaw: S
New current layer <SQUARE>: CIRCLE
?/Make/Set/New/ON/OFF/Color/Ltype/Freeze/Thaw: <RETURN>

Command: CIRCLE
3P/2P/TTR/<Center point>:               Pick a point centered in the upper right quarter of the screen.
Diameter/<Radius>:                      Drag a radius of about 1 inch and pick a point.
```

You should have a yellow square and green dashed circle. Save your drawing by naming it to a new file called WORK. You will use this drawing as the prototype drawing in the next chapter on drawing accuracy.

Saving the WORK Drawing

```
Command: SAVE
File name <CHAPTER2>: WORK        Save with new name, WORK, for use in Chapter 3.
```

Now that you have put WORK safely to rest, you can experiment a little further with creating and modifying layers with a dialogue box.

Using the Layer Control Dialogue Box

If your display supports pull-down menus, you can use the layer control dialogue box (called the modify layer dialogue box in Release 10) to do all the layer setups that we have just done. You can create new layers, rename layers, and use all the other options the LAYER command offers. Using the dialogue box offers the advantage of seeing all the layer information and the settings as they are made. This is a convenient way to set layer data and makes it much easier to keep track of your layers.

The layer control dialogue box is found with the [Layer Control...] item on the [Settings] pull-down menu or by typing the DDLMODES command at the command line. DDLMODES is a *transparent* command, meaning you can use it when you are in the middle of most other commands by prefacing it with a single quote: 'DDLMODES.

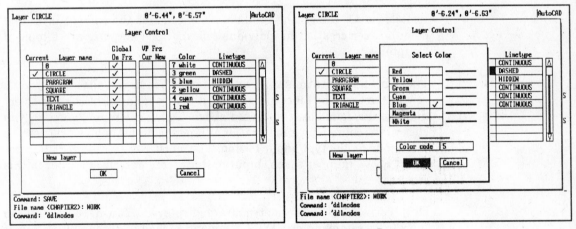

Dialogue Box Showing Current Settings   Color Dialogue Box

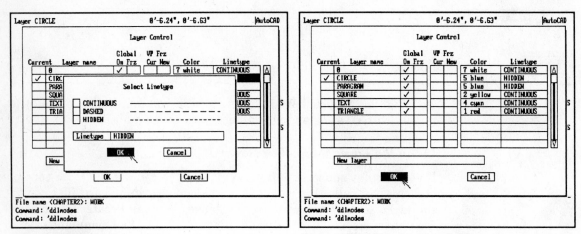

Linetype Dialogue Box   Dialogue Box Showing New Settings

Each row in the layer control dialogue box controls the settings for one layer. There are three groups of settings. In the first group (the block at the left), you control the current layer, on/off visibility, and freeze/thaw regeneration. To set a new current layer, just click next to its name in the Current column. Only one layer can be current, indicated by the check mark. Click in the On or Frz columns to toggle a layer between on/off or freeze/thaw. Any number of layers can be on or frozen at one time, with a check mark indicating on or frozen.

In Release 11, the second (middle) block controls the current layer and default layer creation in individual viewports. Viewports are a topic of Chapter 4.

The third block controls color and linetype. When you click on a layer's row in the Color or Linetype column, it brings up a select color or select linetype dialogue box, illustrated above. To set colors or linetypes, you click in the column next to the color or linetype name, or you can open the color code or linetype input button. You must use the input button for colors above number seven. Input buttons were described earlier in this chapter.

Only currently loaded linetypes are displayed. You have to use the LINETYPE command or LAYER command to load additional linetypes. If there are more linetypes than can be displayed at once, a scroll bar appears at the right side of the select linetype dialogue box. (In Release 10, use the up/down buttons.)

There is also a permanent scroll bar at the right side of the layer control dialogue box, because most real drawings will have more layers than can be displayed at one time.

Each of the layer names is an input button, which you can use to change its layer name. But, don't try to create a new layer with a blank input button — it may seem to work, but it won't. You have to use the new layer input button to create new layers.

Use the following exercise to practice changing color and linetype for the TRIANGLE layer.

Using the DDLMODES Layer Dialogue Box

Pull down [Settings] *Select* [Layer Control...]	The dialogue box is displayed.
Select [3 green]	The color dialogue box opens.
Select [Blue]	Change color to blue.
Select [OK]	Or <RETURN> to close the color dialogue box.
Select [DASHED]	The linetype dialogue box opens.
Select [HIDDEN]	Change linetype to hidden.
Select [OK]	Close the linetype dialogue box.

The dialogue box shows the changes to the CIRCLE layer.

Select [OK]	Or <RETURN> to regenerate with the changes.

The circle is now blue and hidden (smaller dashes).

Command: U	Undoes the changes.

If you can modify a layer so easily, it will come as no surprise that you can individually modify the color and linetype properties associated with any drawing entity.

Setting Color and Linetype by Entity

You've seen how to control an entity's color or linetype by drawing it on an appropriate layer. You also can set color and linetype explicitly by *overriding* the layer's defaults and setting an entity's color and linetype with separate commands.

How an Entity Gets its Color

The COLOR command is in charge of making sure an entity gets the color you want. Entities set to specific colors (instead of BYLAYER), by the COLOR command, are referred to as having *explicit* colors. Explicit colors are not affected by the layer the entity is on or by changes to the layer. When a new entity is created, AutoCAD checks the current setting of COLOR, and assigns that color to the new entity. Existing entities are not affected by the COLOR command, only entities created after the color is set.

You can set color to any valid color name or number. (Remember you can have 1 to 255 colors, but only the first seven have names.) Setting color by layer is AutoCAD's default condition. When color is set to BYLAYER, AutoCAD doesn't store new entities with a specific color. Instead, it gives new entities the color property by layer, which causes entities to adopt the color of whatever layer the entity is on.

➡ *NOTE: There is also a BYBLOCK color. We will cover BYBLOCK assignments when we get to the blocks chapter.*

Take a look at the color setting right now. Change the color to red using the COLOR command. You will see that the default color is set to BYLAYER. After you change the color, draw another circle to see how the explicit color settings override the layer setting.

Using the COLOR Command

```
Select [SETTINGS] [COLOR:]            Or just type COLOR.
Command: COLOR
New entity color <BYLAYER>: RED     New entities will be red.

Command: CIRCLE                       Draw a circle below the first circle.
```

Your drawing should show a red dashed circle in addition to your green dashed circle and yellow square.

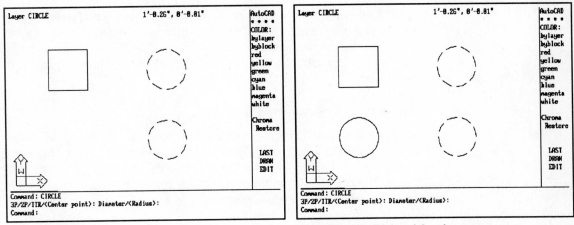

Second Circle Is Color Red   Third Circle is Red and Continuous

How an Entity Gets its Linetype

After this colorful discussion, you might have guessed that linetype settings have a similar control. Take a look at the LINETYPE command. The Set option lets you set an explicit linetype that overrides the layer's default for all entities that you create after you change the setting. Linetype can also be set to BYLAYER to use the layer's default.

LINETYPE Options

? — Displays a listing of all the linetypes currently defined in the drawing.

Create — Allows user to create a linetype.

Load — Loads linetype from a user-specified file. The default ACAD.LIN file has 27 linetype definitions.

Set — Sets the linetype to be used for all new entities until reset.

Using the LINETYPE Command

```
Command: LINETYPE
?/Create/Load/Set: S
New entity linetype (or ?) <BYLAYER>: CONTINUOUS
?/Create/Load/Set: <RETURN>
Command: CIRCLE          Draw another circle.
```

You should have three circles. The last one is drawn with a red continuous line, even though it is on the CIRCLE layer which is set to green and dashed.

➡ *NOTE: Explicit color and linetype settings stay in effect even when you change current layers. We do not generally recommend mixing explicit color and linetype settings with layer settings — it can get too confusing. Try to stick with one system of control or the other, with few exceptions.*

Changing Entity Properties

The COLOR and LINETYPE commands only change the properties for new entities drawn *after* you change the color and linetype settings. However, you can change the properties of existing entities by using the CHPROP (CHange PROPerties) command. After you select the objects to change, AutoCAD prompts you for the properties to modify. You can change the following properties with CHPROP:

- Color

- Layer

- Linetype

- Thickness

Thickness is a property associated with 3D — more about that in a later chapter.

Try changing a circle using CHPROP.

Using CHPROP to Change Layers and Color

```
Command: CHPROP                                          Select or type.
Select objects:                                          Select the green (first) circle.
1 selected, 1 found.
Select objects: <RETURN>
Change what property (Color/LAyer/LType/Thickness) ? LA
New layer <CIRCLE>: SQUARE                               Circle has layer SQUARE properties.
Change what property (Color/LAyer/LType/Thickness) ? C
New color <BYLAYER>: 1                                   1 is the color number for red.
Change what property (Color/LAyer/LType/Thickness) ? <RETURN>    Circle turns red.
```

Obviously, you can't always determine how an entity will be created by looking at the layer name on the status line. You need a way to check the current settings. You have two ways: the entity creation modes dialogue box and the STATUS command.

Controlling Properties With the DDEMODES Dialogue Box

The entity creation modes dialogue box, accessed by [Entity Creation...] on the [Options] pull-down menu or the DDEMODES command, can be used to view or change the current color, layer name, linetype, text style, elevation, or thickness. (In Release 10, it's [Entity Creation...] from the [Settings] pull-down menu.) It can be used transparently during most commands, like 'DDEMODES. Each of the modes has its own input button.

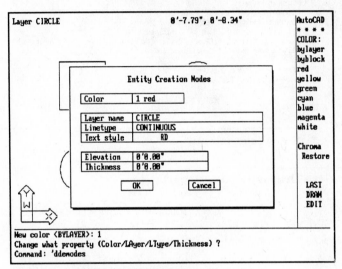

Entity Creation Modes Dialogue Box

We will use this dialogue box later in the book when we begin working with blocks and drawing symbols.

For a more complete listing of everything you wanted to know about your drawing but were afraid to ask, try the STATUS command.

Using the STATUS Command

You can check your current entity properties defaults with the STATUS command, but it can't change them. The STATUS command flips to the text screen. Try it now; type STATUS in response to the command prompt.

```
11 entities in CHAPTER2
Model space limits are X:  0'-0.00"   Y:  0'-0.00"  (Off)
                        X:  0'-11.00"  Y:  0'-8.50"
Model space uses        X:  0'-2.00"   Y:  0'-1.52"
                        X:  0'-8.98"   Y:  0'-7.00"
Display shows           X:  0'-0.00"   Y:  0'-0.00"
                        X:  1'-0.27"   Y:  0'-8.50"
Insertion base is       X:  0'-0.00"   Y:  0'-0.00"  Z:  0'-0.00"
Snap resolution is      X:  0'-1.00"   Y:  0'-1.00"
Grid spacing is         X:  0'-0.00"   Y:  0'-0.00"

Current space:        Model space
Current layer:        CIRCLE
Current color:        1 (red)
Current linetype:     CONTINUOUS
Current elevation:  0'-0.00"  thickness:  0'-0.00"
Axis off  Fill on  Grid off  Ortho off  Qtext off  Snap off  Tablet off
Object snap modes:   None

Free disk: 14403584 bytes
— Press RETURN for more —
```

Status Screen Display

Using STATUS to Get a Drawing Status Report

Command: **STATUS**   Flips to text mode and shows a screen full of information.
-- Press RETURN for more --
Press the <RETURN> key, then hit the Flip Screen key to get back to graphics.

Command: **QUIT**   After examining the screen, quit.

Exit AutoCAD with a 0 from the main menu.

The status report shows your drawing limits at the top of the screen. About halfway down, it lists the current layer, current color, and current linetype. The status text screen carries additional information about your settings. These settings will become more important to you as you read through the book. For now, just feel comfortable knowing that you can look at the information and that AutoCAD is keeping track of all that stuff for you.

If entity properties seem a bit confusing, don't worry — just start with simple controls. Use layers with the default BYLAYER setting to control your drawing color and linetype. Wait until you start editing complex drawings, then use COLOR, LINETYPE, and CHPROP sparingly for exceptions where you need more flexibility.

Summing Up

What you've seen so far is typical of AutoCAD setup commands. AutoCAD begins new drawings by reading many default settings from a prototype drawing named ACAD.DWG. Setting up a drawing file requires setting up units, limits, and a working set of layers as a good foundation for future drawing. AutoCAD tries to save you time by offering defaults and wildcard options in place of elaborate keyboard entry during your setup.

There are several keys to establishing a good drawing setup. Use drawing scale factor to set your drawing limits for your electronic sheet size. You also can use AutoCAD's automatic setup routines to select your final sheet size and to set your limits. You can scale text, linetype, and symbols using your drawing scale factor.

Organize your layers for different object types. Adopt a layer-naming convention that lets you organize your names with wildcards. The current layer is the active drawing layer. The status line always shows the current layer. Default drawing properties for color and linetype are set BYLAYER. You can explicitly override BYLAYER color and linetype with the COLOR and LINETYPE commands. You can also change properties associated with existing entities by using the CHPROP command. If you are uncertain about what properties are current in your drawing, use the entity creation modes dialogue box or STATUS command to help you keep track.

Setting up is well and good, but we're getting anxious to try out some drawing basics.

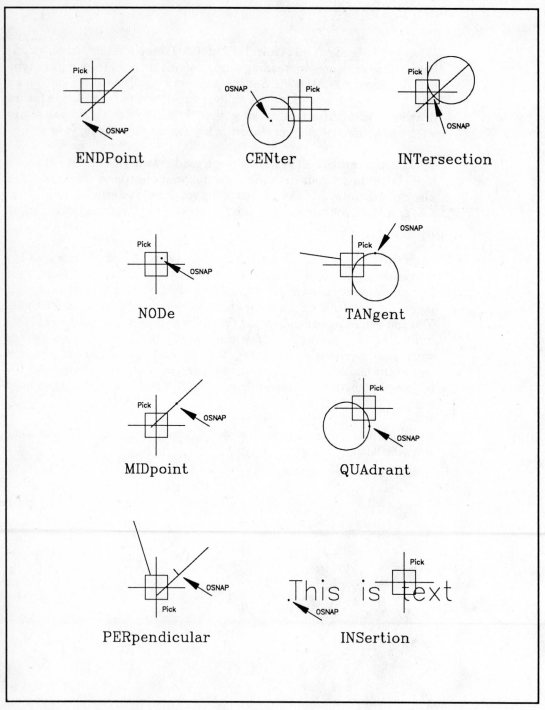

OSNAP Targets and the Points They Pick

CHAPTER 3

Drawing Accurately

COORDINATE ENTRY AND CONTROL

Given a straight edge and a rule, a draftsperson can locate a point on a drawing sheet with some degree of accuracy and use that point as a location for drawing more objects. In this chapter, you will learn how AutoCAD's electronic tools replace the draftsperson's manual tools for locating points and maintaining drawing accuracy.

Some benefits from using AutoCAD's tools stand out immediately: no eraser shavings, always having the right scale ruler, never having to borrow your 30-60 triangle back from your neighbor. Other benefits, however, are not as apparent: 100 percent accurate straight edges and triangles, precise mathematically defined curves, and electronically flexible graph paper to trace over as a guide.

Electronic Drawing Aids

The first step in getting accurate drawings is to locate your drawing points. How do you locate your drawing points accurately? One way is to type your coordinates in. You might know some of the coordinate values to start a drawing. However, you rarely have such complete information that you can type in all your drawing points. Besides, this would be grueling, tedious work and prone to typing errors.

Most of the time you *pick* your drawing points. As you saw in the last chapter, it's hard to pick accurately without some kind of help. AutoCAD gives you two ways to control the movement of your pointer so you can select accurate pick points. The first method is to use the *grid* and *snap* functions, and the second is to use the *object snap* functions, commonly called osnap.

How Grid and Snap Work

If you pick your drawing points without some form of control, AutoCAD must approximate the coordinates of your pointer location. These are generally numbers like 2.3754,4.6835. Even if you visually align the crosshairs with the grid or other objects, you can seldom accurately locate the point that you want. Grid acts as a visible template on your screen showing you where a set of points are located, but it does not round the input points to accurate locations. Snap acts as an invisible grid template that controls the points that you can select with your pointer. If you set snap to 0.5, then you can only select points that fall on 0.5 increments.

You control your pick points by coordinating your grid and snap. If you set them equally, then you can only select grid points. If you set your snap increments to half your grid increments, then you can only select grid points or points halfway between grid points. You control the accuracy of your point selection with snap and visually keep track of where you are snapping with your grid.

Object Snap Points

As your drawing becomes more complex, not all drawing points are going to fall on grid and snap points. Points on arcs, circles and intersections of angled lines are obvious examples. AutoCAD offers osnap (Object SNAP) as a means to control pick points on objects. Osnap is sometimes called geometric snap. It helps to think of drawing objects as having *attachment* points. Lines have mid and endpoints; circles have center, quadrant, and tangent points. When you draw, you often *attach* lines to these points.

AutoCAD's osnaps are geometric filters that let you select your drawing attachment points. For example, if you want to draw to an intersection of two lines, you set the osnap to filter for intersections, and pick a point close to the intersection. The point will snap to the intersection of the lines, not something close to the intersection, but *the* intersection! While it takes a little time to get used to setting osnaps, they are the best way to maintain geometrically accurate drawings.

Tools for Making Accurate Drawings

You will find the GRID, AXIS, SNAP, and OSNAP commands on the [SETTINGS] screen menu. The current settings of these commands can be toggled on and off with function and control keys. The [Settings] pull-down menu also contains toggles for snap and grid, and the [Assist] pull-down menu includes the OSNAP command and all of its options. Snap, grid, and axis can also be controlled with the DDRMODES (DRawMODES) command and its drawing tools dialogue box on the [Settings] pull-down menu. DDRMODES is a transparent command, so you can make these settings in the middle of other commands.

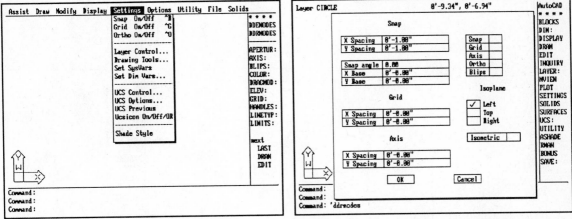

Settings Screen and Pull-Down Menus   *DDRMODES Drawing Tools Dialogue Box*

Using Drawing Aids

We are going to use the WORK drawing we saved in Chapter 2 to help us learn how to use AutoCAD's drawing aids. Use your IA.BAT file to get back into the AutoCAD drawing editor. If you are using the IA DISK, you'll use a technique of starting a new drawing equal to one of the drawings from the disk. This is similar to the equal sign you used to create a new prototype drawing in Chapter 1 with AutoCAD's original defaults, except this time your new drawing will use the defaults from another drawing. AutoCAD will essentially begin with a copy of the other drawing and give it the new name you specify. As you make your way through the drawing exercises, you can select from the screen or pull-down menu items, or type the commands as you need them.

Reloading the WORK Drawing File

     Begin a NEW drawing named WORK=IA6WORK.

     Use the WORK drawing from Chapter 2.

Load AutoCAD with your IA.BAT batch file to get the main menu.

```
Enter selection: 2          Edit an EXISTING drawing.
Enter name of drawing: WORK

Command: ERASE              Clean up any stray entities, like the four lines of the square.
Select objects:            Click on each entity to select, leaving only the green circle at
                           upper right.
```

```
Select objects: <RETURN>
```

Command: **LAYER**   Use the ? option to verify that your drawing settings are the same as those shown in the table below.

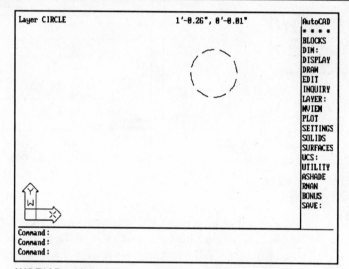

WORK Drawing

Your screen should look like the WORK Drawing illustration, showing a single circle in the upper right of your graphics drawing area. Verify that your drawing settings are the same as those shown in the WORK Drawing Settings table. Your current layer is CIRCLE.

UNITS	Engineering, 2 decimal places, 2 fractional places for angles, defaults all other settings.
LIMITS	0,0 to 11,8.5

Layer Name	State	Color	Linetype
0	On	7 (white)	CONTINUOUS
CIRCLE	On/Current	3 (green)	DASHED
PARAGRAM	On	5 (blue)	HIDDEN
SQUARE	On	2 (yellow)	CONTINUOUS
TEXT	On	4 (cyan)	CONTINUOUS
TRIANGLE	On	1 (red)	CONTINUOUS

WORK Drawing Settings

Let's start by drawing a few points on the CIRCLE layer.

Controlling Drawing Points

The POINT command is the simplest drawing command that inputs a drawing point. Try it with the coordinate values shown below. To see the actual point entity, you need to redraw your screen after you enter the point.

Using the POINT Command

```
Select: [DRAW] [next] [POINT:]          Or type POINT to make the point.
Command: POINT Point: 3,6.25            In the upper left quarter of your screen.

                                        A small blip appears at that point.

Command: REDRAW                         Leaves only a dot.
```

First, a mark appeared on your screen at the coordinate values you input. This mark was actually larger than the point that you placed. It was the construction marker (blip) for the point. Your redraw cleared the construction marker and left a small green dot on the screen. (It may be hard to see if your screen has a white background.) This is a true drawing point you can osnap to. You can be certain of its location because you input the *absolute* coordinate values. Absolute coordinates are explicitly entered coordinates.

How Accurate Are Pick Points?

When you pick a point on the screen with your pointer, it is much more difficult to get accurate points. To help track your pointer, turn on your coords by pressing the <F6> key or <^D>. Take a look at the status line and see what the digital readout of your coordinates says. Move your pointer around; the status line should display the current X,Y location of your crosshairs.

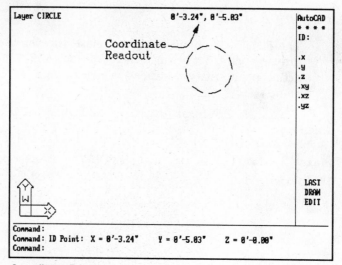

Coordinate Readout

Now, try the following exercise to see how accurately you can pick your drawing points. To test your pick point, use an inquiry display command called ID. Select [ID:] from the [INQUIRY] screen menu or type it in. Then *try* to pick the point given in the exercise.

Using ID to Test Pick Points

Make sure your coords are toggled on with <^D> or <F6>.

```
Select: [INQUIRY] [ID:]              Use coordinate readout to position your crosshairs.
ID Point:                            Try picking a point at exactly 0'-3.25",0'-5.00".
X = 0'-3.24"      Y = 0'-5.03"      Z = 0'-0.00"
                                     Your pick points may be different.
```

The ID command shows the X, Y, and Z position of your pick point. Try a few more points. You will quickly find it's nearly impossible to pick the point you want accurately. Without some form of controlling your picks, a drawing can quickly turn into a sea of inaccurate points.

➡ *NOTE: Even if ID and the coordinates display claimed the point was exactly at 3.25,5.00, if you changed your units to six or eight decimal places, you would find that it was really rounding off an inaccurate point.*

Grid and Axis Displays

The first step to getting accurate points is to set up templates that help you see points on the screen. AutoCAD has two such templates: the grid and the axis display. Both grid and axis can be set and toggled on/off with the DDRMODES drawing tools dialogue box. The most useful of these two tools is the grid.

Setting Up a Grid

A grid is a frame of reference, a series of construction points that appear on the screen but are not part of the drawing file itself. You set up a grid with the GRID command. Set up a one-inch grid, then prove to yourself that grid points do not actually control input points by moving your crosshairs around and trying to pick one with ID.

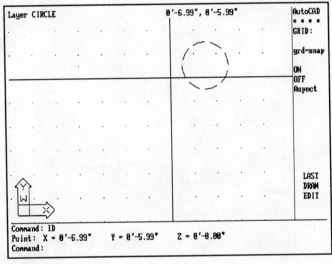

My First Grid

Using GRID to Set Up a Grid

Select: **[SETTINGS] [GRID:]**   Or type GRID.
GRID Grid spacing(X) or ON/OFF/Snap/Aspect <0'-0.00">: **1**

Command: **ID**
Point: Try to pick 7.00,6.00.
X = 0'-6.99"   Y = 0'-5.99"   Z = 0'-0.00"   Still not precise.

Grid is just a visual aid. It doesn't affect point entry or the movement of the pointer. When you set your grid spacing, avoid setting dense grids. A too-dense grid gets in the way and redraws slowly.

➤ *TIP: Turning a grid on not only helps you visualize distances on the screen, it also shows your drawing limits.*

You are not limited to creating rectangular grids. You have several options in setting up your grid. You can, for example, change your grid spacing to give different X,Y aspect ratios. The illustration below shows a grid with a 2X:1Y aspect ratio.

```
Layer CIRCLE                        1'-0.26", 0'-0.01"           AutoCAD
                                                                 * * * *
  .    .    .    .    .    .    .    .    .    .    .             GRID:

  .    .    .    .    .    .    .    .    .    .    .             grd=snap

  .    .    .    .    .    .    .  /   \  .    .    .             ON
                                  (     )                        OFF
  .    .    .    .    .    .    .   \   /  .    .    .            Aspect

  .    .    .    .    .    .    .    .    .    .    .

  .    .    .    .    .    .    .    .    .    .    .

  .    .    .    .    .    .    .    .    .    .    .

  .    .    .    .    .    .    .    .    .    .    .

  .    .    .    .    .    .    .    .    .    .    .             LAST
 Y                                                               DRAW
 W                                                               EDIT
  X>  .    .    .    .    .    .    .    .    .    .

Horizontal spacing(X) <0'-1.00">:
Vertical spacing(X) <0'-1.00">: .5
Command:
```

Grid With 2X:1Y Aspect Ratio

Here are your options for setting the GRID command.

GRID Options

ON — Turns grid on.

OFF — Turns grid off.

Snap — Changes the grid spacing to match the current snap setting.

Aspect — Allows different spacing for vertical and horizontal.

spacing (X) — A value followed by an X creates a grid that is a multiple of the current snap setting.

➤ *NOTE: A <^G> or <F7> acts as an on and off toggle for the grid.*

➡ *TIP: If your grid takes too long to redraw, it's too dense. Try a coarsely spaced grid coordinated with a finely spaced axis.*

AutoCAD's Axis Ruler

Another way to help you eyeball accurate screen locations is to use an axis ruler. An axis acts like a manual drafting machine, giving you tick marks across the bottom and right side of your screen.

You can select [AXIS:] from the [SETTINGS] menu, use the AXIS command, or use the drawing tools dialogue box. The axis prompt, shown in the illustration, is virtually identical to grid, and the command behaves the same way.

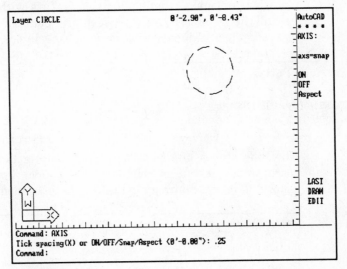

```
Layer CIRCLE                    0'-2.90", 0'-8.43"        AutoCAD
                                                          * * * *
                                                          AXIS:

                                                          axs=snap

                                                          ON
                                                          OFF
                                                          Aspect




                                                          LAST
                                                          DRAW
                                                          EDIT

Command: AXIS
Tick spacing(X) or ON/OFF/Snap/Aspect <0'-0.00">: .25
Command:
```

AutoCAD's Axis

Notice that the lower and right boundaries of the screen have a built-in ruler with tick marks at .25-inch spacing and a longer tick at every inch. Use these ruling lines to help you locate your crosshairs movement. It's best to coordinate your grid and axis spacing. For example, set grid to one and axis to .125 to help you eyeball 1/8-inch increments between grid points. Although axis helps keep track of where you are, it does not affect point entry itself. An axis provides reference marks only at the screen edges and won't work in viewports. Using a grid is the easiest and most popular way to locate drawing points.

A grid provides a good set of reference points, but you still can't *pick* the point you want accurately. This is about to change. This may be the last time you'll see freely moving crosshairs. To whip the pointer into shape, you need *snap*.

Setting Snap Points

Snap sets up the smallest increment AutoCAD will recognize when you move the pointer around. When you set snap on and set a spacing value, notice that your screen cursor has a jerky motion. It jumps from snap point to snap point instead of tracking smoothly. Think of setting snap as setting your smallest drawing increment. When you set your snap spacing values, all drawing pick points are forced to multiples of your snap values.

It's good practice to set your snap to some fraction of your grid spacing. AutoCAD normally aligns your snap points with the grid. It's easy to eyeball the 1/4 or 1/5 points between grid points as you draw. Try setting your snap to 0.25 inch, or 1/4 your grid spacing.

Using SNAP to Set Snap Points

Select: **[SETTINGS] [next] [SNAP:]**
Snap spacing or ON/OFF/Aspect/Rotate/Style <0'-1.00">: **.25**

Now, the status line says "Snap," indicating that snap is on and the coordinates readout is rounded to 1/4 inch. Try moving the pointer around. The crosshairs jump to the snap increments.

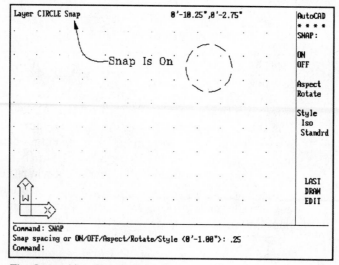

The Status Line Shows Snap On

➡ *NOTE: Snap has a toggle: <^B> or <F9>. You'll find this toggle helpful when you are trying to get to a point that is not snappable. Use <^B> in the middle of other commands when you want to turn snap off (or on).*

Using Snap Points to Draw Objects

Once you set your snap, you can draw accurately as long as what you want to draw is on a snap point. The status line will show the correct crosshairs position as it rounds the X,Y values to 0.25 inches.

Let's draw a 2" x 2" square with the lower left corner at 0'-7.50",0'-1.00". Use the coords readout to help you pick the points given in the exercise below.

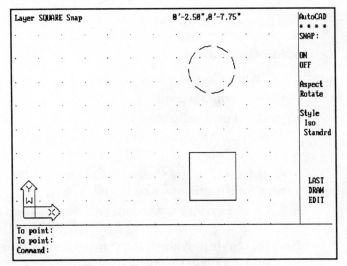

A Square Drawn With Snap

Using Snap to Draw a Square

Command: **LAYER**	Set layer SQUARE current.
Command: **LINE** From point:	Watch the coords display. Pick absolute point 7.50,1.00.

The coords display now shows a distance and angle, which we'll play with soon. But for now, toggle coords with <F6> or <^D> to show crosshairs position as X,Y.

To point: To point:	Pick absolute point 9.50,1.00. Pick absolute point 9.50,3.00.

```
To point:                      Pick absolute point 7.50,3.00.
To point:                      Pick absolute point 7.50,1.00.
To point: <RETURN>             End LINE command.
```

When you are done, your screen should look like the illustration above.

As you work with grid and snap, you will find that you need to adjust your grid and snap settings as you zoom to work in greater detail. If you start with a snap at 1 unit and a grid at 5 units on a whole drawing, you may need to reset your snap to 0.25 units and your grid to 1 unit when you zoom to work on a portion of the drawing. You can coordinate your snap and grid spacing to suit your needs. Make it a practice to set your grid and snap and leave them on most of the time. If you don't pick your drawing points with snap (or osnap) on, you won't get accurate drawings.

You have several options in setting your snap spacing. Here is the list:

SNAP Options

Snap spacing — A value indicating the snap setting.

ON — Turns snap on.

OFF — Turns snap off.

Aspect — Allows a different increment spacing for the vertical and horizontal snap.

Rotate — Changes the angle and base point (origin) of the snap. Also changes the grid and axis to match.

Style — Provides a standard or isometric snap.

Note that Style provides a standard snap and an isometric snap. You can use isometric snaps to control isometric drawing planes. We will show you how isometric snaps work later in this chapter.

➥ *NOTE: We won't show the grid in most of the illustrations in this book, but you should generally keep it on.*

Using Ortho Mode as a Special Snap

When you are drawing horizontal and vertical lines, you can place an additional constraint on your pointer movements by setting a special *ortho* mode on. Ortho stands for *orthogonal*, and limits your pointer movement to right angles from the last point. This means that any lines you enter with the pointer when ortho is on will be aligned with the snap axes. In effect, you can only draw right angles.

Ortho is easy to use and handy any time you are faced with drawing sets of horizontal and vertical lines. Try turning ortho on and drawing another square around the square you just drew. To turn ortho on, type the ORTHO command, or use either <^O> or <F8> as toggles. You can also use the drawing tools dialogue box. After you draw the square, undo it and toggle ortho off; you will use this drawing later on to try out osnaps.

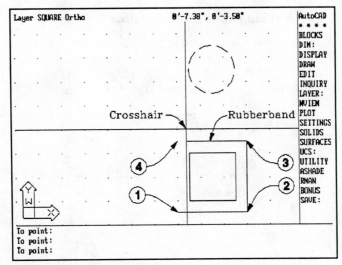

Drawing a Square With Ortho

Using Ortho to Draw a Square

Toggle ortho on with <^O> or <F8> and snap off with <F9>.

Command: **LINE**	
From point:	Pick ① near 7.00,0.50.
To point:	Pick ② near 10.00,0.50.
To point:	Pick ③ near 10.00,3.50.
To point:	Pick ④ near 7.00,3.50.
To point: **C**	C closes series of lines and ends command.
Command: **U**	Undo removes the four lines you just drew.

Toggle ortho off with <^O> or <F8>.

When you turn ortho on, Ortho appears on the status line and <Ortho on> shows on the prompt line. As you draw the square, you find that your cursor is limited to vertical and horizontal movement, making it easy to get true 90-degree corners. The rubber band cursor that normally trails from the last point to the intersection of the crosshairs instead goes from the last point to the nearest perpendicular point on the X or Y crosshairs.

➡ NOTE: *If you toggle a mode like ortho, snap, or grid in the middle of a command, and later undo the command, the toggled setting is also undone.*

Checking Your Drawing Aids Settings

While you have used individual axis, grid, and snap commands to help you construct these shapes, you can also set these drawing aids using the DDRMODES command. Check your settings by comparing them to the Drawing Tools Dialogue Box illustration.

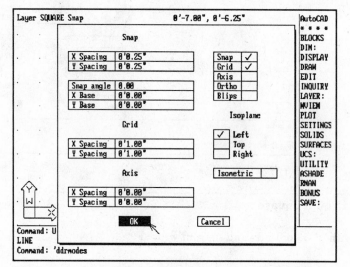

The Drawing Tools Dialogue Box

Coordinate Entry

When you enter coordinates from the keyboard, they override the snap and ortho drawing controls, but not object snap. You often use coordinate entry when you are setting up drawings or when you are drawing at specific points or known distances relative to known points.

➡ NOTE: *The Z distance or Z angle is always assumed to be zero unless it is specified with another value.*

Absolute Coordinates

When you know the exact coordinates of your point or its distance and angle from the 0,0 drawing origin, you can simply type in the coordinates in one of several formats. These are all known as absolute or explicit coordinates.

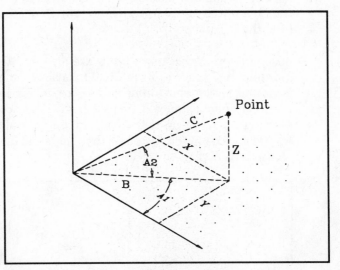

Various Forms of Absolute Coordinate Entry

Absolute Cartesian coordinates treat coordinate entry as X and Y displacements from 0,0 (or X,Y,Z from 0,0,0 in 3D). For example, 6,5,4 places a point 6 units along the positive X axis, 5 units along the positive Y axis, and 4 units along the positive Z axis from the 0,0,0 base point. The default position for 0,0 is at the lower left of your limits and drawing screen, but you can set it anywhere you like with the UCS command. If your displacement is positive, you don't need to use a + sign. Negative displacement is left and down on the screen. You must use a - sign for negative displacements. In the above illustration, Cartesian points are located using the distances X, Y, and Z.

Absolute Polar coordinates also treat coordinate entry as a displacement from 0,0 but you specify the displacement as a distance and angle. For example, 2<60 is 2 units from 0,0 along a line at 60 degrees from the X axis in the X,Y plane. The distance and angle values are separated by a left angle bracket (<). Positive angles are counterclockwise relative to 0 degrees as a horizontal extending to the right of 0,0. Ninety degrees is vertically above, 180 degrees is horizontally left. See the illustration below.

Absolute Spherical coordinates are 3D polar coordinates, specified as a distance and two angles. The first angle is from 0,0 in the X,Y plane and the second angle is the angle towards the Z axis up or down from the X,Y plane. In the above illustration, a point is located using spherical coordinates by distance C and angles A1 and A2. For example, 2<60<45 specifies a point 2 units from the 0,0,0 origin along a line at 60 degrees from the X axis in the X,Y plane and at 45 degrees up towards the Z axis from the X,Y plane.

Absolute Cylindrical coordinates are also for 3D use. They're like polar coordinates plus a height in the Z axis above or below the X,Y plane. As indicated in the above illustration, a point is located using cylindrical coordinates by distance B, angle A2, and distance Z. For example, 2<60,3 specifies a point 2 units from the 0,0,0 origin along a line at 60 degrees from the X axis in the X,Y plane that angles up to a point 3 units vertically above the X,Y plane.

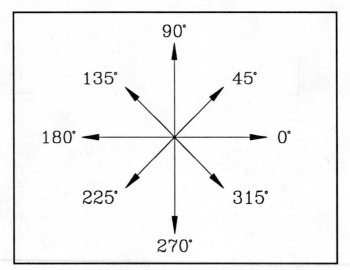

Default Units Angle Directions

Relative Coordinates

Very often, the point you want to enter has a known X,Y or X,Y,Z distance or known distance and angle from a previous point, but its relative displacement from 0,0 is unknown. Any of the above methods of entering coordinates can also be used *relative* to the last previous point entered in your drawing instead of relative to 0,0. To enter a relative point, you simply enter an @ symbol before the first number.

Relative Cartesian coordinates treat the last point of coordinate entry as a temporary 0,0. If you want to add a horizontal line segment that is two units in the X direction and one in the Y from the previous point, you type @2,0. Relative polar coordinates also treat the last point as 0,0, but you specify your point displacement with a distance and angle. For example, @2<60 is 2 units at 60 degrees.

If you want to enter a new point at the last point, you could use a zero distance, like @0,0 or @0<*nn* (where *nn* could be any angle). This is the same as the last point. But there is a simpler way. You can just enter the @ sign without any number or angle and AutoCAD interprets it as specifying the last point.

➥ *TIP: You often want to draw relative to a point that is not the last point used in the drawing. Just use the ID command to pick the point you want to work relative to and it will become the new last point. You can also check and change the last point with the LASTPOINT system variable.*

Using Absolute Coordinates

Let's review absolute Cartesian coordinates, which you've already used several times, and try absolute polar coordinates as we draw a triangle at the upper left of the screen.

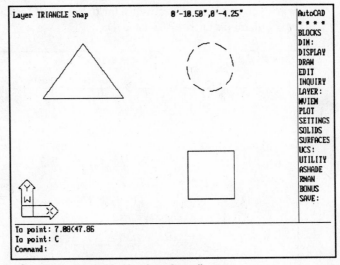

Triangle Drawn With Absolute Coordinates

Specifying Absolute Points

Continue working in the WORK drawing.

Command: **LAYER**	Set layer TRIANGLE current.

Command: **LINE**	
From point: **1.25,5.25**	Absolute Cartesian.
To point: **3,7.5**	Absolute Cartesian.
To point: **7.08<47.86**	Absolute polar.
To point: **C**	Closes it.

These were simple points. In a real drawing, they'd be harder to calculate and we wouldn't be there to give them to you. And if you examined the drawing database closely, you'd find that the third point (five times the square root of 2 at 45 degrees) doesn't exactly align with the first. Absolute coordinates are great for locating the first point of an object in the drawing, but relative coordinates usually serve you better for subsequent points. And, often, relative polar coordinates can be easily picked with the cursor.

Tracking and Picking Polar Coordinates

Often, the precision of the snap, grid, and ortho tools is sufficient for accuracy, but it would be easier to draw if you knew how far the cursor is from the last point. You can use the pointer to pick polar coordinates. You track your pointer movements for polar input by toggling coords into polar readout mode with <F6> or <^D>.

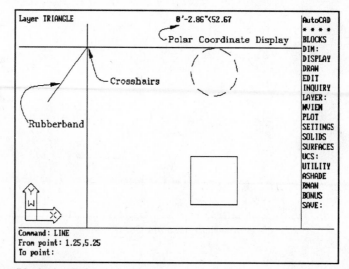

Displaying Polar Coordinates

Coords has three modes. The default mode is static coordinates, or off. Static coordinates display an X,Y point, which is updated only when a new point is picked.

When you toggle <F6> once, you get the second mode where the X,Y display is constantly updated as you move the cursor. This second, constantly updated mode has a split personality in most commands. When the crosshairs pull a rubber band line around, such as in a LINE command, the second mode automatically switches into a polar *dist<angle* readout relative to the last point. This is the most frequently used mode because it lets you pick the initial point for a command with absolute X,Y coords and pick subsequent points with relative polar points.

The third mode locks the coords into X,Y display. This works only within a command that shows a polar readout. Then, pressing <F6> once more locks it into X,Y mode. If this sounds confusing, it is! Do what we do, which is toggle once or twice until we get the coords display we want.

Drawing With Relative Coordinates

Let's try relative, Cartesian, and polar coordinate entry by drawing a parallelogram. We'll use both keyboard and cursor to specify relative polar coordinates. Use the following exercise sequence for your input values.

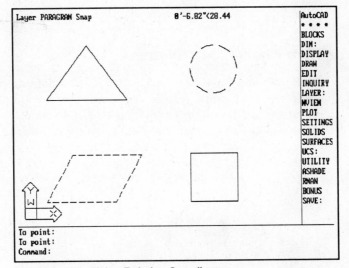

Parallelogram Using Relative Coordinates

Using Relative Coordinates to Draw

Continue from the previous triangle exercise. You'll work relative to its last point.

Command: **LAYER**   Set layer PARAGRAM current.
Command: **LINE**

Toggle coords once if needed with <F6> or <^D> so they update the X,Y display as you move.

From point: Use the coords to pick absolute Cartesian coordinates
                     0'-4.25",0',1.00".

The coords change to polar display. Toggle once more so they lock into X,Y mode.

To point: **@2.25<60**   Relative polar coordinates.
To point: **@-3,0**   Relative Cartesian coordinates.

Toggle coords twice more so they track in polar mode.

To point: Using the coords, pick relative polar coordinates @ 0'-2.25"<240.00.
To point: Using the coords, pick relative polar coordinates @ 0'-3.00"<0.00.
To point: **<RETURN>**

➡ *NOTE: Don't let the coords readout fool you. It displays with as much or as little precision as you set in the UNITS command. A polar readout is rarely precise at angles other than 90-degree increments. For example, 2.10<60 is more likely 2.0976325 at 60.351724 degrees.*

Let's turn and look at the world sideways.

Creating Your Own Coordinate System

So far you have been using AutoCAD's default coordinate system, the *world* coordinate system. You can create your own coordinate system using the UCS command. The UCS command lets you position the 0,0 origin anywhere you wish, so that you can work relative to any point you wish. You can also rotate the X,Y (and even Z) axes to any angle in 2D or 3D space. While the UCS was developed for 3D, it can be extremely useful for 2D drawing applications.

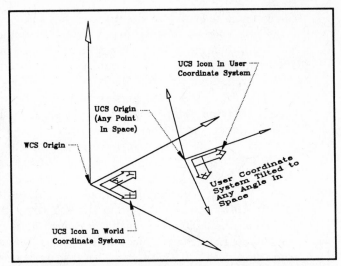

User Coordinate System and World Coordinate System

We will show you two examples. The first uses UCS to change the location of the 0,0 origin point and the direction of the X and Y axes in your drawing. The second changes the location of 0,0, keeping the X and Y directions the same as the default directions. Drafting in 2D, you frequently encounter cases where you have drawing data relative to 0,0 positions. Large sets of offset data or datum-dimensioned work are common examples. To handle this type of drawing, you can set your UCS, input the drawing data, then return your UCS to its original (default) world setting.

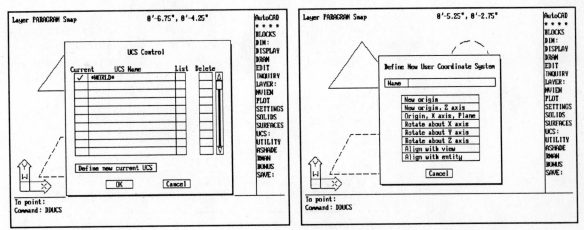

UCS Control Dialogue Box   *Define a New Current UCS Dialogue Box*

You can modify or change the current UCS with either the UCS command or the UCS control dialogue box, the DDUCS command. The [UCS:] item on the root screen menu brings up a menu of UCS options, which includes [DDUCS:]. The [UCS Control...] item on the [Settings] pull-down menu also brings up the dialogue box. The [Define new current UCS] button on the UCS control dialogue box brings up the sub-dialogue box illustrated above. The [Settings] pull-down menu includes several other UCS-related items. [UCS Options...] is an icon menu of preset 3D UCS orientations. [UCS Previous] restores the most recent previous UCS. And [Ucsicon On/Off/OR] toggles the UCS icon through its settings.

The UCSICON (the X,Y arrow at the lower left) helps you keep track of the UCS. It shows the orientation of the X,Y axes. It can be set to appear aligned on the 0,0,0 origin of the UCS, if there is room on screen. A plus mark appears in the UCS icon at the origin, when the icon is set to the origin and it can fit there. If it can't fit on screen at the origin, it will appear at the lower left, without a plus mark. The UCS icon's appearance is controlled by the UCSICON command.

Make sure your UCSICON (the X,Y arrow at the lower left) is on, then use the UCS command to rotate your drawing's coordinate system 90 degrees and set the 0,0 origin near the lower right corner. When you specify the coordinates of a new UCS, you specify them in terms of the current coordinate system. Use the coords display to pick the new origin.

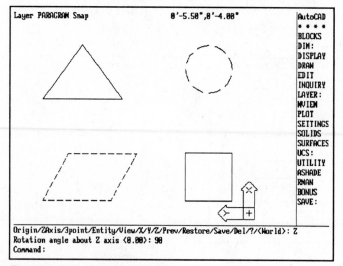

The New User Coordinate System

Using UCS to Create a User Coordinate System

```
Command: UCSICON
ON/OFF/All/Noorigin/ORigin <ON>:OR          Set UCS icon to origin.

Command: ZOOM                               Zoom out to see UCS icon jump to origin.
All/Center/Dynamic/Extents/Left/Previous/Vmax/Window/<Scale(X/XP)>: .9
Command: U                                  Undo to zoom back.

Command: UCS                                Move Origin to lower right corner.
Origin/ZAxis/3point/Entity/View/X/Y/Z/Prev/Restore/Save/Del/?/<World>: O
Origin point <0,0,0>: 10.25,.5              Pick absolute point 10.25,.5 as coords of new UCS.

Command: UCS                                Rotate about the Z axis 90 degrees.
Origin/ZAxis/3point/Entity/View/X/Y/Z/Prev/Restore/Save/Del/?/<World>: Z
Rotation angle about Z axis <0.00>: 90
```

To see the effect of the changed origin, move your crosshairs around and watch your coords display. They should show 0,0 at the lower right corner, a *vertical* X direction and a *horizontal* Y direction.

While offsetting the origin is straightforward, you might ask what rotating the UCS around the Z axis has to do with your 2D drawing. Imagine that you're standing on the X axis, looking down at your drawing, with your left arm extended to the left to grip a pole rising up from 0,0. Walk forward through 90 degrees, kicking the X axis along with you. You just rotated about the Z axis 90 degrees.

Try out the new UCS by making a border around your drawing. Use the following sequence as a guide.

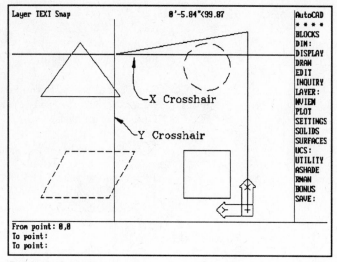

Border in Progress

Drawing a Border in a UCS

Command: **LAYER**	Set layer TEXT current.
Command: **LINE**	
From point: **0,0**	Lower right corner of border.
To point:	Pick relative polar coords @ 7.50<0.00.
To point:	Pick relative polar coords @ 9.75<90.00. Notice "up" is left now!
To point:	Pick relative polar coords @ 7.50<180.00.
To point:	Pick relative polar coords @ 9.75<270.00.
To point: **<RETURN>**	End the line.
Command: **UCS**	Set UCS back to World, the default.
Origin/ZAxis/3point/Entity/View/X/Y/Z/Prev/Restore/Save/Del/?/<World>: **<RETURN>**	

Try changing the location of your UCS origin to about midway up your drawing, then input some text.

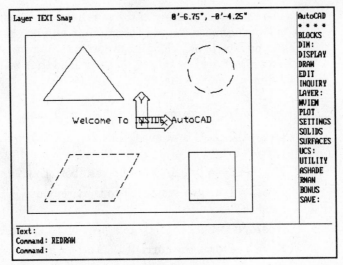

Text Centered at Current UCS Origin

Using UCS to Demonstrate Changed Origin Point

```
Command: UCS                                        Set UCS to center of drawing.
Origin/ZAxis/3point/Entity/View/X/Y/Z/Prev/Restore/Save/Del/?/<World>: O
Origin point <0,0,0>: 5.5,4.25                      The current coordinates of the new UCS.

Command: DTEXT

Justify/Style/<Start point>: C
Center point: 0,0
Height <0'-0.20">: .25
Rotation angle <0.00>: <RETURN>
Text: Welcome To INSIDE AutoCAD                      Our favorite text.
Text: <RETURN>

Command: REDRAW                                      Clean up the display.
Command: UCS                                         Set UCS back to the world coordinate system.
Origin/ZAxis/3point/Entity/View/X/Y/Z/Prev/Restore/Save/Del/?/<World>: <RETURN>
Command: LAYER                                       Set layer 0 current.
Command: SAVE                                        Save with the name BASIC, for later use, then quit.
```

Check your drawing. Your screen should look like the illustration above. Each shape should be on its appropriately named layer, with the color and linetype of the layer. Your grid should be one unit and snap .25 units. If needed, make corrections and save it again as BASIC. We'll use this drawing again in the following exercises and in the next chapter on display controls.

As you can tell by looking at the command prompt line, the UCS command is one of the more complex commands and has several options. We will show you how to use all of these options when we discuss 3D in Part Two. Meanwhile, here is a subset of the options that will get you through most two-dimensional applications.

Subset of UCS Options (for 2D Applications)

Origin — Lets you specify a new X,Y,Z origin point relative to the current origin.

Z — Lets you rotate the X,Y axes about the Z axis.

Prev — Lets you step back to the previous UCS, up to ten previously used UCSs.

Restore — Sets the UCS to a previously saved UCS.

Save — Stores the current UCS under a name that you specify.

Del — Removes a saved UCS.

? — Displays a list of saved UCSs by name, point of origin, and orientation.

<World> — The default, sets the UCS to the world coordinate system.

Here are the UCSICON command options to control the display of the UCS icon.

UCSICON Options

ON — Makes the UCS icon visible.

OFF — Removes the UCS icon.

All — Displays the UCS icon in all viewports — see the next chapter.

Noorigin — Displays the UCS icon in the lower left corner of viewport instead of at the origin.

ORigin — Displays the UCS icon at the point of origin (0,0,0).

If you want to take a coffee break, this is a good stopping point. In fact, whenever we save or quit a drawing, you can figure that's a safe breaking point. For the rest of the chapter, we are going to use the BASIC drawing as a scratch drawing to see how osnaps work.

Osnaps — Snapping to Entities

Snap is great when what you want to draw fits the snap increments. And, between the various ways for absolute or relative coordinate entry, you can draw almost anything. But when you need to align new points, lines, and other objects with geometric points on entities you've already drawn, you need an easier way.

For example, let's say you want to start a new line at the exact endpoint of one of the lines on the screen and it doesn't fall at a snap point. Or what if you want to pick a tangent point to a curve? Or pick the intersection of two lines that don't fall on a snap point? You need osnap! The OSNAP command lets you precisely edit existing entities or precisely add new entities to existing entities by providing a choice of geometric points that you can *osnap* to.

Using OSNAP to Pinpoint a Crosshairs Location

AutoCAD's OSNAP command and filter modes calculate the *attachment* points you need to make accurate drawings. You tell AutoCAD which osnap attachment mode(s) to use, such as INT for INTersection. Then, when you pick a point or enter coordinates near the geometric point you want, AutoCAD osnaps to the precise attachment point.

In a dense drawing, there might be several suitable attachment points close to your pick point. When osnapping to an INTersection, AutoCAD may indeed find an intersection, but not necessarily the intersection you want. Osnap uses a tolerance or *target* box for identifying the points it considers. This tolerance is controlled by an *aperture* box, an electronic bull's-eye that homes in on osnap points. AutoCAD only considers the osnap for objects that fall within the aperture. Just how large you should set the aperture depends on what you are selecting, how you are zoomed, your display resolution, and your drawing density.

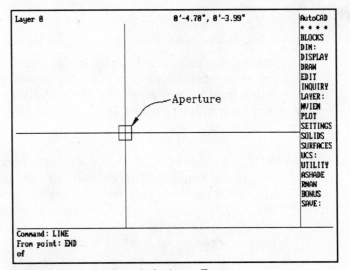

OSNAP Turns the Crosshairs Into a Target

➡ *NOTE: Some display adapters, those that use display list (virtual screen technology) to provide instantaneous pans and zooms, take over control of the aperture setting. See your display adapter manual for information if this is the case.*

The OSNAP Targets illustration on the facing page of this chapter shows you all the filter modes for picking different attachment points on objects. The basic geometric shapes in your BASIC drawing will let you exercise all these osnap options.

Setting the Aperture and Picking a Point

Let's get started by setting the aperture to control the size of the crosshairs bull's-eye that osnap uses to zero in on target objects. You can type the APERTURE command or use the [APERTUR:] selection from the [SETTINGS] screen menu. While you are at it, change your current layer to layer 0, using it as a scratch layer.

Using APERTURE to Set the Osnap Target

Edit an EXISTING drawing named BASIC=IA6BASIC.

Edit an EXISTING drawing named BASIC.

```
Command: APERTURE
Object snap target height (1-50 pixels) <10>: 5
```

A pixel is the smallest *dot* that can be displayed on your screen. Four or six pixels (the default value is ten) give a good target size. The size is measured from the center, so five pixels make a ten-pixel high aperture box. Try a few different values to see how comfortable you feel with larger and smaller apertures.

➡ *NOTE: A small aperture size finds points faster and more accurately in crowded drawings, but the crosshairs are harder to line up. A large aperture is easy to line up, but is slower and less accurate in a crowded drawing. If you have 1024 x 768 or greater screen resolution, you may want to set the aperture size to eight or ten instead of the five specified in the exercise above.*

Overrides vs. Running Mode

You can use osnaps as single pick *override* filters, or set a *running* osnap mode that remains in effect until you are prompted for object selection or you turn it off. You select osnaps as *overrides* (which interrupt the current running mode) from the [Assist] pull-down menu, or the [* * * *] item that appears near the top of the screen menu. You can find the OSNAP command on the [Assist] pull-down or the [SETTINGS] screen menu. The osnap options are the same for both interrupts and running modes.

```
Assist  Draw  Modify  Display  Settings  Options  Utility  File  Solids
Help!                                                              HELP
                                                                  CENter
Cancel                                                            ENDpoint
                                                                  INSert
Osnap: <node>                                                     INTersec
CENter                                                            MIDpoint
ENDpoint                                                          NEArest
INSert                                                            NODe
INTersection                                                      PERpend
MIDpoint                                                          QUAdrant
NEArest                                                           QUICK,
NODe                                                              TANgent
PERpendicular                                                     NONE
QUAdrant                                                          CANCEL:
Quick,<node>                                                      U:
TANgent                                                           REDO:
NONE                                                              REDRAW:
                                                                  SETVAR:
FILTERS      >                                                      LAST


Command:
Command:
Command:
```

[Assist] and [* * *] Osnap Menus*

➡ *TIP: If you type the osnap modifiers, you just type the first word or first three or four characters like ENDPoint or PERpendicular. When using ENDPoint, get in the habit of typing ENDP, not END, to avoid accidentally ENDing your drawing.*

Using OSNAP as a Single Pick Filter

To learn how overrides work, use NODe and ENDPoint to draw a line from the point entity (your first point) in the triangle to the corner of the triangle. NODe osnaps to a point entity, not the triangle's geometric node. The resulting drawing will look like the OSNAP NODe and ENDPoint illustrations. Pick the osnap options from the [Assist] pull-down menu, tablet menu, [* * * *] screen menu, or type them at the keyboard.

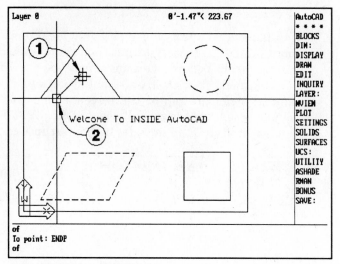

OSNAP NODe and ENDPoint

Using OSNAP NODe and ENDPoint

Command: **SNAP**	Turn snap off.
Command: **LINE**	
From point: **NOD**	Type NOD for node.
of	Pick point ① near point entity in triangle.
To point: **ENDP**	Type ENDP for endpoint.
of	Pick point ② near corner of triangle.
To point: **<RETURN>**	

Congratulations! You've successfully osnapped.

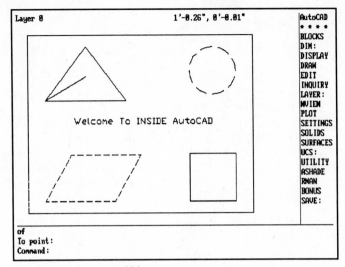

Completed Osnapped Line

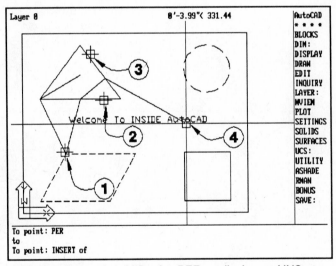

OSNAP INTersection, MIDpoint, PERpendicular, and INSert

Continue the exercise to see how the remaining osnaps work.

Completing the OSNAP Options

```
Command: LINE
From point: @          Starts line from last point.
To point: INT          Type INT for intersection.
of                     Now pick ① near intersection of parallelogram.
To point: MID          Type MID for midpoint.
of                     Pick ② or anywhere on base line of triangle.
To point: PER          Type PER for perpendicular.
of                     Pick ③ or anywhere on right side of triangle.
Select: [****] [INSert] Try the screen menu of OSNAPs.
To point: INSERT of    Sets mode and the menu changes back.
                       Pick ④ or anywhere on the text.
```

See the illustration below for the following points.

```
To point: TAN          Type TAN for tangent.
of                     Pick ⑤ on upper left side of circle.
To point: CEN          Type CEN for center.
of                     Pick ⑥ or anywhere on circle.
To point: QUA          Type QUA for quadrant.
of                     Pick ⑦ near bottom of circle.
To point: NEA          Type NEA for near.
of                     Pick ⑧ or anywhere on line from text to circle.
To point: <RETURN>
```

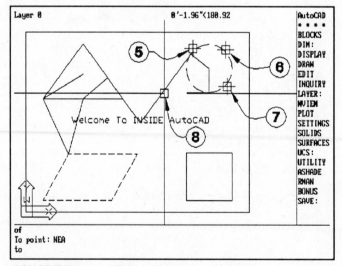

OSNAP TANgent, CENter, QUAdrant, and NEAr

Your drawing should look like the Completed Osnaps illustration.

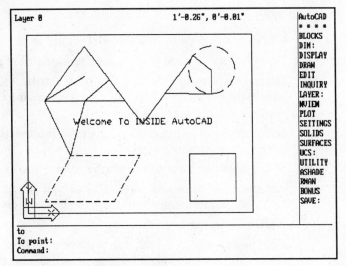

```
Layer 0                        1'-0.26", 0'-0.01"      AutoCAD
                                                       * * * *
                                                       BLOCKS
                                                       DIM:
                                                       DISPLAY
                                                       DRAW
                                                       EDIT
                                                       INQUIRY
                                                       LAYER:
                                                       MVIEW
                                                       PLOT
          Welcome To INSIDE AutoCAD                    SETTINGS
                                                       SOLIDS
                                                       SURFACES
                                                       UCS:
                                                       UTILITY
                                                       ASHADE
                                                       RMAN
                                                       BONUS
                                                       SAVE:

to
To point:
Command:
```

Completed Osnaps

Using QUIck to Optimize OSNAP

AutoCAD goes through a lot of work trying to find the correct object to osnap to when you are using an OSNAP command. In fact, AutoCAD searches every object on the screen to find all objects crossing the aperture box. Then it calculates potential points for all of these objects to find the *best* (closest) fit for your osnap request. This can take a bit of time when you have a lot of objects.

You can optimize or shorten the osnap search process by keeping the aperture reasonably small to keep extraneous objects out of the target. Or you can use the QUIck osnap option. QUIck lets AutoCAD take the most recently created object that meets your osnap criteria instead of doing an exhaustive search and comparison to find the closest. You invoke QUIck by using it as a prefix for other osnap option(s), like QUI,INT for a quick intersection.

QUIck may sometimes let you down if the first fit that AutoCAD finds is not the one you want. In that case, simply cancel what you are doing and start the osnap process again without the quick modifier. Here is the complete osnap options list, including the QUIck modifier.

OSNAP Options

CENter — Snaps to the center of an arc or circle.

ENDPoint — Snaps to the nearest endpoint of a line or arc.

INSert — Snaps to the origin of text, attributes and symbols (block or shape) that have been inserted into the drawing file. More about blocks, shapes, and attributes later.

INTersection — Snaps to the nearest intersection of any combination of two lines, arcs or circles.

MIDpoint — Snaps to the midpoint of a line or arc.

NEArest — Snaps to the nearest point on an entity. This will generally be an endpoint, tangent, or a perpendicular point.

NODe — Snaps to a point entity.

PERpendicular — Snaps to a point on a line, arc, or circle that, for the picked entity, would form a perpendicular (normal) line from the last point to the picked entity. The resulting point need not even be on the entity.

TANgent — Snaps to a point on an arc or circle that forms a tangent to the picked arc or circle from the last point.

QUAdrant — Snaps to the closest 0-, 90-, 180-, or 270-degree point on an arc or circle.

QUIck — Forces all other osnap options to quickly find the first potential target, not necessarily the closest. QUIck finds the potential point that is on the most *recent* qualified object in the target box.

NONe — Removes or overrides any running osnap.

➡ *NOTE: In the above list, line and arc don't refer to only line and arc entities, but include each edge or segment of solid, trace, 3Dface, viewport, polygon mesh, or polyline entities. Polylines are treated as if they have zero width. Some of these entities may not be familiar to you, but we'll cover them in later chapters.*

In the exercises, you used OSNAP as an override in the middle of the line command to fine tune your line endpoints. This override mode temporarily sets up an osnap aperture condition to complete a task at hand. Often, you'll repeatedly use the same mode or combination of modes so AutoCAD lets you set running modes.

Using a Running Mode Osnap

Setting up osnap conditions to be in effect until you change them is called a *running mode*. You set a running mode with the OSNAP command. Running mode osnaps remain in effect until you replace them with another running mode setting or temporarily override them. Unlike SNAP, GRID, and ORTHO, the OSNAP command is not transparent, but, fortunately, overrides are. Use the NONe override to temporarily suppress a running mode.

➥ *NOTE: If a running osnap is on, the crosshairs will have a bull's-eye aperture during your point entry and object selection.*

Try putting a diamond in the square using a running osnap mode.

Using a Running Osnap to Put a Diamond in a Square

```
Command: OSNAP
Object snap modes: MID          Type MID for midpoint.

Command: LINE
From point:                     Pick point ① on the top line.
To point:                       Pick point ② on the right line.
To point:                       Pick point ③ on the bottom line.
To point:                       Pick point ④ on the left line.
To point:                       Pick point ⑤ on the top line.
To point: <RETURN>
```

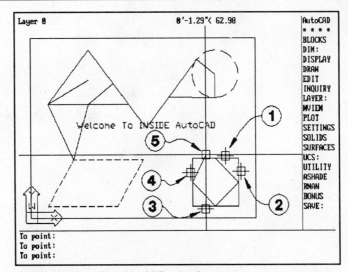

Drawing With a Running MIDpoint Osnap

You can specify two or more modes at once and AutoCAD will find the calculated point of whichever is the closest to the crosshairs. Specify multiple modes by separating them with commas, like END,MID,CEN.

➡ *TIP: INT,END,MID will cover most cases.*

Use the override mode whenever the need arises. Set up a running osnap when you know that you will be repeatedly using the same osnap mode(s).

REDRAW and BLIPMODE for a Clean Screen

As you worked through the osnap exercises, you probably noticed that when you enter a point on the screen (either with a pointer or keyboard entry), AutoCAD places a small cross (blip) on the screen. As you draw, filling up the screen area with real drawing entities (like lines and circles), you also get a screenful of clutter from construction markers. A few blips are great for keeping an eye on where you've been (or might want to go again), but they are a distraction when they accumulate. You will also find as you draw, erase, and move entities, that pieces of lines and entities seem to disappear. Usually, they're still there, but when you erase or move an entity that overlaps another, it leaves a gap in the underlying entity's screen representation.

Use the REDRAW command to clean up the screen, redraw underlying entities and get rid of blips. Let's try it.

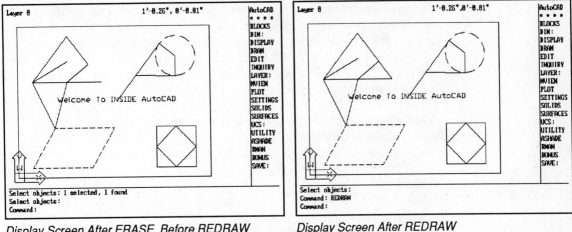

Display Screen After ERASE, Before REDRAW   Display Screen After REDRAW

Using REDRAW to Clear Up the Screen

```
Command: ERASE
Select objects:
Select objects: <RETURN>
```
Pick point on line from triangle to the center of text.
It's gone. So is part of the triangle — or is it?

```
Command: REDRAW
```
The screen redraws, the blips are gone and the triangle's okay.

```
Command: QUIT
```
You don't need to save this drawing.

➡ *TIP: If the grid is visible, you can do a redraw without typing or picking the command. Toggling grid twice with <^G> or <F7> causes a redraw. You also can issue a transparent redraw with 'REDRAW.*

If you find you just don't need blips, you can use the BLIPMODE command to suppress construction markers. You can keep AutoCAD from drawing these temporary markers by typing BLIPMODE OFF or selecting [BLIPS:] from the [SETTINGS] screen menu.

Summing Up

You have seen that one of the tricks to accurate drawing is to use relative and polar points, with coords for reference. You use grid to give you a frame of reference and snap to limit your crosshairs and picks to preset increments. If you need to draw at 90-degree increments, toggle ortho on. If you need to align your coordinate system with your drawing, you can change your UCS. Many users find it helpful to jot down notes or make up a checklist to keep track of these display settings.

To construct geometrically accurate objects, use coordinate entry and use osnap for snapping to objects. You can invoke the OSNAP command temporarily as an override to any point-picking command. A running osnap mode sets up a full-time mode and aperture that you can still override. Try to find a good aperture setting to control the reliability and speed of your osnap searches.

Throughout the rest of this book, you will see coordinates given in response to prompts with the exercises. You can type them, or you can pick the coordinates with the pointing device if you are sure the pick is accurate. Remember crosshairs position is only accurate with snap on, or with osnap. Use osnap at every opportunity you can. Your drawing productivity will improve and you can be confident that your work is accurate. Now that you've had a chance to play around with osnaps, you can move on to learning how to get around in AutoCAD.

CHAPTER 4

Getting Around

MAKING A SMALL DISPLAY SCREEN DO THE WORK OF A BIG PIECE OF PAPER

Whether you've set your drawing limits to represent 2 by 3 feet or 2000 by 3000 feet, your display screen is not large enough to give you a one-to-one view of your drawing file. In this chapter, you will learn to use AutoCAD's set of electronic tools to control where you are in your display, where you are going, and how you will get there. Your display becomes a *viewport* into your drawing, zooming in, out, and around. You will learn to use *multiple viewports* to see several parts of your drawing simultaneously, and to scale the viewports to different sizes for eventual plotting.

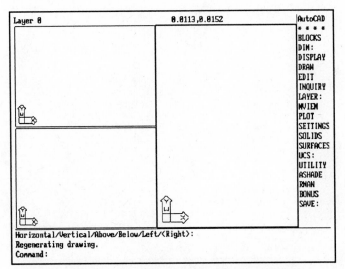

Screen Divided Into Three Viewports

The Benefits of Getting Around

AutoCAD's display controls make your drawing life easier. AutoCAD's basic display controls, like *zoom* and *pan*, function just as they do in photography. The ZOOM command lets you magnify your drawing to do detailed work. PAN lets you slide your drawing from side to side so that you can work on large objects without having to return to a full screen view to find where you are. Simple controls, like *redraw* and *regen*, let you clean up your screen or display the most current view of your drawing.

To make working on your drawings easier, you can open multiple viewports on the screen to display your model at different scales and from different viewpoints. You can also use these viewports to display areas of your model that would normally not be visible on the screen together, such as both ends of a long part. For example, you can see your entire object in a single window while you zoom in to work on a drawing detail in a second window. Or you can keep a parts schedule in one window while you check your drawing annotations in another. You can even set many of AutoCAD's settings, such as snap, grid, and ucsicon (and even layers in Release 11) differently in each viewport. When you save your drawing, your viewport setup is saved with it so you don't have to create the viewports each time.

You will find the view control tools on the [DISPLAY] screen menu and the [Display] pull-down menu.

Display Screen and Pull-Down Menus

Display Control Setup

You don't need an elaborate drawing to get a feel for display controls; the simple geometric shapes in the BASIC drawing you saved in Chapter 3 will work well enough to get you around the display screen. If you are using the IA DISK, you have the BASIC drawing as IA6BASIC.DWG.

AXIS	GRID	SNAP	ORTHO	UCS	UCSICON
Off	On	On	Off	World	On

UNITS	Engineering, 2 decimal places, 2 fractional places for angles, defaults all other settings.
LIMITS	0,0 to 11,8.5

Layer Name	State	Color	Linetype
0	On/Current	7 (white)	CONTINUOUS
CIRCLE	On	3 (green)	DASHED
PARAGRAM	On	5 (blue)	HIDDEN
SQUARE	On	2 (yellow)	CONTINUOUS
TEXT	On	4 (cyan)	CONTINUOUS
TRIANGLE	On	1 (red)	CONTINUOUS

BASIC Drawing Settings

Display Control Setup

Begin a NEW drawing named BASIC=IA6BASIC.

Edit an EXISTING drawing named BASIC from Chapter 3, and make sure the drawing has the settings shown in the BASIC Drawing Settings table.

Your screen should look like the BASIC Drawing illustration.

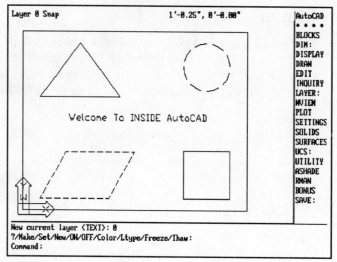

BASIC Drawing

Controlling Screen Display With ZOOM

Suppose you want to look more closely at the triangle on the screen. To do this, you need to *zoom* in on the drawing. The most common way to tell AutoCAD what part of the current screen you want to enlarge is to show a box or *window* around the area of interest. ZOOM Window zooms in on your drawing.

Using ZOOM Window to Look More Closely

Step through a zoom window example. Use the illustration as a guide to picking your window corners. You don't need to pick exact coordinates; just show a rough area you want to see in more detail.

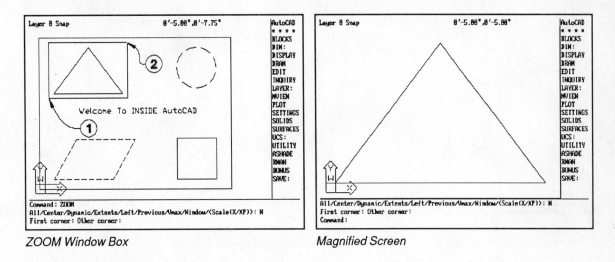

ZOOM Window Box   Magnified Screen

Using ZOOM Window

```
Command: ZOOM
All/Center/Dynamic/Extents/Left/Previous/Vmax/Window/<Scale(X/XP)>: W
First corner:                    Pick point ①.
Other corner:                    Pick point ②.
```

Notice that after you pick the first corner, instead of the normal crosshairs, your cursor changes to a *rubber band* box. As soon as you pick the other corner, AutoCAD repaints the screen with the area you enclosed in the window. The corners that you picked guide AutoCAD in setting up the zoomed-in display. This display will usually not be exactly the same shape as your original window because AutoCAD maintains its X and Y screen ratio regardless of your corner locations.

Try zooming closer to the upper point of the triangle, picking two more window corners, and letting AutoCAD redraw the screen. Use the Second ZOOM Window illustration as your guide.

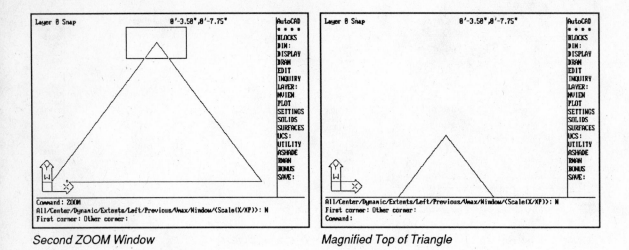

Second ZOOM Window   Magnified Top of Triangle

Picking a ZOOM Window

```
Command: ZOOM                          Zoom to upper point of triangle.
All/Center/Dynamic/Extents/Left/Previous/Vmax/Window/<Scale(X/XP)>: W
First corner:                          Pick the lower left corner.
Other corner:                          Pick the upper right corner.
```

How far can you zoom in? Let's say you drew the entire solar system at full scale — it's about seven billion miles across. If you drew it with enough detail, you could zoom in far enough to read this book on your desk, thanks to AutoCAD's 14 significant digits of precision. Try zooming in on your drawing if you want, before we zoom back out.

Okay, you can get in. How do you get back out? Use ZOOM All.

ZOOM All is the easiest way to get back to the full display of your drawing file.

Using ZOOM All

```
Command: ZOOM
All/Center/Dynamic/Extents/Left/Previous/Vmax/Window/<Scale(X/XP)>: A
Regenerating drawing.
```

Your screen should be back to where you started. When AutoCAD does a ZOOM All, it regenerates and repaints the screen with everything in the drawing file. If you have drawn within your drawing limits, ZOOM All takes you to your limits. If you have exceeded your limits, ZOOM All zooms beyond the limits to display everything in your drawing file.

Other ZOOM Options

ZOOM Window and ZOOM All will get you in and out, but you have several other zoom options at your fingertips. Here's the complete list.

ZOOM Options

All — Zooms out to limits, or everything in the drawing file, whichever is greater. ZOOM All always regenerates the drawing, sometimes twice.

Center — Magnifies the screen around a center point with a given height or magnification factor.

Dynamic — Temporarily displays the whole drawing (or as much as it can without a regen), letting you graphically select any portion of the drawing as your next screen view.

Extents — Gives the tightest possible view of everything in the drawing file.

Left — Sets a new lower left corner and zooms to a height or by magnification factor.

Previous — Restores the last zoom setting. Remembers up to ten previous magnifications.

Vmax — Zooms out as far as possible without causing a regen. (Not in Release 10.)

Window — Uses a rectangular window to select a drawing area to display on the screen.

<Scale(X/XP)> — Uses a numeric zoom factor to determine magnification. A magnification factor of 1 displays a view of the drawing limits. A value less than 1 zooms out from the limits, and greater than 1 zooms in. The magnification X modifier gives zooms relative to your current view. For example, 2X gives a display twice as large as the last display. The XP modifier (not in Release 10) scales the view relative to paper space. Paper space is covered in detail later in this chapter.

➥ *NOTE: Zooms will occasionally require a drawing regeneration. ZOOM All and Extents always cause a drawing regeneration. If you can use a ZOOM Previous or ZOOM Vmax, you will avoid the regeneration.*

Keeping Track of Zoom Displays

Every time you zoom in or out, AutoCAD keeps track of the previous display. In fact, AutoCAD remembers up to ten zooms. Try the Left and Center options, then use Previous to step back out.

Using ZOOM Left, Center, and Previous

```
Command: ZOOM                                Use the Left option to zoom an area surrounding the text.
All/Center/Dynamic/Extents/Left/Previous/Vmax/Window/<Scale(X/XP)>: L
Lower left corner point:                     Pick absolute point 2.50,2.00.
Magnification or Height <0'-8.50">: 4.5
```

```
Command: ZOOM                                Zoom Center on the W in Welcome.
All/Center/Dynamic/Extents/Left/Previous/Vmax/Window/<Scale(X/XP)>: C
Center point:                                Pick a point on the W.
Magnification or Height <0'-4.50">: .5
```

```
Command: ZOOM                                Zoom Previous to return to the complete text.
All/Center/Dynamic/Extents/Left/Previous/Vmax/Window/<Scale(X/XP)>: P
Command: ZOOM                                Use Previous again to return to the start.
All/Center/Dynamic/Extents/Left/Previous/Vmax/Window/<Scale(X/XP)>: P
```

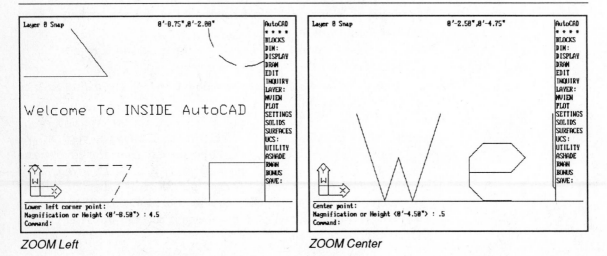

ZOOM Left   ZOOM Center

If all went well, you should end up where you started. Your screen should show a zoomed-out view of your drawing.

➥ *NOTE: Previous does not necessarily zoom out. It zooms to the previous zoom view setting.*

You may have noticed a speed difference in zooms that regenerate the screen and those that do not. In a complex drawing, this can be a considerable time difference. To control when it occurs, you need to understand how zoom works.

Zoom, Regen, Redraw and the Virtual Screen

To understand the ZOOM command, you need to understand the relationship of redraw, regen, and the virtual screen. When you load a new drawing or use the REGEN command, AutoCAD recalculates the current view to its full 14 places of precision. It calculates this as if it were a 32,000 x 32,000 pixel display screen, the *virtual screen*. This is a *regen*. Then it translates this calculated image to your actual display screen and *redraws* the screen. AutoCAD can do a redraw very quickly, several times as quickly as a regen. This translation is all that occurs when you use the REDRAW command, toggle the grid, turn on layers, or change other settings that cause a redraw.

Many zooms require only a redraw, not a regen. As long as you do not zoom outside of the current virtual screen, or zoom so far into tiny detail that AutoCAD can't accurately translate from the virtual screen, it won't regenerate. When a zoom occurs without a regen, it occurs at redraw speed.

The key to fast zooming is to avoid regens. Zooming in is usually no problem, but the easiest way to control this when zooming out is to use ZOOM Dynamic.

ZOOM Dynamic Gives You More Display Control

You have used the basic two-step process of zooming in on your drawing with a window and zooming back out with a ZOOM All. But what if you want to magnify a small portion of your drawing while you are already zoomed in to a different section? There is another option called ZOOM Dynamic that lets you control and display your zoom window in a single step without having to do a ZOOM All.

There are really three display subsets. When you work with a dynamic zoom, these subsets are shown on your screen. Here are the display sets:

- The drawing extents. Everything in the drawing file.

- Generated area. A portion (up to all) of the drawing file that AutoCAD has regenerated. This is the virtual screen.

■ The current screen view. A portion (up to all) of the generated data that currently appears on the screen.

When you select a dynamic zoom, you can see all three of these areas graphically on the screen before making a decision on what your next screen view will be.

Take a look at the ZOOM Dynamic Control Screen illustration. You see four rectangular areas outlined on the diagram. The first three show the entire drawing extents (white or black), the currently generated virtual screen (four red corners), and the current view screen (green or magenta). (The extents will be the limits unless you have drawn beyond the limits.)

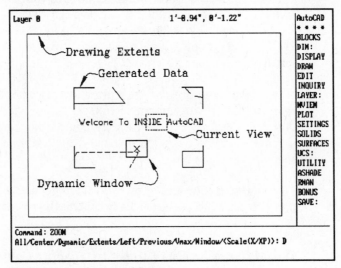

ZOOM Dynamic Control Screen

The fourth rectangular area is a dynamic window (white or black) that moves with your pointer. Use this dynamic window to select the next screen view you want to see.

If you select your next screen view from within the area bounded by the *generated* data, the next screen view will appear on the screen in redraw speed. If you select your next screen view to include data from outside the currently generated data, your zoom will require a regeneration of the entire drawing file as AutoCAD calculates the part of the drawing file you want to see in your next view. When you move the pointer outside the generated drawing file area, a little hourglass appears on the lower left part of the screen indicating that regeneration will occur. If you zoom in beyond about 50X, AutoCAD must regenerate the drawing.

Try a ZOOM Dynamic. First zoom All and then zoom in to magnify your drawing three times. This ensures we all start out the same. Then call up the ZOOM Dynamic display.

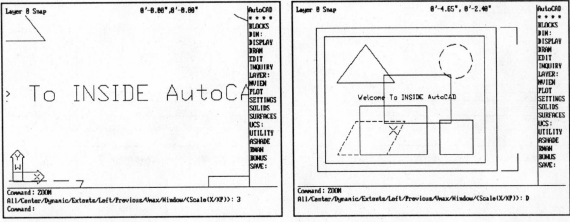

Screen Magnified Three Times   Beginning of ZOOM Dynamic

Using ZOOM Dynamic

```
Command: ZOOM                    Zoom All.
Command: ZOOM                    Use a scale factor of 3 to magnify display.
All/Center/Dynamic/Extents/Left/Previous/Vmax/Window/<Scale(X/XP)>: 3

Command: ZOOM                    Now get the dynamic zoom display on the screen.
All/Center/Dynamic/Extents/Left/Previous/Vmax/Window/<Scale(X/XP)>: D
```

Your screen should look like the Beginning of ZOOM Dynamic illustration. When you move your pointer around, it *drags* the dynamic viewing window around the screen as if it were held by the X handle in the middle of the window. Your pointer also controls the size of the window. When you press your pointer button, you get an arrow that controls the size of your window. Then, when you move the arrow to the right, you make the window larger. Left makes it smaller.

When the dynamic window is the size you want, press the pointer button again to lock in the size. You can toggle between controlling the dynamic window size and its location with the pointer button.

Once you have windowed the next viewing screen that you want, press the <RETURN> key while holding the dynamic viewing window in place to select it. AutoCAD will zoom. Use the illustrations as a guide in the exercise sequence.

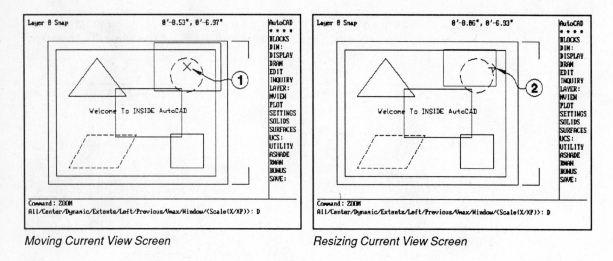

Moving Current View Screen

Resizing Current View Screen

Controlling a ZOOM Dynamic

`All/Center/Dynamic/Extents/Left/Previous/Vmax/Window/<Scale(X/XP)>:` **D**

Move the dynamic window around with the X handle ①.
Press the pointer button to switch to dynamic window size.

Stretch or shrink the dynamic window by moving horizontally ②.
Press the pointer button to switch to dynamic window location control.

Line up the dynamic viewing window to enclose the circle ③.
Hold the pointer in place and press the <RETURN> key. AutoCAD zooms.

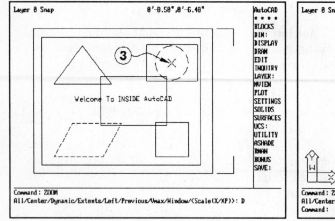

Viewing Window Enclosing the Circle

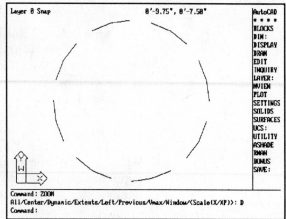

Display After Dynamic Zoom

➡ *NOTE: It is possible to shrink the dynamic window so far that you see only the arrow or X. You will have to enlarge the window with the pointer to regain control.*

➡ *TIP: You can do your own style of dynamic zoom by simply using the normal zoom options and cutting them short. For example, you can start a ZOOM Previous and cut it short with a <^C> as soon as you see enough to decide where to go next. Then follow it with your intended zoom.*

When you are done, try zooming back out with a ZOOM Extents. ZOOM Extents and All both zoom out as far as needed, even beyond the limits, to display everything in the drawing file. Unlike All, which never zooms to a smaller area than the limits, ZOOM Extents zooms to the smallest area possible that will display all entities in the drawing.

Using ZOOM Extents

```
Command: ZOOM                                    ZOOM Extents magnifies screen to edge of border.
All/Center/Dynamic/Extents/Left/Previous/Vmax/Window/<Scale(X/XP)>: E
```

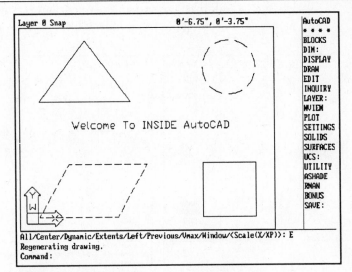

ZOOM Extents

Your screen should look like the ZOOM Extents illustration.

➡ *TIP: Always use a ZOOM Extents just before you end your drawing session. It will act as a check to let you know if you have drawn anything outside your limits. You can cut it short with a <^C>.*

As you may have noticed, you can use ZOOM Dynamic to move your current view from side to side without changing the magnification. This is called *panning*. There is also a PAN command just for panning.

Using PAN to Slide a View

Frequently, you will need to move your drawing sideways (or up, or down). Say you are working on a zoomed-in area and want to see the part of the drawing file that is just a little to the left. What view control do you use? Use PAN. PAN acts just like a camera pan. It lets you move around the drawing file at your current magnification.

To make PAN work, you need to supply AutoCAD with a *displacement*. You define a displacement by specifying two points. These two points determine a vector giving the distance and direction of your pan. When you give two points to identify a displacement, you specify a point where AutoCAD will pick up the drawing (first displacement point) and then specify another point where the drawing will be placed (second displacement point). Your display crosshairs trail a line from the first to the second displacement point, showing you the pan path.

Use PAN to isolate the square in the upper left corner of your screen. When you are done, your screen should look like the View After Pan illustration.

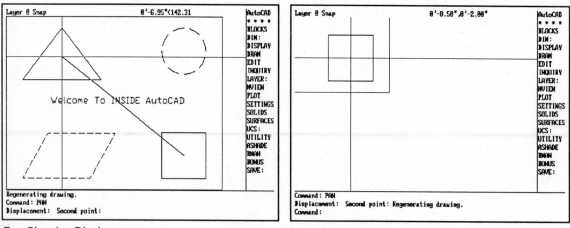

Pan Showing Displacement   View After Pan

Using PAN for Display

```
Command: PAN
Displacement:                          Pick first point in square.
Second point:                          Pick second point in triangle.
```

➡ *NOTE: Using ZOOM Dynamic with a constant window size functions like the PAN command. You can also do limited panning with the Center and Left zoom options by defaulting the height.*

Using VIEW to Name and Save Working Displays

As you work on a drawing, you will find that your zooms and pans frequently return to the same few drawing views. It would certainly save time if you could save and recall your zooms and pans.

Suppose that you are going to concentrate your work on the square for the next few hours. Periodically, you will want to zoom out to work in other areas, but most of the time you will be zoomed in to the square. Rather than having to show a window around the square every time you want to zoom to this area, you can store this window, give it a name, and call it up whenever you need it.

A stored window is called a *named view*. To store a window, use the VIEW command to name and store it. You can select [VIEW:] from the [DISPLAY] screen menu, or you can type it at the keyboard. Here's an exercise to test AutoCAD's VIEW command and to save SQUARE as a named view.

Using VIEW to Save and Restore a View

```
Command: ZOOM                          Zoom to an area just surrounding the square.

Command: VIEW
?/Delete/Restore/Save/Window: S
View name to save: SQUARE

Command: ZOOM                          Zoom All to test the view.

Command: VIEW                          Now restore it.
?/Delete/Restore/Save/Window: R
View name to restore: SQUARE
```

When you are done, your display should show the restored square.

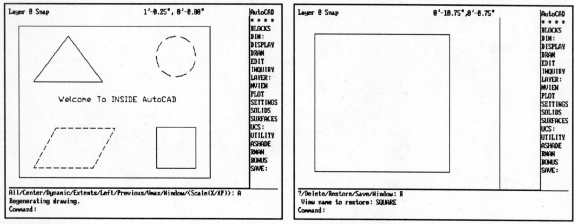

Current Display   Saved and Restored View Named SQUARE

➥ *TIP: Useful named views would be L for Limits or A for All. Both are quick and easy to type and can be used instead of ZOOM All to avoid regens. Use a view called PLOT for consistency in plotting.*

The VIEW command has five options.

VIEW Options

? — Displays a list of all named views, and whether they exist in paper space (P) or model space (M). Paper space and model space are covered later in this chapter.

Save — Lets you name the current view and stores its size and center point.

Restore — Redisplays the named view that you specify.

Delete — Prompts you for the name of a view to delete from the library of named views.

Window — Lets you name and save a view that you specify with a window (not necessarily the current display).

➥ *NOTE: You can rename an existing view with the RENAME command.*

➥ *TIP: If you zoom Center .8X, then save the view as A or ALL, you will give yourself a margin of safety in avoiding zoom and pan regenerations. Then use VIEW Restore All instead of ZOOM All.*

Keeping the Right Image Generated

As your drawing files become larger, you will need to control the screen size and resolution of your drawing. This means that you have to be conscious of just how much of your drawing you want AutoCAD to keep active at any one time. In using dynamic zooms, you have seen that AutoCAD keeps three different sets of drawing data active: the drawing extents, generated data, and the screen view.

When your drawing file is small and uncomplicated, all these subsets are usually one and the same. But as your drawing file gets larger, only portions of the file are generated, and it is more efficient to show only portions of your drawing on the screen. Going from one screen view to another within the generated portion of the drawing file with a PAN or ZOOM is usually done with redraw (fast) speed. However, calling up a screen view that contains non-generated data requires a regen of a different set of data and takes more time.

VIEWRES Controls Smooth Curves and Regeneration

The AutoCAD VIEWRES (VIEW RESolution) command controls the speed of your zooms and regenerations in two ways. First, it turns *fast zoom* on and off. Fast zoom means that AutoCAD maintains a large virtual screen so it can do most pans and zooms at redraw speed. If fast zoom is off, all pans and zooms cause a regen. Second, it determines how fine to generate curves. When circles or arcs are tiny, AutoCAD needs only a few straight lines on the screen to fool your eye into seeing smooth curves. When arcs are larger, AutoCAD needs more segments (or vectors) to make a smooth arc. The VIEWRES circle zoom percent tells AutoCAD how smooth you want your curves, and AutoCAD determines how many segments are needed to draw what is to be shown on the screen.

Try altering the smoothness of the circle on the screen by generating fewer segments. To see the effect, you need to change the circle's layer to a continuous linetype.

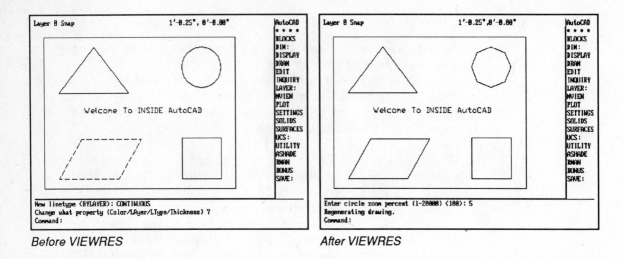

Before VIEWRES   After VIEWRES

Using VIEWRES to Control Resolutions

Command: **ZOOM**   Zoom All.
Command: **CHPROP**   Change the circle's linetype to continuous.

Command: **VIEWRES**
Do you want fast zooms? <Y>: **<RETURN>**
Enter circle zoom percent (1-20000) <100>: **5**
Regenerating drawing.

Command: **VIEWRES**   Set zoom percent back to 100.

The trade-off for fast zoom is that when a regen is required, it will take longer than if fast zoom is off, because it regenerates a larger area.

➥ *NOTE: If you turn fast zoom off, ZOOM Dynamic and all other pans and zooms will always cause a drawing regeneration. Although turning fast zoom off is rarely advisable, it may be more efficient when zooming large text-filled drawings or doing work that often causes regens even if fast zoom is on. Also, if set to a high number, VIEWRES may cause slow regenerations.*

Controlling Data Generation With REGEN and REGENAUTO

You've seen that the VIEWRES command and some zooms cause AutoCAD to regenerate the drawing. When the drawing file is full of many entities, particularly text, arcs, and circles, this regeneration will take a long time.

You can force a regeneration of the screen and drawing file with the REGEN command. You might choose to do so to make AutoCAD recalculate the virtual screen at a particular current view so that your dynamic zoom screen just shows the portion of the drawing that you are interested in. Try a regeneration now by typing REGEN or selecting it from the [DISPLAY] menu.

Using REGEN to Regenerate a Drawing

```
Command: REGEN
Regenerating drawing.
```

➡ *TIP: Freezing layers keeps extraneous data from being regenerated. Thaw the layers when you need them.*

Using REGENAUTO to Control AutoCAD's Regeneration

When you zoom, pan, or view, you usually want AutoCAD to make sure that everything in the drawing file is represented accurately on the screen. However, since regeneration in large drawings may take a long time, you may not want AutoCAD to regenerate when you are busy drawing or editing.

You can control when AutoCAD regenerates the drawing with the REGENAUTO command. When REGENAUTO is off, AutoCAD avoids regeneration unless absolutely necessary. When necessary, AutoCAD will first stop and ask if you want to regenerate. However, the REGEN command always overrides REGENAUTO and forces a regeneration.

The disadvantage to turning REGENAUTO off is that reset linetype scales, redefined symbols, and changed text styles won't automatically display with their new settings until you regenerate. Once you are comfortable with these items in AutoCAD, this is a small penalty to pay for the time savings of keeping REGENAUTO turned off in complex drawings.

➡ *NOTE: QTEXT is a command that displays text on the screen as only a box outline so that the screen will regenerate quickly. We will show you how QTEXT works in the chapter on text entities.*

Transparent PAN, ZOOM, and VIEW

You can use the PAN, ZOOM, and VIEW commands, as well as REDRAW, while you are in the middle of most other AutoCAD commands. These *transparent* commands are triggered by a leading apostrophe (′). Recall that you can get transparent ′HELP the same way.

Draw a line and try a transparent ′VIEW and ′ZOOM. Look for the double angle bracket at the command prompt line. The double bracket shows that the current command is suspended.

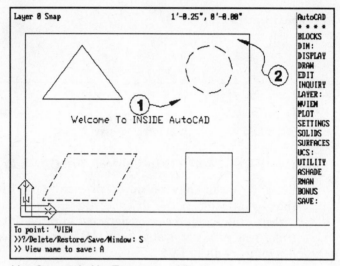

Layer 0 Snap   1'-0.25", 0'-0.00"

Welcome To INSIDE AutoCAD

AutoCAD
* * * *
BLOCKS
DIM:
DISPLAY
DRAW
EDIT
INQUIRY
LAYER:
MVIEW
PLOT
SETTINGS
SOLIDS
SURFACES
UCS:
UTILITY
ASHADE
RMAN
BONUS
SAVE:

To point: 'VIEW
>>?/Delete/Restore/Save/Window: S
>> View name to save: A

Line Suspended by Transparent View

Using Transparent VIEW and ZOOM

Command: **ZOOM**   Zoom All.

Command: **LINE**   Pick any point in the triangle.

To point: **′VIEW**   Type a leading apostrophe for transparency.
                                                 Note the >> prompt indicating that another
                                                 command is suspended.

>>?/Delete/Restore/Save/Window: **S**
>>View name to save: **A**   Saves the current view as A for All.
Resuming LINE command.

To point: **′ZOOM**   Transparently window the circle.
>>Center/Dynamic/Left/Previous/Vmax/Window/<Scale(X/XP)>: **W**
>>First corner: Pick first corner point ①.
>>Other corner: Pick second corner point ②.
Resuming LINE command.

To point: Pick any point within the circle.
To point: **′VIEW**   Restore the view A for All.

```
>>?/Delete/Restore/Save/Window: R
>>View name to restore: A                    Back to the whole view, without a regen.
Resuming LINE command.

To point: <RETURN>

Command: QUIT                                Leave the drawing unchanged.
```

So far, all the display controls you've used have looked in on your drawing with a single viewing screen or viewport. Next, we'll see how you can create multiple views of your drawing and display them on the screen simultaneously. In effect, you divide your screen into windows called *viewports* and display different views of your drawing in each of them.

Displaying More Than One View at a Time

You've been working in a viewport all along — a single viewport that covers the entire drawing area of your screen. Multiple viewports work just as if you divided your drawing screen into rectangles, making several different drawing areas instead of one. You can have up to 16 viewports visible (and create as many as you want) at one time. (In Release 10, you are limited to four viewports created and displayed on DOS machines, or 16 on UNIX and other machines.) You still retain your screen and pull-down menus and command prompts area.

You can work in *only* one viewport at a time. This is called the *current* viewport. You set the current viewport by clicking on it with your pointer. When a viewport is current, its border will be thicker than the others. When you work within a viewport, use your normal display controls just as if you were working with a single screen. You can zoom and pan, set a grid and snap, and those settings are retained for that viewport. The key point, however, is that the images shown in multiple viewports are multiple images of the same data. You're not duplicating your drawing — just putting its image in different viewports.

Because the viewports look onto the same *model* or drawing, you *can* draw from viewport to viewport. You can start a line in one viewport, click to set another viewport current, and then complete the line. AutoCAD will rubber-band your line segment across the viewports.

Multiple viewports are essential in 3D modeling to give you concurrent views of your model from different viewpoints. For example, you can display plan, elevation, and isometric views of your model on the same screen. Viewports also offer advantages over a single view display in some common 2D drafting situations. When you are faced with the problem of detailing different areas of a large drawing or you need to keep one area of your drawing (like a title block or bill of materials) in constant view, use viewports to divide your screen.

There are two types of viewports available in AutoCAD — *tiled* viewports and untiled (*paper space*) viewports (which are actually entities). (Release 10 is limited to tiled viewports.) Since untiled viewports offer several advantages over tiled viewports, let's first take a look at the environment in which untiled viewports work. It's called paper space.

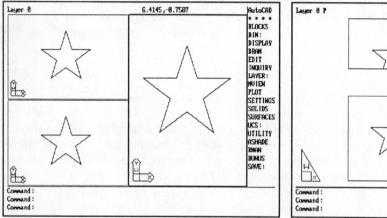

Tiled Viewports

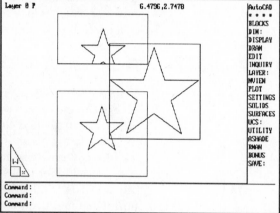

Untiled Paper Space Viewports

Understanding and Using Paper Space and Model Space

Model space is the drawing environment that exists *in* any viewport, whether it is a single full-screen viewport, one of several tiled viewports, or a viewport entity in paper space. Model space was the only drawing environment that was available for drawing in AutoCAD Release 10. Release 11 adds a new environment called *paper space*. Think of paper space as an infinitely large sheet of paper upon which you can arrange viewports that look onto your model. While model space is a three-dimensional environment, paper space is a two-dimensional environment for arranging views of your model for drawing within or plotting.

Whether you are creating two-dimensional or three-dimensional models, you will do most of your drawing in model space. You'll draw in paper space when you add standard items like title blocks and sheet borders and some types of dimensioning or annotation. Paper space dimensioning and annotation is essential in 3D work.

There is no way to view paper space other than in plan view, which reinforces the two-dimensional nature of paper space. You can actually draw 3D objects in paper space, but with no way to view them, it makes little sense to do so.

Working in Paper Space

Along with paper space comes a new type of viewport — paper space viewports. Paper space viewports can be any size; they do not have to touch (be tiled), and they can even overlap one another. Think of viewports as glass windows into your drawing that can either be opened or closed. If you are in paper space, the window is closed and you can't reach through it to make changes to the entities behind it. But you can move and edit the window frame itself. When you are in model space, the current viewport window is open and you can get at the entities shown inside to edit them or draw more. But you can no longer make changes to the window frame — just to the entities inside. And, you can't have more than one of those windows open (current) at a time.

You can draw anything in paper space that you can draw in model space, except that 3D objects will look flat. Paper space is like another semi-independent drawing that overlays your entire group of viewports. What you draw in paperspace appears *over*, but not *in*, your viewports. You can osnap from paper space to the model-space contents of the underlying viewports, but you cannot osnap from model space to paper space.

When you are working in paper space, viewports are like any other entity. For example, you can edit the boundary of the viewport itself. Indirectly, that can affect the view of the model shown in the viewport. If you make the paper space viewport larger by stretching it, you might see more of the model. If you make the paper space viewport smaller, some of the model might disappear behind the boundary of the viewport. You can use the MOVE command to grab a viewport and move it around on the screen without affecting other viewports. You can change the color of a viewport's boundary box using CHPROP, and you can erase a viewport just like any other AutoCAD entity. But all this happens in paper space.

When you drop back into model space, you can select individual viewports and edit individual entities that show up in those viewports. But, you can't edit the viewport frame's size, color, or other attributes.

Paper Space Viewports vs. Tiled Viewports

So what's so special about paper space viewports? You can work on simultaneous multiple views of your drawing in tiled viewports. But there are restrictions on how you can size tiled viewports, while you can resize and place paper space viewports however you like. Paper space viewports also allow you to selectively control layers by viewport, rather than globally in all tiled viewports. This lets you freeze a layer in one viewport while leaving it thawed in another.

Because paper space viewports let you do everything that tiled viewports do, and then some, we recommend going directly to paper space.

The Command Set for Paper Space Viewports

We'll use three primary commands and one system variable to enter and use viewports in paper space. The TILEMODE system variable must be set to 0 (off) to take you into paper space. Then use the MVIEW command to create viewports. To enter model space so you can work within these viewports, use the MVIEW command. And, to return to paper space to edit viewports, add title blocks or annotation, or set up for plotting, use the PSPACE command.

Entering Paper Space and Creating Viewports

When you begin a drawing in AutoCAD, the display shows a single viewport by default, unless you are using a prototype drawing that has been set up for multiple viewports. The system variable TILEMODE is set to 1 (on) by default, which gives you only tiled viewports. To enter paper space, TILEMODE must be set to 0. If you are in paper space, setting TILEMODE back to 1 will place you back in model space with one or more tiled viewports.

To switch to paper space, select the [Mview] option from the [Display] pull-down menu. Selecting [Mview] changes from the [Display] pull-down menu to the [Mview] pull-down menu. It also sets TILEMODE to 0 (meaning paper space viewports), and executes the MVIEW command. You can also access the MVIEW command from the [DISPLAY] screen menu or type it from the command line.

Let's take a look at an example using the BASIC drawing from Chapter 3 or IA6BASIC.DWG from the IA DISK. We'll enter paper space, create a few paper space viewports, then draw some lines and experiment with object selection in paper space.

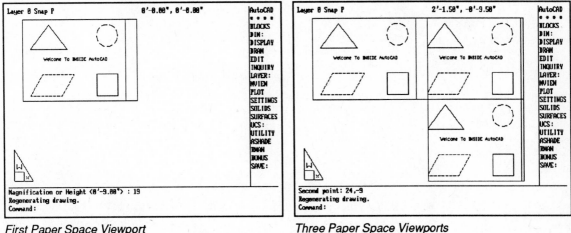

First Paper Space Viewport   Three Paper Space Viewports

Creating Viewports in Paper Space

Begin a NEW drawing again named BASIC=IA6BASIC.

Edit an EXISTING drawing named BASIC, and make sure the drawing
has the settings shown in the BASIC table near the start of this chapter.

```
Command: TILEMODE          (TILEMODE is set automatically when you select [Mview]).
New value for TILEMODE <1>: 0
Entering Paper space.  Use MVIEW to insert Model space viewports.
Regenerating drawing.
```

The drawing has disappeared because there are no paper space viewports to display it in yet.

```
Command: MVIEW             Fit a single viewport to the full screen.
ON/OFF/Hideplot/Fit/2/3/4/Restore/<First Point>: F
```

> The screen looks like before you started, except for a triangular *paper
> space icon*, a P on the status line, and a border around the single
> viewport.

```
Command: ZOOM              Zoom Center with center point 12,0 and height 19.
                           You see the viewport like a window surrounded by paper space, as
                           illustrated.
```

```
Command: MVIEW             Let's make some more viewports, as shown in the illustration.
ON/OFF/Hideplot/Fit/2/3/4/Restore/<First Point>: 2
Horizontal/<Vertical>: H
Fit/<First Point>: INT
of
                           Pick upper right corner of viewport.
```

```
Second point: 24,-9
Regenerating drawing.
```

```
Command: SAVE                   Save the drawing.
```

```
Command: LINE                   Draw a few lines across the screen. They cut right across viewports.
```

```
Command: ERASE
Select objects:                 Select the lines.
Select objects:                 Try to select the circle or text. You can't.
Select objects: <RETURN>
```

➡ *NOTE: You don't have to be in paper space to use MVIEW. If you are in model space, AutoCAD temporarily switches to paper space to create the viewports.*

The MVIEW command gives you other options for creating and controlling viewports in paper space. Here is a listing of them.

MVIEW Options

<First Point> — The default option lets you create a viewport using two points. You pick two points to define a rectangular boundary, and the viewport is created to fill that area.

ON — Turns on the model view inside the viewport. When on, the default, AutoCAD displays the model and includes the viewport when it regenerates.

OFF — Turns off the model view inside the viewport. When the viewport is off, you can move, resize, and otherwise edit the viewport in paper space without having the model view visible inside the viewport. This saves time when AutoCAD regenerates.

Hideplot — Turning Hideplot on in a viewport causes a hidden-line removal to occur on that viewport when it is plotted from paper space. This doesn't change the way the model is displayed in the viewport.

Fit — Creates a single viewport to fill the display, however large it happens to be.

2 — Allows you to create two viewports within a rectangular area you specify, either horizontal (one above the other), or vertical (side by side).

3 — Allows you to create three viewports in a rectangular area, making them side by side, stacked on top of each other, or with a larger viewport above, below, to the left, or to the right of two smaller ones.

4 — Creates four viewports in a rectangular area, either by specifying the area, or fitting the four viewports to the display.

Restore — Translates a tiled viewport configuration created with the VPORTS command into individual paper space viewports.

➡ *NOTE: The viewports created with the Fit option will appear tiled, but you can move them apart and resize them using commands such as STRETCH and MOVE.*

➡ *NOTE: The MVSETUP bonus program included with AutoCAD can set up multiple viewports, adjust limits, and insert a title block. It can be accessed from the [BONUS] screen menu if you select [BONUS] [next] and [MVSETUP].*

Well, now you have multiple viewports. What do you do with them?

Drawing in Multiple Viewports

We'll try a simple exercise, entering model space and setting the upper left viewport current. Then we'll zoom to get a better view of the triangle and draw a line from the center of the triangle to the circle on the right. We'll traverse the rest of the drawing, drawing to the approximate center points of the square and parallelogram, and close the line up to the triangle.

If you have Release 10, you can still do this exercise. Just do the exercises in the Using Tiled Viewports section at the end of this chapter, then come back and try this. Your screen won't quite match the illustrations, but will be similar.

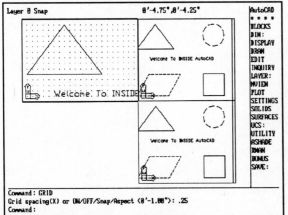

Left Viewport Zoomed, With Small Grid

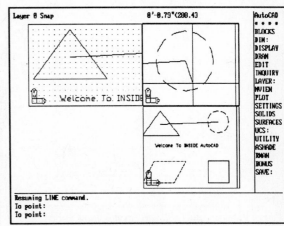

Upper Right Viewport With First Line

Drawing With Multiple Viewports

Continue in the BASIC drawing.

Command: **MSPACE**   You enter model space. (Skip this command in Release 10.)
                              The paper space icon disappears and each viewport gets a UCS icon.
                              The upper right was created last, so it is current and has a fat border.

Move the cursor. Notice it's a crosshair when over the current viewport, but an arrow elsewhere.

Pick a point in the upper left viewport, making it current.

Command: **ZOOM**   Use a window to magnify triangle and a bit of the text.
Command: **GRID**   Set grid to .25.

Command: **LINE**
From point: Start line from approximate center of triangle.

Pick a point in the upper right viewport, making it current.

To point: **'ZOOM**   Do a transparent zoom window around circle.
Resuming LINE command.

To point: Continue line to approximate center of circle.

Make bottom right viewport current.

To point: Continue line to approximate center of the square.
To point: Continue line to approximate center of the parallelogram.
To point: **C**   Line closes in the triangle.

When you are done, the upper viewports should show portions of the completed lines and the bottom viewport should show it all.

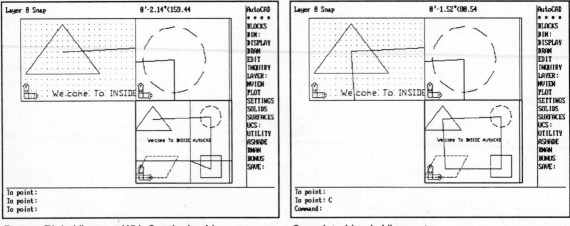

Bottom Right Viewport With Continuing Line   *Complete Line in Viewports*

We just kind of slapped those viewports up on screen. They're fine for drawing, but we could edit them to make better use of our screen's space.

Editing Paper Space Viewports

In model space, any actions you take such as erasing, copying, and so on, affect the model in the current viewport, not the viewport itself. When you are working in paper space, the only entities you can access are the boundary boxes around each viewport, and any entities you may have created or inserted in paper space itself. That's the key to understanding viewports in paper space: when you are working in paper space you can't make any changes to the model — just to the viewport. To make changes to the model, you have to re-enter model space. But there are times when you will want your edit commands to change the viewport itself, rather than the model that is displayed inside it. For example, you might have created a viewport that isn't quite large enough to display all of the view that is supposed to appear in it to a certain scale. So, you would use AutoCAD's STRETCH command to resize the viewport while in paper space.

AutoCAD recognizes the boundary box around the viewport as a single entity. If you select one line of the boundary box, the entire viewport is selected. Because the viewports are recognized as single entities, you can move, copy, erase, and scale them. (These editing commands will be covered in detail in the chapter on editing — for now just follow the exercise steps.)

You can also place the viewports on different layers. If the color for a viewport is set to BYLAYER, the boundary box will display at whatever color has been assigned to the layer. Or, you can change the color of the boundary box lines by using the CHPROP command and providing an explicit color for the viewport. Changing the layer or color of the boundary does not affect the image inside the viewport, just the boundary box. If you want to plot a drawing without plotting the viewport boundary boxes, place the boundaries on a layer that can be turned off for plotting.

Let's go back to the BASIC drawing that was modified in the last exercise, and use AutoCAD's editing commands to change the viewports. If you have already quit the drawing, load it in again using option 2 from the main menu. Use the illustration for your pick points.

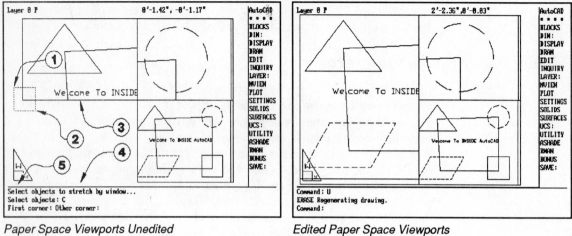

Paper Space Viewports Unedited   Edited Paper Space Viewports

---

Editing Paper Space Viewports

Continue in the BASIC drawing.

Command: **PSPACE**   Make sure you are in paper space.

Command: **STRETCH**
Select objects to stretch by window...
Select objects: **C**
First point: Pick point ① near left viewport.
Second point: Pick point ②, enclosing bottom left corner of viewport.
Select objects: **<RETURN>**
Base point: Pick point ③ on bottom edge, by which to stretch viewport boundary.
New point: Stretch the viewport down to make it twice its original size
                                   and click on ④ aligned with bottom of bottom right viewport.

Command: **MOVE**   Move all the viewports into positive X,Y coordinate space.
Select objects: Select all three viewports by picking each on one boundary box line.
Select objects: **<RETURN>**
Base point or displacement: Pick point ⑤ outside bottom left of left viewport.
Second point of displacement: **0,0**

Command: **ZOOM**   All.

Command: **CHPROP**   Change color of upper right viewport's boundary box.
Select objects: Pick the boundary box for the viewport.
Select objects: **<RETURN>**
Change what property (Color/LAyer/LType/Thickness) ? **C**
New color <BYLAYER>: **RED**
Change what property (Color/LAyer/LType/Thickness) ? **<RETURN>**

Command: **ERASE**   Erase the bottom right viewport.
Select objects: Pick viewport No. 3.
Select objects: **<RETURN>**

Command: **U**	Undo the erasure.
Command: **SAVE**	Save the drawing.

You can see how easy it is to change paper space viewports. Just remember that if you want to change the viewport, you have to be in paper space. If you want to change the model, you have to be in model space.

Controlling Layer Visibility With VPLAYER

Normally, freezing a layer makes that layer disappear from every viewport on the screen. That's because the LAYER command affects layers globally. With paper space viewports (not tiled viewports), you can control the layer visibility in individual viewports, using the VPLAYER (ViewPortLAYER) command.

Unlike freezing layers with the LAYER command, VPLAYER only affects how layers appear in a single viewport. This allows you to select a viewport and freeze a layer in it, while still allowing the contents of that layer to appear in another viewport. VPLAYER settings only affect the visibility of layers in viewports when TILEMODE is set to 0 (paper space viewports). If you switch back to a single or tiled model view by setting TILEMODE to 1 (model space), the global layer settings take precedence over any VPLAYER settings.

The VPLAYER command can be executed from either paper space or model space. If you are in model space and use the select option, it temporarily switches to paper space so you can select a viewport. We'll try it from model space to demonstrate.

Let's use the BASIC drawing again to experiment a little with the VPLAYER command. If you have already quit the drawing, reload it. At the end, we'll set TILEMODE back to 1 (on) and see the screen change back to a single tiled viewport, as it was before we started on our paper space journey.

Controlling Layer Visibility with VPLAYER

Continue in the BASIC drawing, or reload it. Make sure you're in model space.

```
Command: VPLAYER
?/Freeze/Thaw/Reset/Newfrz/Vpvisdflt: F        Freeze.
Layer(s) to Freeze: CIRCLE
All/Select/<Current>: S                         Select.
Switching to Paper space.
```

```
Select objects: 1 selected, 1 found          Select upper right viewport.
Select objects: <RETURN>
Switching to Model space.

?/Freeze/Thaw/Reset/Newfrz/Vpvisdflt: F
Layer(s) to Freeze: PARAGRAM
All/Select/<Current>: S
Switching to Paper space.
Select objects: 1 selected, 1 found          Select lower right viewport.
Select objects: <RETURN>
Switching to Model space.

?/Freeze/Thaw/Reset/Newfrz/Vpvisdflt: F
Layer(s) to Freeze: TEXT
All/Select/<Current>: S
Switching to Paper space.
Select objects: 1 selected, 1 found          Select left viewport.
Select objects: <RETURN>
Switching to Model space.

?/Freeze/Thaw/Reset/Newfrz/Vpvisdflt: <RETURN>
Regenerating drawing.

Command: TILEMODE                             Set to 1 and you'll revert to a single tiled viewport.

Command: SAVE
```

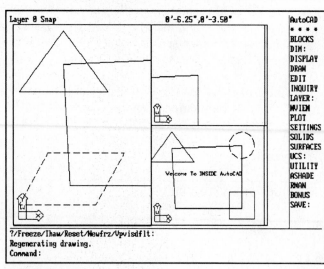

BASIC Drawing After VPLAYER

Compare your display with the illustration. Notice that even though a layer is frozen in each of the viewports, the data on it still appears in the other viewports.

The VPLAYER command gives you a number of options for selectively controlling layer visibility, as well as creating new layers. The following is a list of options available in VPLAYER.

VPLAYER Options

? — If you enter a question mark, AutoCAD prompts you to select a viewport, then displays the names of layers in that viewport that are frozen. If you happen to be in model space, AutoCAD will switch temporarily to paper space to let you select a viewport.

Freeze — Allows you to specify one or more layers to freeze in the selected viewport. You can answer the prompt with a single layer name, a list of layer names, or a wildcard specification to affect a number of similarly named layers.

Thaw — Allows you to thaw a layer, turning its display back on again. As with Freeze, Thaw lets you respond with single or multiple layer names, as well as wildcard specifications.

Reset — Restores the default visibility setting for one or more layers in the selected viewport. See the following explanation of Vpvisdflt for more information on default visibility settings.

Newfrz — Gives you a quick way to create layers without exiting the VPLAYER command. By default, layers you create this way are frozen and you must thaw them with the Thaw option before they will be visible.

Vpvisdflt — Lets you set the default visibility of one or more layers. Say you freeze a layer in several viewports and thaw the same layer in others. The Vpvisdflt setting for that layer determines the initial display mode (frozen/thawed) of that layer in any new viewports you create from that point on.

Dialogue Box Viewport Layer Control

You can also use the layer control dialogue box, the DDLMODES command, to control layers in paper space viewports.

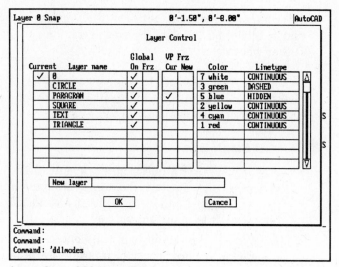

Layer Control Dialogue Box

The VP Frz Cur (ViewPort FReeZe CURrent) column controls the freeze/thaw status of layers in the current viewport. If you are in paper space, the change applies to the paper space view itself, not to any of the viewports within. A check mark means the layer is frozen. Click to change it.

The VP Frz New column controls how layers will be in newly created viewports. If checked, the layer(s) will automatically be frozen in subsequently created viewports. You might choose to do this when setting up several new viewports in a complex drawing.

Next, let's take a look at tiled viewports and converting them to paper space viewports.

Using Tiled Viewports

Most, if not all, of your modeling and drawing can be done using paper space viewports. However, there may be times when you want to use AutoCAD's tiled viewports for model space work. And, if you are using Release 10, tiled viewports are all you have! Bear in mind when you go through the following exercises that all of the drawing features found in tiled viewports, like the ability to draw from one viewport to another, are also inherent in paper space viewports.

The VPORTS command controls tiled viewports. It divides the AutoCAD graphics screen into windows. Like paper space viewports, each tiled viewport contains a unique view of the drawing. Unlike paper space viewports, however, tiled viewports must touch at the edges, and they can't overlap one another. You can't edit, rearrange, or turn individual tiled viewports on or off. The other limitation of tiled viewports is in layer visibility — VPLAYER and the VP Frz columns of the layer control dialogue box don't work in tiled viewports. You have to use the LAYER command or Global column of the layer control dialogue box to freeze layers in tiled viewports, and the corresponding layers in all viewports will be affected.

Tiled viewports are created with the VPORTS command. The TILEMODE system variable must be set to 1 (on). Select [VPORTS:] from the [SETTINGS] screen menu. VPORTS offers several command options that you can use to build your screen display by adding, deleting, and joining viewports. Once you have the viewports you want, you can save and name the group. A group of viewports is called a *configuration*. Use the same naming conventions to name your configuration that you use for layer names. You can have up to 31 characters, and you can use three special characters ($, -, and _) in your names. Saving and restoring named tiled viewports are the only advantages tiled viewports have over paper space viewports, but we'll tell you how to get around this in paper space later in this chapter.

Here are the command options.

VPORTS Options

Save — Stores the current viewport configuration under the name that you specify.

Restore — Redisplays a saved viewport configuration.

Delete — Removes a named viewport configuration.

Join — Combines two adjoining viewports into a single viewport.

SIngle — Makes the current viewport into a single screen.

? — Displays a detailed description of the current viewport in the drawing.

2 — Divides the current viewport in half vertically or horizontally.

3 — Divides the current viewport into three viewports. You can choose from several configuration options.

4 — Divides the current viewport into quarters.

Creative use of the 2, 3, 4, and Join options is often needed to get the arrangement you want. Try using VPORTS to divide your screen into three viewports using the BASIC drawing from Chapter 3 or IA6BASIC.DWG from the IA DISK. First, start a new drawing, or set TILEMODE to 1 in your current drawing. Then divide your screen in half. Next, divide the top half into three viewports. Finally, join the top three viewports into two viewports so that you end up with a configuration of two up and one below. Use the illustrations and the exercise sequence below as guides.

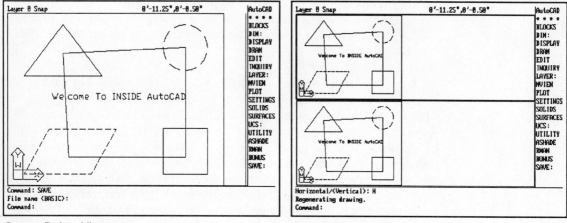

Screen Before Viewports   Screen With Two Viewports

Using VPORTS to Get Multiple Views

Begin a NEW drawing named TILEVP=IA6BASIC.

Edit an EXISTING drawing named BASIC, or continue from the previous exercise.

Command: **TILEMODE**	If continuing with Release 11, make sure it's set to 1 (on).

Command: **VPORTS**   Divide screen in half horizontally.
Save/Restore/Delete/Join/SIngle/?/2/<3>/4: **2**
Horizontal/<Vertical>: **H**
Regenerating drawing.

Command: **VPORTS**   Divide top half into three viewports.
Save/Restore/Delete/Join/SIngle/?/2/<3>/4: **3**
Horizontal/Vertical/Above/Below/Left/<Right>: **V**

Command: **VPORTS**   Join the top left and center viewports.
Save/Restore/Delete/Join/SIngle/?/2/<3>/4: **J**
Select dominant viewport <current>: **<RETURN>**
Select viewport to join: Pick top center viewport.

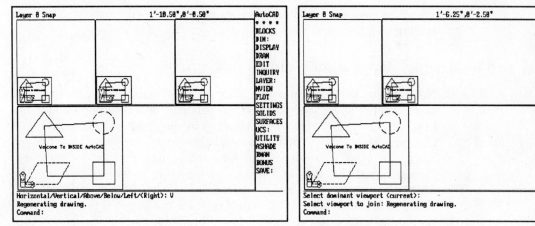

Top Viewport Divided Three Times   Screen With Two Viewports Joined

Now, save your viewport configuration, return your display to a standard single-screen display, and restore the named viewport configuration.

Saving a VPORT Configuration

Command: **VPORTS** Save/Restore/Delete/Join/SIngle/?/2/<3>/4: **S** ?/Name for new viewport configuration: **BASIC**	Save the viewport configuration.
Command: **VPORTS** Save/Restore/Delete/Join/SIngle/?/2/<3>/4: **SI**	Set viewport to single screen.
Command: **VPORTS** Save/Restore/Delete/Join/SIngle/?/2/<3>/4: **R** ?/Name of viewport configuration to restore: **BASIC** Regenerating drawing.	Restore the viewport configuration.

Command: **SAVE**

If you're using Release 10, you can use this configuration and drawing to do the earlier *Drawing With Multiple Viewports* exercise.

➡ *NOTE: You can translate previously saved tiled viewports into paper space viewports. This is primarily for Release 10 users who are switching to Release 11. To do so, use the Restore option of the MVIEW command while in paper space.*

The time it takes to name and save standard working views and viewport configurations is worthwhile if you are using multiple views. As your drawings become more complex, named views will save you time in editing and plotting.

Saving and Restoring Paper Space Viewports

Neither the VPORTS command nor the VIEW command can save and restore paper space viewports. When you save and restore named views in paper space, any viewports currently in the views will be visible, just like any other entity. But if the arrangement of viewports has changed since the view was saved, the former arrangement is not restored. However, you can save and restore paper space viewports by using the BLOCK, INSERT, and MVIEW commands. The BLOCK and INSERT commands are covered in detail in Chapter 9, but here are the steps. We'll try saving and restoring viewports in Chapter 5.

To save an arrangement of viewports: while in paper space, you make a block of the viewport entities you want to save, using an insert base point of 0,0 and any name you like.

To restore a previously saved (blocked) arrangement of viewports: while in paper space, you insert the saved block of the viewport entities using an insert point of 0,0 and prefacing the name with an asterisk. Then you use the MVIEW command to turn them on (they insert turned off), selecting all of the viewports. Of course, before inserting the saved viewports, you would probably want to erase any current viewports.

To save an arrangement of viewports for use in other drawings, you use the WBLOCK command instead of the BLOCK command. To import them into other drawings, use the INSERT and MVIEW commands as previously described. You can also create several groups of viewports in paper space, and pan around to the set you want to work in.

➡ *NOTE: Some early copies of Release 11 may create an extraneous viewport when you reinsert wblocked viewports. If you see an extra image, zoom out, and erase the extra viewport frame, then zoom Previous.*

Using REDRAWALL and REGENALL

When you are using multiple viewports and you want to redraw or regenerate all the ports, use the REDRAWALL or REGENALL commands. The standard REDRAW and REGEN commands only affect the current viewport. REDRAWALL can also be performed transparently.

➡ *NOTE: You can delete the BASIC and TILEVP drawings; we won't be using them again.*

Summing Up

There are many ways to get around an AutoCAD display screen. Display commands frame different aspects of your drawing, while viewports give you multiple views. Here are a few summary tips from experienced users.

Zoom gives you more (or less!) detail. The most common zoom-in method is Window. It is the most intuitive and convenient way to specify what the next screen view will contain. The most common zoom-out methods are All and Previous, or named views. When zooming out, use ZOOM Dynamic or a view named ALL to get you there in a single step. ZOOM Dynamic lets you choose your next zoom display screen. ZOOM Extents gives you the biggest view possible of your drawing file. Use ZOOM Extents at the end of a drawing session to make sure that you haven't drawn outside your limits.

A PAN displacement gives a nearby view while you are still at the same magnification. When getting from one side of the drawing file to another, use ZOOM Dynamic to get the *whole* view and help you locate your next screen view. ZOOM Dynamic is more intuitive than PAN and gives you feedback on how long it will take to generate your requested image. The VIEW command saves and restores zoomed-in windows. Take the time to use names and store views for drawing efficiency.

Watch how and how often you regenerate your drawing file. Doing a REDRAW cleans construction marks off the screen and *refreshes* the image without regenerating the drawing. Remember VIEWRES optimizes display generation by trading looks for speed. The REGEN command gets you the latest look at what's in the drawing file. Automatic drawing regeneration is controlled with REGENAUTO.

Use paper space viewports to get multiple views of your drawing. Use multiple viewports when you need to do detailed (zoomed-in) work while still looking at your whole drawing, or to see a schedule or reference part of your drawing.

Let's get out of our viewing chairs and climb inside AutoCAD. In the next chapter, we'll find out how AutoCAD's drafting tools work, and how they speed up drawing creation.

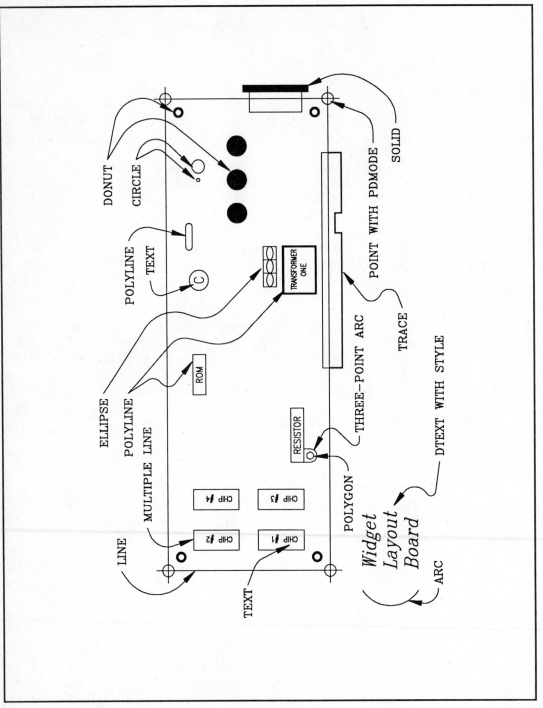

Entities Used in WIDGET Drawing

Setup for WIDGET Drawing

 Begin a NEW drawing named WIDGET=IA6WIDGE.

Begin a NEW drawing named WIDGET and set it up with the settings shown in the WIDGET Drawing Settings table.

```
Command: ZOOM                              Zoom All.
```

If using Release 11, skip the following VPORTS commands. Pick up the exercise again with the TILEMODE command.

```
Command: VPORTS                            (If using Release 10, set up three viewports.)
Save/Restore/Delete/Join/SIngle/?/2/<3>/4: <RETURN>
Horizontal/Vertical/Above/Below/Left/<Right>: A
Regenerating drawing.
```

```
Command: VPORTS                            (If using Release 10, save viewport configuration and
                                           skip rest of this exercise.)
Save/Restore/Delete/Join/SIngle/?/2/<3>/4: S
?/Name for new viewport configuration: 3VIEW
```
If using Release 11, set up the viewports in paper space as shown below.

```
Command: TILEMODE                          Set to 0 (off).
```

```
Command: MVIEW
ON/OFF/Hideplot/Fit/2/3/4/Restore/<First Point>: 3
Horizontal/Vertical/Above/Below/Left/<Right>: A
Fit/<First Point>: F
Regenerating drawing.
Command: BLOCK                             Save the viewport setup.
Block name (or ?): 3VIEW
Insertion base point: 0,0
Select objects: C                          A crossing window (explained in Chapter 6).
First corner:                              Pick a point in lower left viewport.
Other corner:                              Pick a point in right half of upper viewport.
3 found
Select objects: <RETURN>
```

```
Command: INSERT                            Restore the viewports.
Block name (or ?): *3VIEW
 Insertion point: 0,0
 Scale factor <1>: <RETURN>
 Rotation angle <0.00>: <RETURN>
```

```
Command: MVIEW                             Turn the viewports back on.
ON/OFF/Hideplot/Fit/2/3/4/Restore/<First Point>: ON
Select objects: C                          A crossing window.
```

➥ *NOTE: Several of the command items on the [Draw] pull-down menu are modified commands for which you can preset parameters with the [Settings] or [Options] pull-down menus.*

Drawing Goals

The goals for this chapter are two-fold. The first is to learn about the different graphic entities and how they're used. The second is to begin work on a real drawing. You will use graphic entities to build a design, which we call a widget. Then, in the next chapter, you'll use AutoCAD's powerful editing commands to manipulate your drawing by moving, copying, and changing entities quickly and easily.

By the end of the next chapter, you should have a complete widget layout on your screen and a complete understanding of AutoCAD's drawing and editing commands. The widget may show only faint resemblance to a real board layout, but it does contain *all* of AutoCAD's 2D entities. The entities that you will use are shown in the Entities Used in WIDGET Drawing illustration.

Setup for Drawing Entities

To get started, you need to create a new drawing. If you are using the IA DISK, use the IA6WIDGE drawing and name it WIDGET. If you are not using the disk, create the WIDGET drawing with the settings shown in the table below. After you finish your setup, create three viewports, and save your viewport configuration as 3VIEW.

AXIS	COORDS	GRID	SNAP	UCSICON
Off	On	.5	.1	ORigin

UNITS	Engineering, 2 decimal places, 2 fractional places for angles, default all other settings.
LIMITS	0,0 to 11,8.5

Layer Name	State	Color	Linetype
0	On/Current	7 (white)	CONTINUOUS
BOARD	On	2 (yellow)	CONTINUOUS
HIDDEN	On	1 (red)	HIDDEN
PARTS	On	4 (cyan)	CONTINUOUS
TEXT	On	3 (green)	CONTINUOUS

WIDGET Drawing Settings

On paper, your drawing is static. In AutoCAD, graphic entities are *dynamic*. An AutoCAD arc has handles for hauling it around. Text has changeable height, width, and slant. Lines have two endpoints, but when two lines cross, AutoCAD can find the exact intersection.

➡ *NOTE: In addition to the entities illustrated above, AutoCAD has several 3D primitives which are covered in the 3D chapters of the book. Other entities are blocks, attributes, and shapes (covered in Chapter 9) and dimensions (in Chapter 12). You've already learned about viewport entities in Chapter 4.*

Drawing Tools

In the course of setting up your drawing environment, you have already used a core set of drawing commands, the POINT, LINE, CIRCLE, and DTEXT commands. We will formally re-introduce them and their associates, the ARC, PLINE, DONUT, POLYGON, ELLIPSE, TRACE, TEXT, and SOLID commands.

You will find all the drawing commands by selecting [DRAW] on the root screen menu. The [DRAW] screen menu has two pages of commands. Use [next] to get to the second page. [DRAW] appears near the bottom of most screen menus as a convenience to get to the [DRAW] menu. You also can select drawing commands from the [Draw] pull-down menu, or from your tablet menu. In this chapter, we will show the commands to use. Type them or select them by whatever means you prefer.

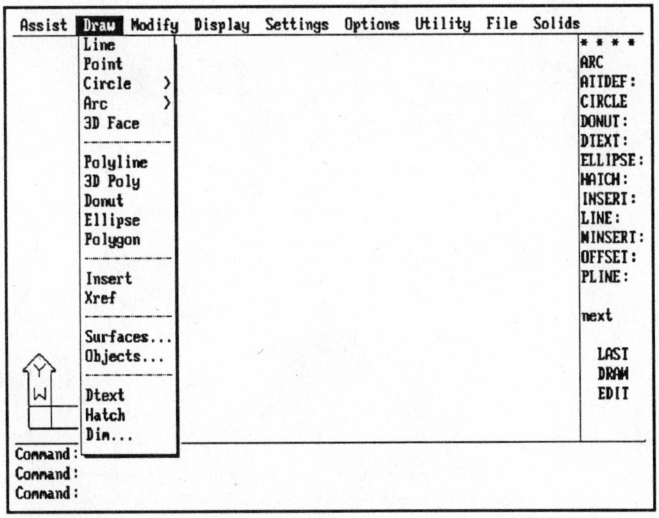

```
Assist  Draw  Modify  Display  Settings  Options  Utility  File  Solids
            Line                                                 * * * *
            Point                                                ARC
            Circle    >                                          ATTDEF:
            Arc       >                                          CIRCLE
            3D Face                                              DONUT:
            ─────────                                            DTEXT:
            Polyline                                             ELLIPSE:
            3D Poly                                              HATCH:
            Donut                                                INSERT:
            Ellipse                                              LINE:
            Polygon                                              MINSERT:
            ─────────                                            OFFSET:
            Insert                                               PLINE:
            Xref
            ─────────                                            next
            Surfaces...
      ⌂     Objects...                                           LAST
    Y                                                            DRAW
    └W      Dtext                                                EDIT
            Hatch
            Dim...
  Command:
  Command:
  Command:
```

Draw Screen and Pull-Down Menus

CHAPTER 5

Graphic Entities

Setup and display controls are really just tools for creating an environment in which to draw. Just as you'll find collections of tools around a manual drafting board for making lines, text, and curves, you will find AutoCAD gives you a collection of electronic tools to perform similar functions. In this chapter, you will learn about the drawing commands — the drawing tools. Each command creates an entity, the most fundamental piece of a drawing. The LINE command creates a line entity; the ARC command creates an arc entity. These drawing entities are sometimes called *graphic primitives*. Primitives are the primary entities from which more complex components, symbols, and whole drawings are built. For example, you might make an annotation bubble symbol from primitive line, circle, and text entities.

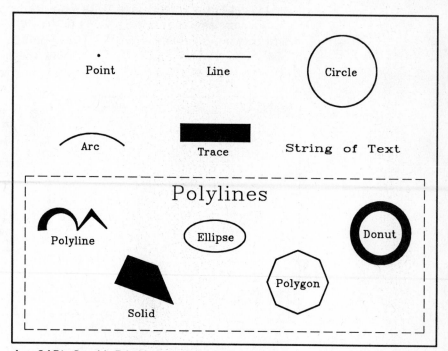

AutoCAD's Graphic Primitives

```
First corner: Other corner:          Pick the same corner points as above.
3 found
Select objects: <RETURN>
Regenerating drawing.

Command: MSPACE                      UCS icons appear in each viewport.
                                     You're in model space.

Command: SAVE                        Save the drawing.
```

Drawing With Viewports 3VIEW

When you are done, your screen should look like the Drawing With Viewports 3VIEW illustration. Your current layer should be layer 0. The crosshairs cursor should be active in the upper viewport because it is current.

From this point on in this chapter, it makes no real difference in the viewports whether you're using Release 10 or Release 11.

Using a Scratch Layer to Experiment

Each exercise in the chapter shows you how to use one or more drawing command options for each graphic entity. As you work through this chapter's exercises, you will use each drawing command. Some commands like ARC, PLINE, and DTEXT have several options that you may want to explore on your own. If you wish, you can make a layer named SCRATCH to experiment on; it will not be used in the basic widget drawing. If your practice entities get in the way, turn layer SCRATCH off.

Using Snaps and Osnaps

The drawing entity exercises show absolute or relative coordinate values for drawing or picking points. These are all snappable (or osnappable) points. You can pick the points on the screen by using your snap and grid, and by following your coords readout. If you are unsure about a coordinate value, you can always pick or type in the value shown in the exercise. If you type the values, omit any trailing zeros or inch marks we show.

The Point's Point

Start with the point. The lowly point is the *most* fundamental drawing entity. Points play a helpful role in building a drawing file. You can use points as drawing reference points. The point itself is sometimes hard to see, but you can control the point display to make points more visible. Lay out the four reference points for the widget board using POINT, then we'll show you how to use the PDMODE system variable to set a point *type* that is easier to see.

A Word About System Variables

AutoCAD stores a long list of system variables with each drawing. System variables give you the opportunity to set defaults for many commands, which AutoCAD stores in the system variable list. You can use the SETVAR command to update the system variable list. This can take less time than changing the default through the command. And some settings can only be changed directly by the system variables. In Release 11, you can either enter the SETVAR command at the command prompt or just enter the variable name as if it were a command. AutoCAD will recognize the system variable by its name and show the current default. Use the SETVAR command to see a list of all the system variables and their current settings by responding with a question mark (?) at the variable name prompt and an asterisk (*) at the variables to list prompt. Release 10 owners cannot enter system variable names directly at the command prompt and must use the SETVAR command.

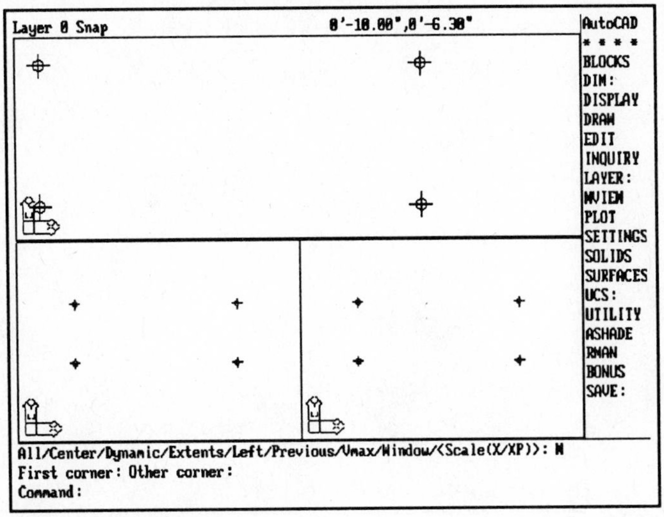

Points With PDMODE

Using PDMODE to Set a Point Type

Command: **POINT**	Now let's make the point.
Point: **2.50",3.30"**	Puts a small blip at the point.
Command: **REDRAW**	Leaves only a hard-to-see dot.
Command: **PDMODE**	(Release 10 users should use the SETVAR command to set PDMODE.)
New value for PDMODE <0>: **34**	Displays points as a circle with a cross in them.
Command: **POINT**	Put points at 2.50,5.80 — 9.50,5.80 — 9.50,3.30.
Command: **REGENALL**	Force a regen to see the first point.
Regenerating drawing.	
Command: **ZOOM**	Use Window to fill top viewport with the points.

Your screen display should look like the Points With PDMODE illustration (above). When you drew the first point, a mark appeared on the screen. This mark was actually larger than the point that you placed — it was simply the construction marker (blip) for the point. The REDRAW cleared the construction marker and left a small, white dot on the screen. That's the default point type.

```
Layer 0                              0.0113,0.0152                AutoCAD
                                                                 * * * *
                                                                 BLOCKS
                         +        X        |                     DIM:
                                                                 DISPLAY
                                                                 DRAW
         O        1      2        3        4                     EDIT
                                                                 INQUIRY
                                                                 LAYER:
                                                                 MVIEW
         ⬡        O      ⊕        ⊗        ⊙                     PLOT
        32       33     34       35       36                     SETTINGS
                                                                 SOLIDS
                                                                 SURFACES
         □        ▢      ⊞        ⊠        ⊡                     UCS:
        64       65     66       67       68                     UTILITY
                                                                 ASHADE
                                                                 RMAN
         ⬜        ⬜      ⊕        ⊠        ⬜                     BONUS
        96       97     98       99      100                     SAVE:

 Command:
 C:PDM
 Command:  Select new point mode <0>:
```

Point Examples

Resetting your point display mode gave you the circle-with-cross points. You can set about 20 combinations of point types with PDMODE. (See the point examples above.) This illustration is an AutoCAD slide which can be displayed with the [Point Type...] selection on the [Options] pull-down menu or the [Complex Points example:] item on the [POINTS] screen menu (select [POINTS:] from the [DRAW] screen menu to get to the [POINTS] menu page). You can also display it with the VSLIDE command; the slide name is ACAD(POINTS). After displaying it with the screen menu or command, use the REDRAW command to restore your screen.

The [Point Type...] selection also prompts for the new PDMODE, or you can type PDMODE or select it from the [POINTS] screen menu.

You control the size of the points with the PDSIZE system variable. Setting PDSIZE to a positive number sets its height in current drawing units. Setting it to a negative number makes its point size a consistent percentage of screen or current viewport height, regardless of zoom. For example, 8 will make points eight units high while -8 will make points 8 percent of the screen or current viewport height. You can use the [Point Size] selection from the pull-down menu, [PDSIZE:] from the screen menu, or just type PDSIZE to change it. (Type SETVAR PDSIZE in Release 10.)

Setting up a reference layer with points or a few lines can help you organize your drawing file for placing other elements. When you are all through with your placements, turn the reference layer off. You can also osnap to a point, which makes them useful to include as osnap nodes in blocks. Blocks are covered in Chapter 9.

The LINE Command — How Two Points Make a Line

You've already used the LINE command several times. Issuing the LINE command to AutoCAD begins a process of recording the two endpoints of a line segment. The two points you identify define a line segment. Remember, there are several ways to enter points.

- Use the pointer and crosshairs to pick points.

- Use SNAP, ORTHO, and OSNAP commands to control your point picking.

- Type coordinates at the keyboard: absolute or relative, Cartesian, polar, spherical, or cylindrical.

In the following exercises, we'll practice using osnaps and the various forms of typed and picked coordinate entry from Chapter 2.

Once a line is created from two endpoints (however they are entered), AutoCAD assumes that you want to continue drawing lines until you end the LINE command and return to the command prompt.

The LINE Command's Options

The LINE command has three useful options: continue, Undo, and Close. The continue option lets you pick up the last point of the most recent line to start a new line segment. A <RETURN> entered in response to the From point prompt lets you continue. Undo eliminates the last line segment of the current command and backs up one point to let you try the line segment again. Close makes a polygon by taking your last endpoint and *closing* it to your first point. Undo and close are achieved by typing a U or a C at the To point prompt.

Here's a little line exercise. Select [LINE] from the [DRAW] screen menu and draw the perimeter of the widget board using osnaps and the Close option.

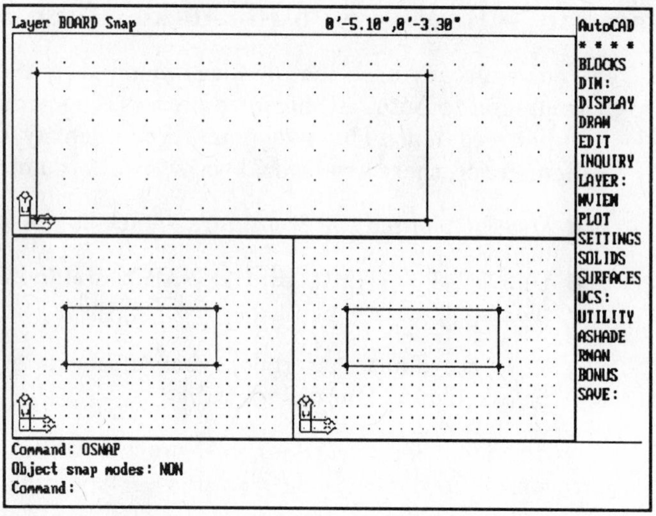

Completed Widget Board Layout

Using LINE With Osnap NODe and the Close Option

Command: **LAYER**	Set layer BOARD current.
Command: **OSNAP**	
Object snap modes: NOD	Sets a running osnap for the points.
Command: **LINE**	
From point:	Pick each of the point entities, in order.
To point: **C**	Close to complete rectangle.
Command: **OSNAP**	
Object snap modes: **NON**	Sets running osnap back to none.

Any time you have drawn a few line segments and want to make them into a polygon, use Close. A C<RETURN> is all you need from the keyboard in response to the To point prompt.

Next, let's use the LINE command's Continue and Undo options. We'll add a port to the widget's right side to see the effects of the Close option.

Using LINE's Undo and Continue Options

Command: **LINE**	
From point:	Pick absolute point 9.30,3.70.
To point: **<Coords>**	Toggle coords to X,Y mode and pick absolute point 9.30,4.50.
To point:	Pick any random point.
To point: **U**	Oops, wrong point. A U undoes it.
To point: **<RETURN>**	Ends command.

```
Command: <RETURN>                    A <RETURN> repeats the command.
LINE From point: <RETURN>            Another continues from last point of last line drawn.

To point:                            Pick absolute point 9.60,4.50.
To point:                            Pick absolute point 9.60,3.70.
To point:                            Pick absolute point 9.30,3.70.
To point: <RETURN>                   Ends command.
```

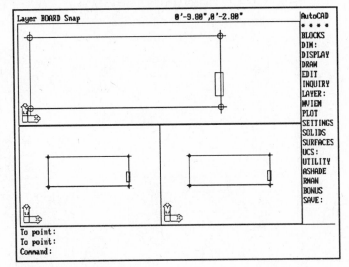

Widget Board With Port

Your screen should look like the Widget Board With Port illustration.

Here is a summary of the LINE options.

LINE Options

<RETURN> — Pressing <RETURN> at the From point prompt starts a new line from the endpoint of the last line or arc drawn.

Close — Uses the From point of the first line segment in the current LINE command as the next To point, making a closed polygon out of the connected segments and ending the command.

Undo — Lets you wipe out mistakes without leaving the LINE command. If you make a mistake, you can undo the last point by picking the screen menu undo selection, or by typing U at the keyboard, then reissuing your next point.

➡ *NOTE: You can keep undoing as long as you are in the LINE command and have not exited the command with a <RETURN>, <SPACE>, or <^C>.*

You've seen how a <RETURN> repeats the previous command. You can also have AutoCAD automatically repeat commands.

MULTIPLE Command

You can automatically repeat commands by preceding them with the MULTIPLE command. Try filling up the left side of the board by drawing four rectangles, using MULTIPLE to repeat the LINE command. We'll call these rectangles RAM chips. As we draw the RAM chips, we'll practice various forms of coordinate entry.

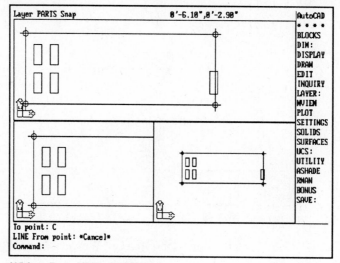

Widget Board With RAM Chips

Using the MULTIPLE Command to Repeat Commands

Click in the bottom left viewport to make it current.

Command: **ZOOM**	Zoom in on left side of board.
Command: **LAYER**	Set layer PARTS current.
Command: **MULTIPLE LINE**	No command prompt is reissued after MULTIPLE.
From point:	Pick absolute point 2.80,3.70.
To point: **<Coords><Coords>**	Toggle to polar display. Pick relative polar point @ 0.70<90.00.
To point: **@.3<0**	Type relative polar point.
To point:	Pick relative polar point @ 0.70<270.00.
To point: **C**	Closes line and MULTIPLE automatically starts a new line.
LINE From point:	Pick absolute point 2.80,4.70.
To point: **@0,.7**	Type relative Cartesian point.
To point:	Pick relative polar point @ 0.30<0.00.

```
To point: @.7<-90                    Type relative polar point (-90=270).
To point: C
LINE From point: 3.4,4.7             Type absolute point.
To point:                            Pick or type relative polar points @.7<90 to @.3<0
                                     to @.7<270 and type C to close it.
LINE From point:                     From absolute point 3.4,3.7 to @.7<90 to @.3<0
                                     to @.7<-90 and C to close.
LINE From point: *Cancel*            Press <^C> to cancel MULTIPLE LINE.
Command: SAVE
```

Your screen should look like the Widget Board With RAM Chips illustration.

TRACE Is a Fat Line

TRACE is a distant cousin of LINE. You draw traces just like you draw lines, with a From point and a To point. But AutoCAD first asks you how wide you want the trace. You can create traces as wide as you want. When drawing traces, AutoCAD lags one segment behind in displaying the trace, calculating the miter angle between the previous trace segment and the next.

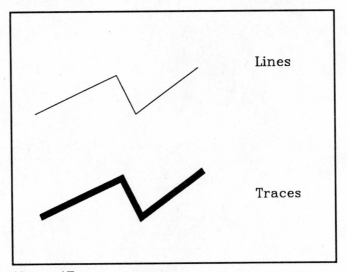

Lines and Traces

Try using TRACE to draw a connector on the lower right side of the widget, typing or picking the points.

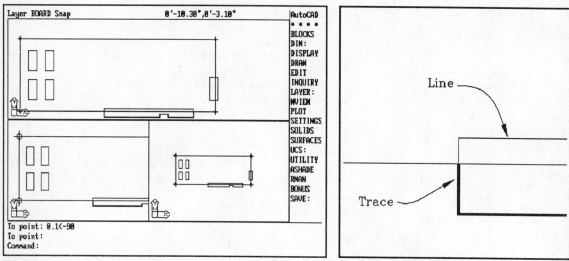

Connector Drawn With TRACE   Detail of Upper Viewport

Using TRACE to Draw a Wide Line

Make the top viewport current.

Command: **LAYER**	Set layer BOARD current.
Command: **TRACE**	
Trace width <0'-0.05">: **.01**	
From point: **5.5,3.3**	
To point: **@.2<270**	
To point: **@2<0**	
To point: **@.1<90**	
To point:	Continue with @.3<0 to @.1<270 to @.9<0 to @.2<90.
To point: **<RETURN>**	
Command: **LINE**	Add interior line from 5.50,3.30 to @.1<90 to @3.2<0 to @.1<-90.
Command: **ZOOM**	Zoom in close to see difference between line and trace.
Command: **U**	Undo the zoom.

You should see a noticeable thickness to the trace. If your drawing has numerous wide traces, it will slow down regens, redraws, and plots. Read about the FILL command, later in this chapter, to see how to temporarily turn off the interior filling of traces and speed things up.

Traces do have some limitations:

■ You can't curve a trace.

- You can't close a trace.

- You can't continue a trace.

- You can't undo a trace segment.

Okay, so TRACE isn't much like LINE, but you get the idea. To create thick lines, we recommend that you use either color assignment to thick plotter pens or the PLINE command (covered later in this chapter), except when you *need* mitered ends.

➥ *TIP: To get a finished end with a miter, draw an extra segment and erase it. The remaining segment will have a mitered end, depending on the direction of the trace that followed.*

➥ *NOTE: Traces are stored like four-sided solids, so osnapping to them is limited. Osnap INT and ENDP both find the corners. Osnap MID finds the middle of any side; you can use it (not ENDP) on the end of a trace to find the original From and To points.*

Arcs and Circles

Unlike lines, arc and circle entities require more than two simple endpoints. You can create arcs and circles in at least a dozen different ways. Regardless of the parameters (like endpoints, angles, directions, or chords) that you enter to create the entity, arcs and circles are stored as the simplest possible geometry. A circle is stored as a center point and a radius. An arc is a center point, a radius, a start angle, and an end angle. Using this geometric information, AutoCAD can regenerate curves at the best possible resolution and smoothness that your system can display or plot.

Getting to Know Circles

If you select [CIRCLE] from the screen menu, you will get another screen menu listing five circle creation methods. Why so many? Different drafting tasks provide different information about where circles should go. Most often you know the center point and the radius or diameter. In these cases, you use this information to create the circle. Here are the circle options.

CIRCLE Options

2P — Lets you pick the two points of the circle's diameter.

3P — Lets you pick any three points on the circumference of a circle.

TTR — Lets you pick two tangent points and a radius. If a circle can exist through these two points, AutoCAD will generate it for you.

<Center point> — Lets you pick the center of the circle and then either use the radius default or diameter option to complete it.

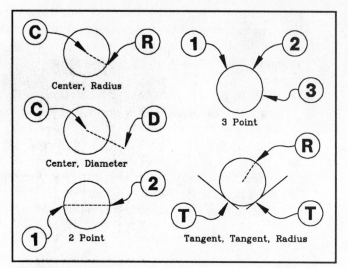

Circle Examples

You can create a circle in at least five ways. Which one do you choose? If you know ahead of time whether you have a radius, diameter, or points, you can pick the correct option from the screen menu. If you haven't thought that far ahead, AutoCAD lets you pick your options in midstream, using keyboard entry.

➤ *NOTE: Notice the difference between Center point / Diameter and 2P. Both let you specify a diameter, but if you pick the second point with Center point / Diameter, it merely shows the diameter's distance and the circle does not draw through the point. When you pick two points with 2P, you see a circle appear between those two points with the distance as the diameter. 2P lets you draw a diameter circle the way most people intuitively think about diameter.*

We'll draw three circles, using MULTIPLE to repeat the command. Try using the default center point/radius, 2P, and center point/diameter options to draw a capacitor near the center of the board and a knob and a small contact (more contacts to follow, next chapter) for a switch on the right side of the board.

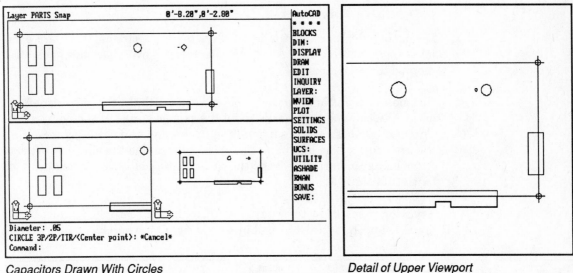

Capacitors Drawn With Circles   *Detail of Upper Viewport*

Using CIRCLE to Draw Capacitors

Command: **LAYER**   Set layer PARTS current.

Command: **MULTIPLE CIRCLE**   Use Center point/radius for capacitor.
3P/2P/TTR/<Center point>: **6.80,5.30**   Center point.
Diameter/<Radius>: **0.15**   The radius.

CIRCLE 3P/2P/TTR/<Center point>: **2P**   Use 2P for center of switch.
First point on diameter: **8.40,5.30**
Second point on diameter: **8.60,5.30**

CIRCLE 3P/2P/TTR/<Center point>: **8.30,5.30**   Use Center point/diameter
                                                                 for contact of switch.
Diameter/<Radius>: **D**
Diameter: **.05**
CIRCLE 3P/2P/TTR/<Center point>: **<^C>**   Cancel the command.

When you pick a center point, AutoCAD gives you the option of selecting a radius or diameter. If you pick a coordinate as the radius, as you did in the example above, you will get a circle through the radius point. A D<RETURN> response instead will show the diameter prompt. Then a coordinate pick will give you a circle by the Center point/diameter method.

Typing 2P, 3P, or TTR <RETURN> will get you one of those options, and AutoCAD will prompt you for the necessary points to complete the circle.

Using Three-Point Arcs

If you thought there were a lot of ways to create circles, there are even more ways to create arcs. AutoCAD offers nearly every possible geometric method to create arcs.

The most straightforward way to enter arcs is with the three-point default of the ARC command. It works about the same way as a three-point circle. The first point is the arc's beginning; the second and third points define the arc's curve. The last point and first point define the chord of the arc. AutoCAD automatically drags the arc, unless you have turned drag off (with DRAGMODE).

Try a three-point arc, to be part of a future logo. Locate the arc just to the lower left of the board, zoomed into your right viewport.

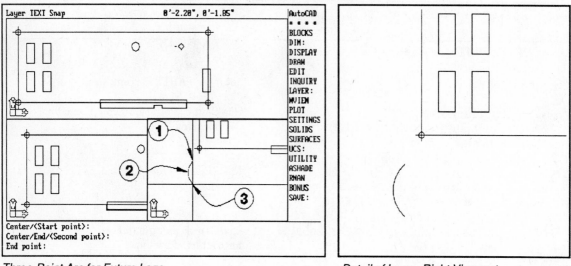

Three-Point Arc for Future Logo   Detail of Lower Right Viewport

Using ARC With Start Point, End, and Direction

Make bottom right viewport current.

Command: **LAYER**	Set layer TEXT current.
Command: **ZOOM**	Zoom to the lower left quarter of viewport.
Command: **SNAP**	Set to 0.05 units.
Command: **ARC**	Three-point.

```
Center/<Start point>:                   Pick absolute point 2.2,2.8. at ①.
Center/End/<Second point>:              Pick second point 2.0,2.35 at ②.
                                        Drag automatically comes on.
End point:                              Pick 2.2,1.9 at ③.
```

Make sure you feel comfortable with the way AutoCAD uses drag to help you decide where the three-point arc is going to fall. After the first two points are entered, drag is automatically turned on. Do you understand why the arc can flip around depending on the third point's placement? Push the pointer around until you do.

Drawing an arc with a start point, an endpoint, and a starting direction (tangentially from the start point) is useful for connecting two parallel lines with an arc. Draw a resistor on the widget using the LINE command. Then use LINE and ARC to draw the mounting tab on the bottom left side of the resistor. Locate the resistor next to the RAM chips in your lower left viewport.

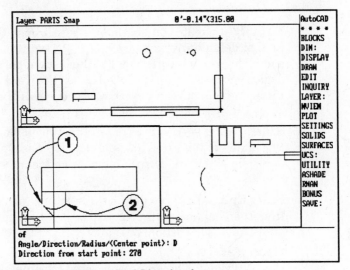

Resistor With Start,End,Direction Arc

Using a Start, End, Direction Arc

Make bottom left viewport current.

```
Command: LAYER                Set layer PARTS current.

Command: ZOOM                 Use Window with corner points at 3.90,3.40 and 5.10,4.20.
Command: VIEW                 Save view as RESISTOR.
```

```
Command: LINE                           Draw rectangle from 4.1,3.9 to @.8<0 to @.2<270 to @.8<180 and close it.
Command: LINE                           Draw line from 4.10,3.60 to @.1<270.
Command: LINE                           Draw line from 4.30,3.60 to @.1<90.


Command: ARC                            A Start,End,Direction arc, using osnaps.
Center/<Start point>: ENDP              Use endpoint osnap.
of                                      Pick endpoint of first line at ①.
Center/End/<Second point>: E            End option.
End point: ENDP                         Drag automatically comes on.
of                                      Pick endpoint of last line at ②.
Angle/Direction/Radius/<Center point>: D        Direction option.
Direction from start point: 270   Type, or drag and pick point at 270 degrees.


Command: ZOOM                           Zoom Previous.
```

There are ten options for the ARC command, which we've grouped by common functions. (See the Arc Examples illustration.)

ARC Options

Default — Creates an arc that passes through three selected points. A further default, invoked by a <RETURN> at the first arc prompt, starts a new three-point arc tangent to the last endpoint of the last line or arc drawn. Similarly, a <RETURN> at the first prompt of the LINE command will start a new line at the end of the last arc. Try some of these arc options on your SCRATCH layer.

Start,Center — Requires an arc starting point and the center point of the radius of the arc. This option group has a third parameter which determines the arc by specifying an endpoint, an angle, or a length of chord.

Start,End — Lets you define the starting and ending points of the arc first, then define how the arc will be drawn. You define the arc with an angle, radius, direction, or center point.

Center,Start — Allows you to first pin down the center of the arc, then the start point. The arc is completed by supplying an angle, length of chord, or endpoint.

You can select any of the ten arc options from the arc, screen, or tablet menus. The options are abbreviated by mnemonic letters. If you're keying arc commands from the keyboard, you'll find the commands have common beginnings according to their class (Start,Center; Start,End, etc.).

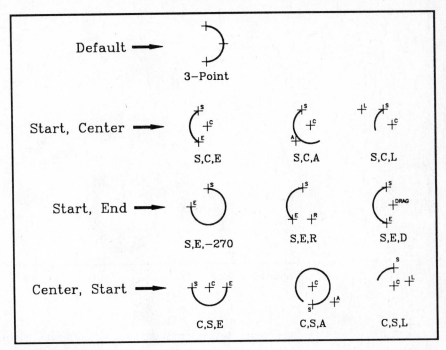

Arc Examples

You can choose your options midstream and select one arc creation method over another by entering ARC and the options from the keyboard. Beginning an arc with a picked point will narrow your construction methods to those that begin with Start; beginning with C will restrict you to options that accept the center point first, and so on.

Polylines Are Sophisticated Lines

You have explored the most common entities, the line, arc, and circle. Given what you already know about entities, how would you create thick lines or thick, tapered lines other than by using the trace command? How would you draw a continuous series of lines and arcs? Can you make a closed polygon with three straight sides (lines) and one curved side?

Before you spend too much time making basic graphic entities work too hard, consider the polyline, or *pline* for short. Instead of creating multiple lines to get a thick one, or creating independent arcs and then connecting them to lines, you can create a polyline.

Polyline Examples

Polylines vs. Lines

Polylines are different from independent line entities that visually appear to be joined by continuing the LINE command. AutoCAD treats a multi-segment polyline as a single drawing entity. Polylines can include both line and curve segments connected at vertices (endpoints). Information such as tangent direction and line width is stored at each vertex.

Polylines offer two advantages over lines. First, as the previous illustration demonstrates, polylines are versatile. They can be straight or curved, thin or wide, one width or tapered. For example, you could draw a curved leader with an arrowhead as a single polyline.

Secondly, the fact that a polyline is a single entity makes editing operations easier and reduces errors when doing crosshatching and 3D work. You can edit a polyline by selecting any segment, since selecting any segment selects all segments. By contrast, if you wanted to copy one of the RAM chip rectangles made up of four individual line entities in the widget drawing, you would have to select each individual line segment. When you crosshatch or create 3D objects from 2D lines, you must have edges that truly connect. (Objects drawn with lines and arcs may appear connected but still have tiny gaps which will cause hatch or 3D errors.) Use polylines to draw any closed or connected object or polygon, particularly if you anticipate hatching it or working with your drawing in 3D.

Using PLINE, try to create another widget rectangle, the ROM chip, in the center of the board.

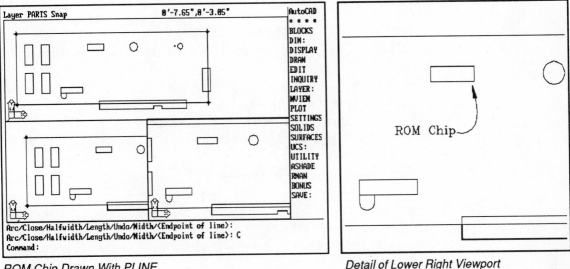

ROM Chip Drawn With PLINE   *Detail of Lower Right Viewport*

Using PLINE to Draw a ROM Chip

Make bottom right viewport current.

Command: **PAN**   Pan or zoom to fill viewport with center of the board.

Command: **PLINE**   Create a ROM chip.
From point: **5.10,5.20**
Current line-width is 0'-0.00"
Arc/Close/Halfwidth/Length/Undo/Width/<Endpoint of line>: **@0,0.2**
Arc/Close/Halfwidth/Length/Undo/Width/<Endpoint of line>: **@.6<0**
Arc/Close/Halfwidth/Length/Undo/Width/<Endpoint of line>:   Pick point @.2<270.
Arc/Close/Halfwidth/Length/Undo/Width/<Endpoint of line>: **C**

Your screen should look similar to the ROM Chip Drawn With PLINE illustration. This new rectangle looks similar to the RAM chips on the left. In the next chapter, you will see that this single ROM chip entity includes all four segments, while the other rectangles are each actually four separate entities.

Since PLINE can draw two basic kinds of segments, straight and curved, you will find that some prompts are similar to the line and arc prompts. When you draw straight polyline segments, you get prompts like

Endpoint, Close, and Undo. Check out the possibilities on the PLINE prompt line.

PLINE Options

Arc — Changes prompt to display arc options.

Close — Draws a straight line segment back to the first point of the polyline.

Halfwidth — Accepts values for half the polyline width for the start and endpoints of the following segment.

Length — Specifies a length of line to be drawn at the same angle as the previous segment. Used immediately after an arc segment, it will produce a tangent line.

Undo — Removes the last segment added to the polyline.

Width — Prompts for the starting and ending width of the following polyline segment. The ending width becomes the default width for all subsequent segments until changed with the Width/Halfwidth option.

<Endpoint of line> — Accepts the next point as the endpoint of the current polyline segment.

Selecting the Arc option presents another set of options, including some familiar arc prompts like Angle/CEnter/Radius, as well as Second pt and Endpoint of arc.

PLINE Arc Options

Angle — Prompts for the included angle of the current arc segment.

CEnter — Prompts for the center point of the current arc segment.

CLose — Draws an arc segment back to the first point of the polyline.

Direction — Allows you to override the default tangent direction.

Halfwidth — Accepts values for half the polyline width for the start and endpoints of the following segment.

Line — Changes prompt to display line options.

Radius — Accepts a radius value for the following arc segment.

Second pt — Accepts the second point of the arc.

Undo — Removes the last segment added to the polyline.

Width — Prompts for the starting and ending width of the following polyline segment. The ending width becomes the default width for all subsequent segments until changed with the Width/Halfwidth option.

<Endpoint of arc> — Accepts the next point as the endpoint of the current polyline segment.

Drawing lines and arcs with PLINE is similar to drawing the equivalent elements with the basic LINE and ARC commands. But there are several important differences. First, you get all the prompts every time you enter a new polyline vertex. Second, there are additional prompts that control the width of the segment, like Halfwidth and Width. When a polyline has width, you can control the line fill by turning FILL on or off. (We will show you how fill works a little later in this section.) Third, you can switch back and forth from straight segments to curved segments, adding additional segments to your growing polyline.

Using PLINE to Draw Arcs and Wide Lines

Try using these extra polyline features by putting two more objects on your widget. Create a diode (a little narrow object with arcs on both ends) by combining line and arc segments. Then, draw a rectangular transformer using a wide polyline. Locate the diode between the circles at the top and the transformer near the bottom center of the board. Continue working in your right viewport. When you start PLINE, the first prompt is for drawing straight segments.

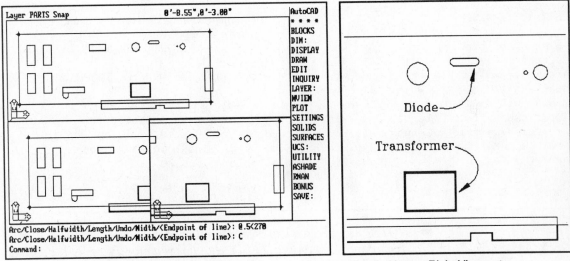

Diode and Transformer Drawn With PLINE   *Detail of Lower Right Viewport*

Using PLINE to Draw a Diode and Transformer

```
Command: PAN                                    Pan or zoom if needed.

Command: PLINE                                  Draw the diode.
From point:                                     Pick absolute point 7.30,5.40.
Current line-width is 0'-0.00"
Arc/Close/Halfwidth/Length/Undo/Width/<Endpoint of line>: @0.30,0
Arc/Close/Halfwidth/Length/Undo/Width/<Endpoint of line>: A          Arc.
Angle/CEnter/CLose/Direction/Halfwidth/Line/Radius/Second pt/Undo/Width/
<Endpoint of arc>: A                            Angle.
Included angle: 180
Center/Radius/<Endpoint>: @0.10<90
Angle/CEnter/CLose/Direction/Halfwidth/Line/Radius/Second pt/Undo/Width/
<Endpoint of arc>: L                            Line.
Arc/Close/Halfwidth/Length/Undo/Width/<Endpoint of line>: @0.30<180
Arc/Close/Halfwidth/Length/Undo/Width/<Endpoint of line>: A          Arc.
Angle/CEnter/CLose/Direction/Halfwidth/Line/Radius/Second pt/Undo/Width/
<Endpoint of arc>: CL                           Close.
```

You can zoom in for a better look, if you wish. Then undo or zoom Previous.

```
Command: <RETURN>                               Repeat command. Draw the transformer
                                                with wide polyline.
PLINE From point:                               Pick absolute point 6.60,3.50.
Current line-width is 0'-0.00"
Arc/Close/Halfwidth/Length/Undo/Width/<Endpoint of line>: W          Width.
Starting width <0'-0.00">: .02
Ending width <0'-0.02">: <RETURN>               Defaults to starting width.
Arc/Close/Halfwidth/Length/Undo/Width/<Endpoint of line>: @0.50<90.00
Arc/Close/Halfwidth/Length/Undo/Width/<Endpoint of line>: @0.70<0.00
Arc/Close/Halfwidth/Length/Undo/Width/<Endpoint of line>: @0.50<270.00
Arc/Close/Halfwidth/Length/Undo/Width/<Endpoint of line>: C

Command: SAVE
```

➤ *NOTE: Because you can create complex objects with polylines, there is
a companion command, PEDIT, that lets you modify a polyline without
redrawing it from scratch. We will cover PEDIT in the next chapter.*

Polylines in Disguise — Donuts, Polygons, and Ellipses

As you might imagine, the DONUT command creates a donut-looking
entity. Donuts can have any inside and outside diameter you like. In fact,
a donut with a 0 inside diameter is a filled-in circle and makes a good dot.

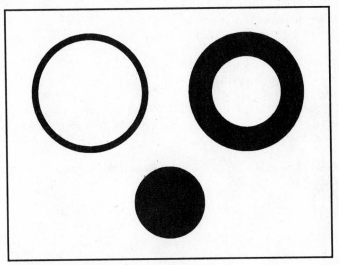

DONUT Examples

Get a cup of coffee and try the donuts! Try putting three filled dots on the
right of the board. Then, put regular donuts at each corner of the widget
as ground holes.

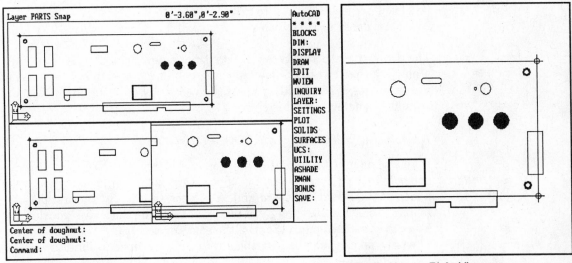

Adding Parts With DONUT   *Detail of Lower Right Viewport*

Using DONUT to Create Donuts

```
Command: DONUT
Inside diameter <0'-0.50">: 0
Outside diameter <0'-1.00">: .3
Center of doughnut:                    Pick absolute point 8.80,4.70.
Center of doughnut:                    Pick absolute point 8.30,4.70.
Center of doughnut:                    Pick absolute point 7.80,4.70.
Center of doughnut: <RETURN>


Command: <RETURN>                      Repeat the command.
DONUT Inside diameter <0'-0.00">: 0.1
Outside diameter <0'-0.30">: 0.15
Center of doughnut:                    Pick absolute point 9.30,5.60.
Center of doughnut:                    Pick absolute point 9.30,3.50.
```

Make the top viewport current.

```
Center of doughnut:                    Pick absolute point 2.70,3.50.
Center of doughnut:                    Pick absolute point 2.70,5.60.
Center of doughnut: <RETURN>
```

As you can see, DONUT keeps on prompting for the center of the donut until you press <RETURN> to exit the command. DONUT or DOUGHNUT, AutoCAD doesn't care which way you spell it.

The donut that AutoCAD constructs is not a new primitive. It is actually a polyline that has the following three polyline properties: it is made of arc segments, it has width (you set the widths by entering the inside and outside diameter), and it is closed.

Drawing Regular Polygons With POLYGON

If you want multi-segmented polygons with irregular segment lengths, use polylines or closed lines. But if you want nice, regular polygons, take a look at the POLYGON command. A polygon is actually another polyline in disguise. POLYGON gives you two ways to define the size of your figure. You can show the length of one of the edges or define it relative to a circle. The polygon can then be inscribed in or circumscribed around the circle.

Six-sided polygons make good hex nuts. Let's put a six-sided polygon in the mounting tab on the bottom of the resistor.

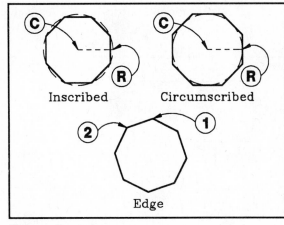

Polygon Examples

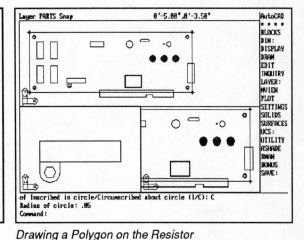

Drawing a Polygon on the Resistor

Using POLYGON to Draw Regular Polygons

Make the bottom left viewport current.

Command: **VIEW**   Restore view RESISTOR.

Command: **POLYGON**
Number of sides: **6**
Edge/<Center of polygon>: **CEN**   Osnap to the center.
of   Pick anywhere on the arc.
Inscribed in circle/Circumscribed about circle (I/C): **C**
Radius of circle: **.05**

When you know the center point, the inscribed or circumscribed method is probably what you need. You'll find the edge method handy for aligning an edge of the polygon with existing objects. The edge method generates a polygon continuing counterclockwise from the two edge endpoints you select.

If you want to see a *slow circle*, do a polygon with 1000 edges.

Last — But Not Least — The Ellipse

The ELLIPSE command creates a polyline in disguise. AutoCAD first prompts you for the major axis, defined by two endpoints or the center and one endpoint. Then you can define the minor axis by distance or rotation, dragging the ellipse if you pick the point or angle. Use the Ellipse Examples drawing as a guide to help you make your ellipses.

Create a rectangle just above the transformer and put three ellipses in it. We'll call the part a jumper.

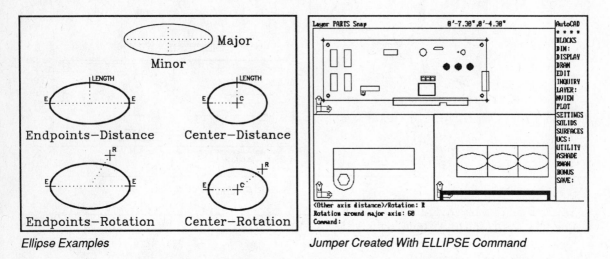

Ellipse Examples

Jumper Created With ELLIPSE Command

Using ELLIPSE to Draw a Jumper

Make the bottom right viewport current.

Command: **ZOOM**	Zoom in close, just above the transformer.

```
Command: PLINE
From point: 6.70,4.10
Current line-width is 0'-0.02"
Arc/Close/Halfwidth/Length/Undo/Width/<Endpoint of line>: W        Set width to zero.
```
    Draw to @0.2<90 to @0.6<0 to @0.2<270 and close.

Command: **LINE**	Snap in two lines, dividing the rectangle in thirds.

Command: **ELLIPSE**	Draw center,distance ellipse in left box.
<Axis endpoint 1>/Center: **C**	Center option.
Center of ellipse:	Pick absolute point 6.80,4.20.
Axis endpoint:	Pick polar point @0.10<0.00.
<Other axis distance>/Rotation:	Pick polar point @0.05<270.00.

Command: **ELLIPSE**	Draw ends,distance ellipse in center box.
<Axis endpoint 1>/Center:	Pick absolute point 6.90,4.20.
Axis endpoint 2:	Pick polar point @0.20<0.00.
<Other axis distance>/Rotation:	Pick polar point @0.05<270.00.

Command: **ELLIPSE**	Draw ends,rotation ellipse in right box.
<Axis endpoint 1>/Center:	Pick absolute point 7.10,4.20.

```
Axis endpoint 2:                    Pick polar point @0.20<0.00.
<Other axis distance>/Rotation: R
Rotation around major axis: 60

Command: SAVE
```

Ellipse is the last of the polyline family. If you want to try more polylines, use your SCRATCH layer as an exploratorium.

SOLID Is a Polygon Filled With Ink

The SOLID command creates a polygon filled with ink or pixels. It's that simple. A solid is a two-dimensional boundary filled with color.

Creating Solids

The SOLID command lets you create a solid filled area. This area is defined by three or four points forming either a triangular or quadrilateral shape. You can construct more complex shapes by continuing to add vertices. The order in which you enter vertices, and the spatial relationship between these points, determines what the solid will look like. You have to be careful not to get a bow tie shape from four points when you really want a quadrilateral. Nine times out of ten, users first create bow ties and butterflies instead of quadrilaterals.

Use SOLID to create a vertical solid at the outer edge of the port on the right side of the widget. Here's the prompt sequence.

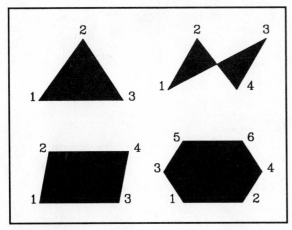

Solid Examples

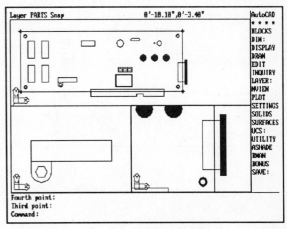

Enhancing the Port With SOLID

Using SOLID to Make a Solid Shape

Command: **ZOOM**	Use Dynamic to magnify an area around the port.
Command: **SNAP**	Set snap to 0.1.
Command: **SOLID**	
First point:	Pick absolute point 9.60,4.60.
Second point:	Pick absolute point 9.70,4.60.
Third point:	Pick absolute point 9.60,3.60.
Fourth point:	Pick absolute point 9.70,3.60.
Third point: **<RETURN>**	

Once they are created, solids and traces are identical except in name. They osnap and fill the same way.

Using FILL Control With Solids, Traces, and Polylines

When turned off, the FILL command temporarily reduces solids, polylines, and traces to single-line outlines of their boundaries. When fill is on, solids, polylines, and traces are filled-in or shaded on the screen and at plotting time. Having fill off decreases redraw, regeneration, and plotting time (you can use off for check plots).

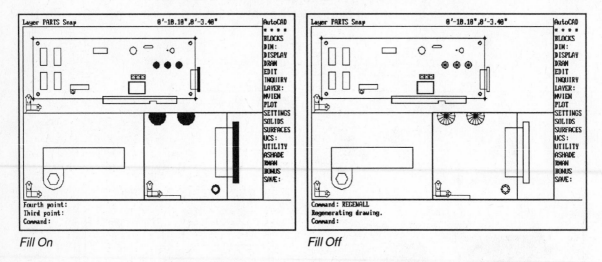

Fill On   Fill Off

Fill is a *toggle*. It is either on or off. Turn the widget's filled entities on and off.

Using the FILL Command

```
Command: FILL
ON/OFF <ON>: OFF           It doesn't affect existing entities until you regenerate.

Command: REGENALL

Command: FILL              Turn FILL back on.

Command: END               End drawing and take a break, or save, regenerate, and continue.
```

Notice the pie-shaped sections in the donuts. When fill is off, each polyline segment shows as an outline.

This is a good resting point. There is one more entity to cover — text. If you have the time, move on. If you are pressed for time, take a break.

A Word About Text and Style

AutoCAD's text has a set of default parameters that define how text is placed and stored. You have to select a beginning point for your text, a height for the characters, and how the text is to be placed and formatted. Then, you key in the characters. You've already used AutoCAD's text in its default form. Before you proceed further with text, you should consider style.

Style Settings

S is for Style, and AutoCAD has it. Think about this: if you had to draw the letter A, you would need 7, 19, or more line strokes, depending on the font. Rather than storing each stroke of each character in each string of text, AutoCAD stores characters as references to their definitions in special files called shape files. Shape files very efficiently store each character definition as a series of *vectors* (line offsets). These shape files are compiled into even more efficient binary SHX files, from which AutoCAD can rapidly extract character information for display. In translating text from the compiled shape files to your screen or plotter, AutoCAD passes the text through several filters to get it to come out the way you want. Text *style* is a set of parameters AutoCAD uses in translating text from a shape into strokes on the plotter or characters on the screen. A text style is a particular named collection of instructions in the current drawing and does not change the original shape file font definition.

As you have seen, AutoCAD supplies you with several default settings. The default style is called STANDARD. This style is defined with the simple TXT font and with default width, rotation angle, and justification (alignment).

Using STYLE to Create and Maintain Text Styles

Use the STYLE command to create new styles or change the parameters for existing styles. Setting your style is really part of the setting up process. We recommend that you set your styles early in the drawing before you get into any intensive text input.

The default TXT font used in the STANDARD style is a bit clunky. Use the following exercise to respecify the font used with your STANDARD style.

Using STYLE to Modify a Text Style

Begin a NEW drawing named WIDGET=IA6WIDG2.

    Edit an EXISTING drawing named WIDGET or continue from the previous exercise.

```
Command: STYLE
Text Style name (or ?) <STANDARD>: <RETURN>          Change the default style.

Existing style.
Font file <txt>: ROMANS
Height <0'-0.00">: <RETURN>
Width factor <1.00>: .8                              Make it a little skinny.
Obliquing angle <0.00>: <RETURN>
Backwards? <N>: <RETURN>
Upside-down? <N>: <RETURN>
Vertical ? <N>: <RETURN>
STANDARD is now the current text style.
```

Now your STANDARD style will use the ROMANS font and be slightly narrower than normal.

To help you graphically select fonts, AutoCAD has three pages of icon menus to select your text styles from. The first two pages are shown in the illustrations below. The third is a set of symbols, and also includes the STANDARD style, as the TXT font item. All of AutoCAD's standard fonts are included in the [Text Font...] icon menus. Selecting a font from the icon menus creates a new style, with the same style name as the font.

To get to these icon menus, select [Dtext Options >] from the [Options] pull-down menu, then select [Text Font...].

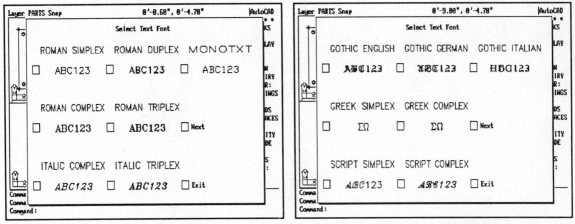

First Icon Menu for Creating Text Styles   Next Icon Menu for Creating Text Styles

Here are the text style options.

STYLE Options

Name — Just a name to help you remember how text drawn in this collection of style parameters will look.

Font — A file of vectors that define letters and symbols with a certain style. When you respecify an existing style with a new font, AutoCAD will regenerate your screen (unless REGENAUTO is off) and replace all the occurrences of that style with the new style. This only affects the font used, not any other options in the style.

Height — The default is zero, which means the TEXT or DTEXT commands will control text height. However, if you set style height to greater than zero, text placed using this style will always default to the height you give here. You will not get a height prompt in the TEXT and DTEXT commands.

Width — A multiplier, normally set to 1, that adjusts the width of characters. With a style width greater than one, you will have fat characters. With a style width less than one, the type will look narrow.

Obliquing Angle — Normally, characters are upright, with obliquing angle = 0. But you can oblique your characters, making them lean forward with a positive slant or backward with a negative one. Be careful: a small angle like 15 or 20 degrees causes a dramatic slant.

Upside-down and **backwards** settings — If you like mirror writing or need to annotate the bottom of something, you can set up a style with upside-down or backwards writing. This also is useful for transparencies or the backs of printed circuit boards. Or just for fun!

Vertical — Any of the standard fonts can be styled vertically.

Text style parameters		
Width factor 0.75 ——► ABC 123		R
Width factor 1.00 ——► ABC 123		O
Width factor 1.25 ——► ABC 123		M
Oblique angle 0 ——► ABC 123		A N S
Oblique angle 10 ——► ABC 123		V
Oblique angle 20 ——► ABC 123		E R
Oblique angle 45 ——► ABC 123		T
Upside down ——► ⱯBC 123		I C
Backwards ——► Ɛⵉⵉ ϽꓭA		A L

Style Examples

Notes on STYLE

Here are some notes on using AutoCAD's STYLE command.

■ AutoCAD's style definitions are maintained in a tables section of the drawing database file. You can store many styles in a single drawing file. They affect only the current drawing.

■ When using the STYLE command, a ?<RETURN> in response to the text style name prompt will give you a list of the styles currently defined and stored in the drawing file.

■ When you give a new name in response to the text style name prompt, AutoCAD creates a new style in the style library.

■ When you give an existing style name in response to the text style name prompt, AutoCAD assumes you want to change or edit the existing style. It prompts you for all the style parameters using the old settings as default prompts.

■ When you change the Font or Vertical option of a style that is currently defined in the drawing file, AutoCAD regenerates the screen. Any existing text of that style is updated with the new style definition. Changes to all other options are ignored for existing text.

➡ *TIP: You needn't bother to define a standard set of styles each time you start a new drawing. You can add your standard styles to your standard prototype drawing (see Chapter 19). Or, you can save them as part of another drawing file and insert them as a block (this won't override any existing definitions in an existing drawing). See Chapter 9.*

Once you have created the styles you want for your drawing, AutoCAD offers two ways to input the text.

Dynamic Text vs. Regular Text

AutoCAD has two text commands, DTEXT and TEXT. Either command places text. The only difference is that DTEXT (you might have guessed it) does it *dynamically*, letting you see each character in the drawing as it is typed.

If you use TEXT, AutoCAD waits for all your text characters and then places the text on the screen when you exit the TEXT command.

To get started with TEXT (and to see the new style definition), let's label the resistor in the lower left part of the widget.

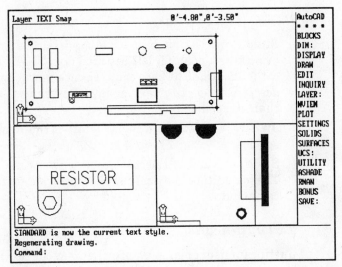

Resistor Labeled With TEXT

Using TEXT to Add Labels

Make the bottom left viewport current.

```
Command: LAYER                                     Set layer TEXT current.

Command: TEXT                                      Label the resistor.
Start point or Align/Center/Fit/Middle/Right/Style: M        Use Middle option.
Middle point:                                      Pick absolute point 4.50,3.80.
Height <0'-0.20">: .1
Rotation angle <0.00>: <RETURN>
Text: RESISTOR                                     The text doesn't appear until you press <RETURN>.

Command: SAVE
```

Notice the prompt options are the same as for the DTEXT command you used earlier. Let's examine them.

Text Formatting Options

The first thing AutoCAD wants to know about the text is how you want to format it. You have several options for formatting your text.

DTEXT/TEXT Options

Start Point — Left-justified is the default. Just respond to the prompt by picking a point for left-justified text. The point picked is the left end of the *base line* (the base of upper-case characters or characters without *descenders*) of the text string. Descenders are the lower part of characters like j or g.

Justify — Displays a menu of all of the available text justification options.

Style — Lets you select from various styles you have previously set. The default is the last STYLE used by text or set by the STYLE command.

Text Justification

Justification (or alignment) specifies how the text is aligned relative to the start and optional endpoint(s) you give it. You've used Middle, Center and the default Left justifications. The justification prompt shows the complete list:

```
Align/Fit/Center/Middle/Right/TL/TC/TR/ML/MC/MR/BL/BC/BR:
```

Let's examine them.

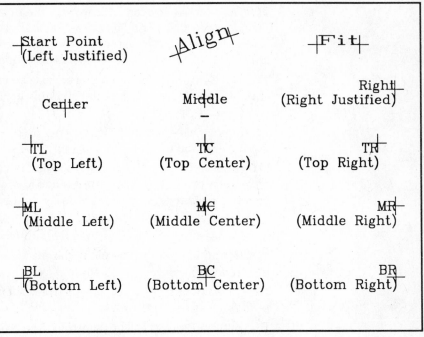

Example Text Justification Options

Justification Options

Align — Give the start and endpoint of the text location. AutoCAD determines the base line angle from your points and fills the distance between the two points with the text string you enter. Align maintains the style's width proportion and adjusts the text height to fit the distance. It overrides the style's height, if set.

Fit — Like Align, you pick the starting point and endpoint of the text string. However, Fit uses the text height you specify and adjusts the text width to fit the distance between the two points. Fit overrides the style's width setting.

Center — The midpoint of the text base line is placed at the point you pick.

Middle — Places the center point of an imaginary rectangle around the text on the point you pick. The vertical position of the text base line will vary, depending on whether the specific text string includes upper-case letters or letters with ascenders (like h and f), or descenders, or both.

Right — Like the left-justified default, except it uses the right justification point you pick as the ending point, at the right end of the base line.

TL (Top/Left) — The top left corner of the first text cell is positioned at the point you pick. The *text cell* is a rectangle enclosing an imaginary character with both ascenders and descenders, or an imaginary upper-case character which also has descenders.

TC (Top/Center) — The point you pick is vertically positioned at the top of the text cells like TL, but the string is horizontally centered on the point.

TR (Top/Right) — The top right corner of the last text cell is positioned at the point you pick.

ML (Middle/Left) — The point you pick is vertically centered on the *upper-case character cell*, at the left end of the string. Regardless of the actual text string, it is calculated as if it contained only upper-case text.

MC (Middle/Center) — The point you pick is vertically centered on the upper-case character cell, at the midpoint of the string.

MR (Middle/Right) — The point you pick is vertically centered on the upper-case character cell, at the right end of the string.

BL (Bottom/Left) — The bottom left corner of the first text cell is positioned at the point you pick.

BC (Bottom/Center) — The point you pick is vertically positioned at the bottom of the text cells like BL, but the string is horizontally centered on the point.

BR (Bottom/Right) — All text characters are placed entirely above and to the left of the point picked.

The TL, TC, TR, ML, MC, MR, BL, BC, and BR justifications are simply the nine possible combinations of the Top, Middle, and Bottom vertical justifications and the Left, Center, and Right horizontal justifications. The default Left and the simple Center and Right justifications are all base line justifications, which could have fit into this same matrix if B wasn't already taken by Bottom! Fit, TL, TC, TR, ML, MC, MR, BL, BC, and BR justified text cannot be used with vertical text styles; the others work vertically or horizontally.

Unlike middle-justified text, which floats vertically depending on the particular character string, TL, TC, TR, ML, MC, MR, BL, BC, and BR justified text maintain their vertical positions regardless of the string entered. Middle is designed to always be centered in both axes, for use in bubbles and similar applications. The other justifications are designed to be consistent for most other applications. (The vertical justification of TL, TC, TR, ML, MC, MR, BL, BC, and BR is not correctly described in early versions of the Release 11 *AutoCAD Reference Manual*, because they were redesigned as the initial manuals were being printed.)

➡ *TIP: If you respond to the DTEXT (or TEXT) start point prompt with a <RETURN>, the new text will start one line below the last text you entered in the drawing. The new text will assume the height, style, and justification of the previous text, even if you have used intervening AutoCAD commands.*

We'll practice several of these justifications as we experiment with the DTEXT command.

Placing Text With DTEXT

DTEXT is easier to use than TEXT. Input for DTEXT is always shown left-justified on the screen regardless of the chosen format. The justification is corrected when the command is finished. You also can reposition the box cursor on the screen at any point during text entry by picking a new point with your pointing device. This lets you place text throughout your drawing with a single DTEXT command. The trade-off for this flexibility in picking new points is the disabling of menus during the DTEXT command.

What happens if you make a mistake entering text? If you are using DTEXT, you can backspace and correct your errors as you type. If you do not realize that you have a mistaken text entry until you see it on the screen, don't panic — all is repairable. We will show you how to edit text in the next chapter. For now, just undo and try again.

We'll try more text input with DTEXT by labeling other parts of the widget. Add text by entering the justifications and starting points shown, and either typing or dragging answers to the height and angle prompts. We'll start on the left, labeling the RAM chips with Middle/Left text.

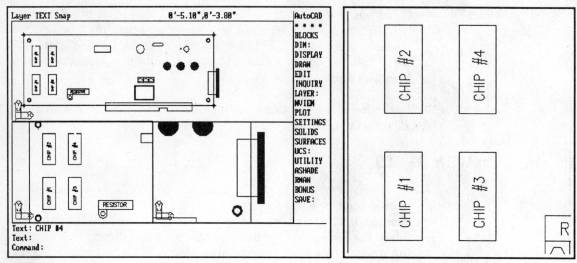

Widget Board With Chip Labels   Detail of Lower Left Viewport

Using DTEXT to Label the Widget Drawing

```
Command: ZOOM                                    Zoom Dynamic to enclose RAM chips.
Command: SNAP                                     Set to 0.05.

Command: DTEXT
Justify/Style/<Start point>: J                    Enter J for the full justification prompt.
Align/Fit/Center/Middle/Right/TL/TC/TR/ML/MC/MR/BL/BC/BR: ML        Middle/Left text.
Middle/left point:                                Pick 2.95,3.8.
Height <0'-0.10">: .08
Rotation angle <0.00>: 90
Text: CHIP #1                                      And move cursor by picking point 2.95,4.8.
Text: CHIP #2                                      And move cursor by picking point 3.55,3.8.
Text: CHIP #3                                      And move cursor by picking point 3.55,4.8.
Text: CHIP #4
Text: <RETURN>                                     Ends DTEXT and redisplays justified text.
```

Whenever you need reminding, you can enter a J at the first text prompt to see the full justification prompt. However, you don't need the full prompt to use any of its justifications. You can enter any of them at the first prompt. Next, try the Middle, Fit, Center, and Middle/Center justifications.

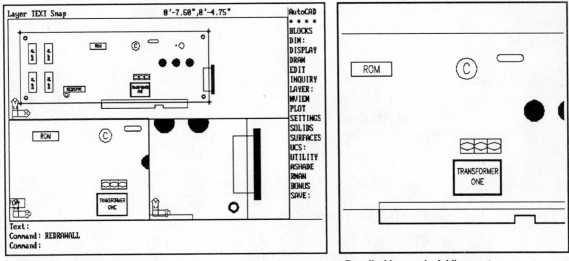

| Widget Board With Text Labels | Detail of Lower Left Viewport |

```
Command: ZOOM                              Pan or zoom Dynamic to the center of the board.

Command: DTEXT                             Label the capacitor circle.
Justify/Style/<Start point>: M             Middle.
Middle point: CEN                          Osnap to center of circle.
of                                         Pick any point on the circle.
Height <0'-0.08">: .15
Rotation angle <90.00>: 0
Text: C
Text: <RETURN>

Command: DTEXT                             Label the transformer.
Justify/Style/<Start point>: F             Fit.
First text line point:                     Pick absolute point 6.65,3.80.
Second text line point:                    Pick polar point @0.60<0.00.
Height <0'-0.15">: .08
Text: TRANSFORMER                          Text is redrawn, squeezed between points.
Text: <RETURN>

Command: DTEXT
Justify/Style/<Start point>: C             Center.
Center point:                              Pick absolute point 6.95,3.65.
Height <0'-0.08">: <RETURN>
Rotation angle <0.00>: <RETURN>
Text: ONE
Text: <RETURN>
Command: DTEXT                             Add label to ROM chip.
Justify/Style/<Start point>: MC            Middle/Center.
Middle point:                              Pick absolute point 5.40,5.30.
```

```
Height <0'-0.08">:                    Pick polar point @0.10<90.00.
Rotation angle <0.00>: <RETURN>
Text: ROM
Text: <RETURN>

Command: REDRAWALL                    To get rid of construction markers.
```

AutoCAD never forgets. Its default prompts during the text commands show your previous parameter settings. You can speed parameter entry by accepting defaults with <RETURN>s.

You also can use snaps and osnaps to help you place your text.

Placing Successive Lines of Text

DTEXT will automatically line up successive lines of text one under the other when you press <RETURN> after each line. If you press <RETURN> at the first text prompt, it will line up under the previous text entered. Let's try it, but first change your text style to one with an oblique slant, to give the widget drawing a title with a unique look.

Defining an Oblique Text Style

Make the bottom right viewport current.

```
Command: ZOOM                         Zoom Dynamic to the logo in the lower left corner of the board.

Command: STYLE                        Create a new style for the title.
Text Style name (or ?) <STANDARD>: TITLE    Name it.
Font file <ROMANS>: ROMANC
Height <0'-0.00">: .2                 Give it a fixed height.
Width factor <1.00>: .8               Make it a little skinny.
Obliquing angle <0.00>: 15            Slant it 15 degrees.
Backwards? <N>: <RETURN>
Upside-down? <N>: <RETURN>
Vertical ? <N>: <RETURN>
TITLE is now the current text style.
```

Now use the TITLE style and have DTEXT automatically line up the words "Widget," "Circuit," and "Board" under one another. When you are done, change your display to a single view and zoom for a good look.

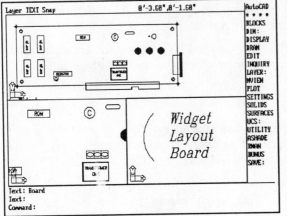

Title Added With Successive Text Lines

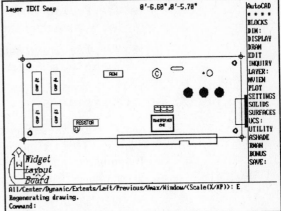

Zoomed Widget Board With Text

Creating Successive Lines of Text

```
Command: DTEXT
Justify/Style/<Start point>:          Pick absolute point 2.50,2.60.
Rotation angle <0.00>: <RETURN>
Text: Widget
Text: Layout
Text: Board
Text: <RETURN>
```

Make the top viewport current.

```
Command: VPORTS          (If using Release 10, set VPORTS to SI for a single screen view.)

Command: TILEMODE        (If using Release 11, set to 1 [on] for a single screen view.)

Command: ZOOM            Zoom Extents to fill the screen.

Command: SAVE
```

Your final screen should look like the Zoomed Widget Board With Text illustration.

We have two more special, quick text topics. But first, here are some tips on text entry.

➧ *TIP: Often you can set height and angle once (say when you are setting up your drawing file), and simply use these defaults for all future text use.*

➧ *TIP: To add a line to existing text, use DTEXT with osnap mode INSert and enter only a space on the first line. Then a <RETURN> will space you down for the next line.*

➨ *TIP: You can enter text upside down by using an angle definition to the left of the starting point (180 degrees).*

➨ *TIP: The default height shown in the TEXT command is rounded off to your units setting and may not accurately display its true value.*

Using Special Text Characters

Occasionally, you may need to use special symbols, or angle text on a drawing. This section describes how to create some common special texts. If you want to try some of the special text examples, use your SCRATCH layer to practice on.

➨ *NOTE: If your special text needs exceed those shown here, see CUSTOMIZING AutoCAD from New Riders Publishing for instructions on creating your own fonts and characters.*

Text Underscore and Overscore

Underscores, superscripts, and special symbols are used regularly in text strings on drawings. You will not find these symbols on standard keyboards. The Special Text Examples illustration shows some special text. The underscored and overscored text in the illustration was typed into the DTEXT command as follows:

Text: **%%u88%%u %%o88%%o**

You can enter the special character switches, %%u (underline) and %%o (overscore), any time you are typing a text string in response to the text prompt.

SPECIAL TEXT CHARACTERS

%%%	Forces single PERCENT sign	%
%%p	Draws PLUS/MINUS symbol	88±
%%u	UNDERSCORE mode on/off	88
%%o	OVERSCORE mode on/off	88
%%c	Draws DIAMETER symbol	88ø
%%d	Draws DEGREE symbol	88°
%%nnn	Draws ASCII character	

Special Text Examples

Angled vs. Vertical Text

Most text reads horizontally from left to right. Sometimes, however, you may want text which is not horizontal.

Usually, you just use the normal DTEXT or TEXT parameters to rotate or align your text at any angle. But occasionally, you want your text to read vertically. You can create a style and give it a vertical orientation. A vertical orientation aligns characters one below the other. You can give all standard AutoCAD fonts a vertical orientation.

Quick vs. Fancy Text

As your drawing file fills up with drawing entities, it takes longer and longer to zoom, redraw, or regenerate the screen. Sooner or later, you'll want to cut down the regeneration time. AutoCAD offers two options for speeding up text display. First, you can do all your text work in a simple font such as TXT while you are creating the drawing and for test plots. When it comes time for final plotting, you can enhance the drawing by replacing the simple font with a more elegant one such as ROMANC. You save time during initial drawing editor work, but your drawings still come out well with the last-minute font change.

➡ *NOTE: Font character definitions differ in width, and font respecification doesn't attempt to compensate, so you may find the new fancy text will not fit where you placed the old simple text.*

A second option (and one we recommend to speed regeneration time) is to use AutoCAD's QTEXT command. QTEXT (for Quick TEXT) lets you temporarily replace the screen display of text with a rectangle outlining its position.

The QTEXT Command

QTEXT is available from the keyboard or from the [SETTINGS] screen menu. It does not replace text until the next regeneration. Try *qtexting* the widget drawing.

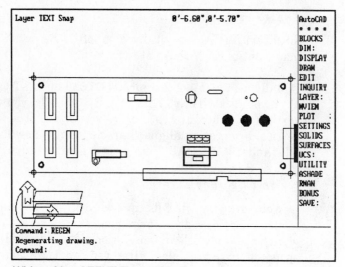

Widget After QTEXT Turned On

Looking at QTEXT

```
Command: QTEXT
ON/OFF <Off>: ON

Command: REGEN                          The text is replaced with boxes.
Regenerating drawing.

Command: QTEXT                          Turn QTEXT off.

Command: END
```

The text will regenerate when you reload the drawing in the next chapter.

Notice that QTEXT did not accurately represent the justification and text line lengths. To do so, AutoCAD would have to do the full text display calculations, and that would save little time over normal text display.

Summing Up

In this chapter you've covered a lot of material. Congratulate yourself on a whirlwind tour of graphic entities. Screen and tablet menus are becoming friends, like road signs in a new town. While the number of side streets for different drawing commands may seem endless, you're beginning to understand how the primary drawing commands will get you almost all the way to your destination.

You may put aside learning additional commands and options until you need them or have some extra time to explore AutoCAD further. If you like Sunday drives into the country, AutoCAD lets you wander through some of the less frequently used commands without letting you go too far astray. We invite you to master the ten different ways to create an arc!

Here are some reminders about entities you have used.

Points are useful reference locaters for a later osnap. They can be displayed in various sizes and styles.

Lines are the pillars of the drawing community. Connected lines are the norm, a <RETURN> stops a connected line run. Continue starts a line at the last endpoint. Close makes a polygon by returning a connected line series to the first point. Take advantage of TRACE's mitered edge to get angled ends for fat lines. Otherwise, you will find PLINE superior to TRACE for every other purpose.

CIRCLE requires minimal information to generate full circles. Center point/radius is the most common circle creation method. A three-point arc is the most convenient to create. The start,center series is also useful.

Polylines let you create single graphic elements composed of linear and curved segments. Donuts, polygons, and ellipses are made from polylines.

Text gets to the screen through a filtering process that controls style, justification, height, and rotation. DTEXT dynamically places text as you key characters at the keyboard. Style gives you flexibility in creating typestyles that are tailored to your needs. The justification options give control over placement. Keeping text on its own layer or using QTEXT keeps redraw and regeneration times to a minimum as drawing files expand.

You can think ahead about the sequence for entering SOLID vertices. But we bet you'll get a bow tie anyway!

Onward

In this chapter you began earnest work on a real drawing. You will be relieved to know that every entity that you used here works the same in a 3D drawing, although AutoCAD has a few more graphic entities especially designed for 3D which you will see in a later chapter.

While widgets may not be your thing, you have already mastered setting layers, drawing lines and circles, and inserting text. By the end of the next chapter, this drawing will be a complete, four-layer, full-color widget layout drawing.

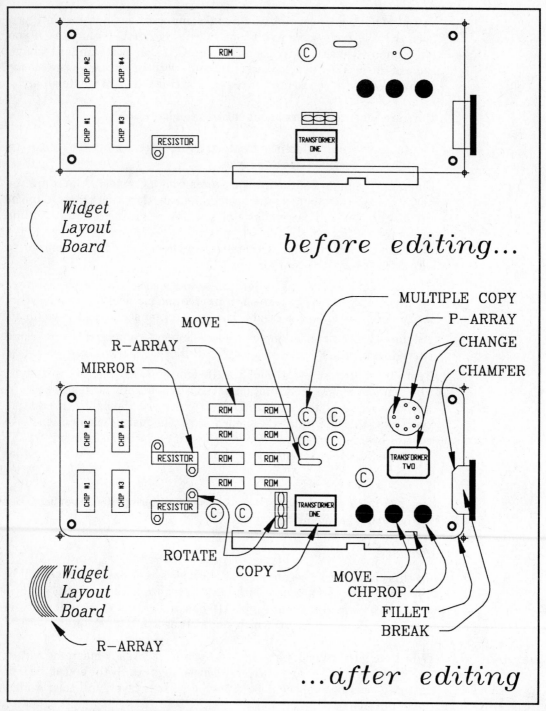

Widget Drawing Before and After Editing

CHAPTER 6

Introduction to Editing

IF AT FIRST YOU DON'T SUCCEED, TRY EDITING

You Edit More Than You Create

As you go through the book's examples, you may feel like saying, "Give me a drafting board, a straight edge, and a compass and I can beat this CAD system in a flash!"

It just isn't so. While some draftspeople may be able to create original linework faster than AutoCAD, it is safe to say that no human can revise and print new clean drawing sets faster than AutoCAD (and an organized user). The one certainty in the drawing business is *change*. Change this! Change that! Drawing revision numbers keep mounting! Becoming familiar with AutoCAD's editing functions is critical to your successful use of AutoCAD.

So far you have spent most of your tutorial time creating new drawing entities. Beginning with this chapter, you'll see how easy it is to modify your drawing with AutoCAD's editing commands. You may find yourself spending more time editing existing drawings than creating new ones.

The benefits of editing are pure and simple. Editing allows you to quickly and easily stay on top of changes, and to create multiple objects with minimal original entry.

Editing Activities — Changing, Copying, and Erasing

What types of activities will you encounter in editing a drawing?

Three basic activities stand out: changing, copying, and erasing. You can change an existing entity's location, layer, and visual properties like color and linetype. You also can *break* entities, deleting portions of line and arc segments. You can copy entities, either one at a time or in a swoop (array) of creation. You can erase entities, getting rid of previous mistakes.

There are more advanced editing functions, like trimming, extending, stretching, and scaling, as well as some editing *construction* techniques. We will cover these advanced functions in the following chapters. And, we will cover 3D variations on these editing commands in the book's 3D chapters.

The Editor's Toolkit

Most of the editing commands you will use are gathered on the [EDIT] screen menus and the [Modify] pull-down menu. There are also settings for the CHAMFER, FILLET, DIVIDE, and MEASURE commands on the [Options] pull-down menu.

[EDIT] Screen and [Modify] Pull-Down Menu

This chapter covers the basics of editing. You'll change both the spatial (location) and appearance (color and linetype) properties of existing entities. We have broken down the basic editing commands into two groups. The first group includes MOVE and ROTATE, which relocate entities; COPY and MIRROR, which duplicate entities; and ARRAY, which makes multiple copies. The second group includes the BREAK, CHAMFER, and FILLET commands. These commands delete portions of objects. In addition, we will review how to delete whole entities with ERASE.

How Editing Commands Work

Most editing commands involve a four-step process. You have to think about what kind of edit you want to do, which objects you want to edit, and how you want to edit them. The process works this way:

- Select the editing command

- Select the entities

- Enter parameters and pick points

- Watch the edit occur

Selecting an editing command puts you in an object selection mode. To get the objects you want, most commands require you to group one or more objects. This group is called the *selection set*.

The Selection Set

There are about a dozen ways to collect objects for editing, including picking individual objects and using a window. If you make an error at the select objects prompt, AutoCAD will prompt you with all the available modes. As you select objects, AutoCAD sets up a *temporary* selection set and highlights the objects on the screen by temporarily changing their color, blinking them, or giving them dotted lines. This way you can confirm what you've selected to edit. Once you have selected all desired objects, a <RETURN> continues the editing command. One of the goals for this chapter is to give you practice using a variety of the myriad options available for collecting selection sets.

Basic Selection Set Options

Object pick — The default is to select by picking individual objects. Picking finds the most recently created object that falls within or crosses the pick box. If snap and osnap are used together, AutoCAD snaps first, then osnaps from that snapped point.

Window — Pick the corners of a window to group the objects you want and it selects only those objects that are totally enclosed in the window.

Last — Adds the last object created to the selection set.

Crossing — Works like Window, except it also includes any object which is partially within (or crossing) the window. If your display hardware supports pull-down menus, Crossing will use a dashed or highlighted box.

Remove — Switches to Remove mode, so you may select objects to be removed from the selection set (not from the drawing).

Add — Switches from the Remove mode back to normal, so you may again add to the selection set.

Multiple — Lets you pick multiple objects in close proximity and speeds up selection by allowing multiple selections without highlighting or prompting. An extra <RETURN> is required to complete the multiple selection and return to normal object selection.

Previous — Selects the entire previous selection set (from a previous command) as the current selection set.

Undo — Undoes or reverses the last selection operation. Each U undoes one selection operation.

When do you use which mode? Object picking is quick and simple, even for picking three or four objects, and it requires no mode setting. Last and Undo are obvious. Previous is great for repeated operations on the same set of objects, like a copy and rotate operation.

Choose between Window and Crossing, depending on which will best extract the group you want from the crowd. Sometimes selecting more objects than you want is inevitable; that is why the Remove mode exists. And Add just gets you back to normal.

➡ *NOTE: The Window selection process ignores the portions of objects that fall partly outside the current viewport or screen display. If all visible portions of an object are within the Window box, it will be selected.*

AutoCAD has a preference for finding the most recently created object. Sometimes objects are so close to each other that you can't pick the one you want; AutoCAD just keeps finding the same most recently created object over and over again. In those cases, you can use Multiple to pick repeatedly and it will only find the recent object once. Then you can use Remove to remove the recent object if you don't want it.

➡ *NOTE: There are a number of editing commands, such as FILLET (which you will see later in this chapter), and TRIM and EXTEND (next chapter), that require individual entity selection part or all of the time. In these cases, you must select your objects by picking them.*

There are three other selection set options: BOX, AUto, and SIngle. These are designed primarily for use in menus and offer no real advantages over the above when specifying modes from the keyboard.

Advanced Selection Set Options

BOX — Combines Window and Crossing into a single selection. Picking the points of your box (window) from left to right is the same as a Window selection; right to left is the same as a Crossing selection.

AUto — Combines individual selection with the BOX selection. This selection acts just like BOX except if the first pick point finds an entity, that single entity is selected and the BOX mode is aborted.

SIngle — Works in conjunction with the other selection options. If you precede a selection with SIngle, object selection will automatically end after the first successful selection, without the <RETURN> normally required to exit object selection.

When specifying modes from the keyboard, you obviously know how you intend to select the object(s), so you can use Window, Crossing or just pick the object rather than use BOX or AUto. And it's easier to just hit that last <RETURN> from the keyboard than to enter SI<RETURN> in advance.

➡ *TIP: Create a button menu with AUto object selection programmed onto a button and you can do all of your object selection without using the keyboard or other menus. See Chapter 19 or, for greater detail, get CUSTOMIZING AutoCAD from New Riders Publishing.*

Setting Up for Editing

This chapter uses the WIDGET drawing that you created in the last chapter, or IA6WIDG3.DWG from the IA DISK. You'll create a new file called WIDGEDIT in which you'll try out the editing options.

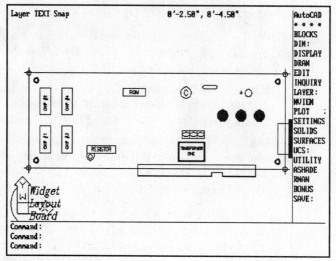

Setting Up for Editing

Setup for Editing the WIDGEDIT Drawing

 Begin a NEW drawing named WIDGEDIT=IA6WIDG3.

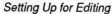 Begin a NEW drawing named WIDGEDIT=WIDGET and confirm the settings shown in the setup table below.

Command: **ZOOM**   Zoom Center with a height of 6 for a little elbow room to work in.

AXIS	COORDS	GRID	SNAP	UCSICON
Off	On	.5	.1	OR

UNITS	Engineering, 2 decimal places, 2 fractional places for angles, default all other settings.
LIMITS	0,0 to 11,8.5
ZOOM	Zoom Center, height 6"
VIEW	Saved as RESISTOR

Layer Name	State	Color	Linetype
0	On	7 (white)	CONTINUOUS
BOARD	On	2 (yellow)	CONTINUOUS
HIDDEN	On	1 (red)	HIDDEN
PARTS	On	4 (cyan)	CONTINUOUS
TEXT	On/Current	3 (green)	CONTINUOUS

Setup for Editing the Widget Drawing

You should have a full screen view of the widget. The following exercises do not make use of the viewports stored with the widget drawing, but you can use viewports in the exercises if you want to. You can restore Release 10 viewports with VPORTS or Release 11 viewports with TILEMODE=0. Your current layer is not important to the exercises. Editing commands work on any layer! If you want additional practice using individual editing commands, use a layer named SCRATCH, set it current, create some new entities to practice on, and practice the editing command. When you are done, undo, erase, or freeze the SCRATCH layer and take up again where you left off.

MOVE — Some Quick Moves With AutoCAD

Making a move is quite simple. You grab what you want, and move it where you want it. Try moving the solid donuts using a Window selection. When you are prompted for a *base point* or *displacement,* pick a base point. After you pick this point, you can *drag* the selection set with your pointer and pick a second displacement point to place the objects.

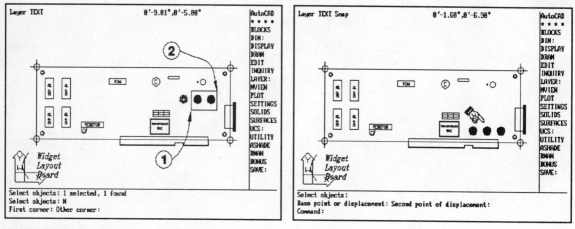

Selecting Donuts With Window for MOVE   ☞ *Moved Donuts*

Selecting and Windowing Donuts to Move

Command: **MOVE**	Crosshairs change to a pick box.
Select objects: **?**	Any wrong input gives you a full prompt.
Invalid selection	
Expects a point or Window/Last/Crossing/BOX/Add/Remove/Multiple/	
Previous/Undo/AUto/SIngle	
Select objects:	Pick the far left donut.
1 selected, 1 found.	
Select objects: **W**	Put window around the two right donuts.
First corner:	Pick first corner at ①.
Other corner:	Pick second corner at ②.
2 found.	All the donuts are highlighted.
Select objects: **<RETURN>**	This tells AutoCAD you are through selecting.
Base point or displacement:	Pick any point near the donuts.
Second point of displacement:	Pick polar point @1.00<270.00 and the move takes place.

As you can see, moving is easy. In the default Select Objects mode, the crosshairs cursor changes to a small square pick box. A selection window is similar to a zoom window. After you collect your donuts with a window, they are highlighted. You tell AutoCAD you're through collecting by pressing <RETURN> in response to the select objects prompt. When you are through selecting, pick your displacement points and your donuts are moved.

➡ *TIP: You can change the pick box size by changing the system variable PICKBOX. Just type PICKBOX (or use the SETVAR command in Release 10). You can also change it transparently in the middle of a command with 'SETVAR or 'PICKBOX, but the change won't take effect until the second following pick.*

Displacement and Drag

When you change the location of objects that you have collected in a selection set, you use a displacement. If you know the absolute X,Y or polar displacement, you can enter it at the base point or displacement prompt. For example, either 0,-1, or 1<270 (don't preface it with an @) would duplicate the move we just did. Then you enter a <RETURN> instead of a value at the second point prompt to tell AutoCAD to use the first value as an absolute offset.

Often you want to show a displacement by entering two points, as we just did. Think of the first point (base point) as a *handle* on your selection set. The second point is where you are going to put the handle of the set down. The displacement is an imaginary line from the base point to the second point. AutoCAD calculates the X and Y differences between the base and second points. The new location of the object(s) is determined by adding this X,Y displacement to its current location.

AutoCAD does not actually draw a displacement line; it gets the information it needs from the displacement points. When you pick displacement points on the screen, AutoCAD shows you a temporary rubber band line trailing behind the crosshairs from the first point to the second.

As you just saw when you moved the donuts, an image of the selection set also follows the crosshairs. This is called *dragging*. It provides a visual aid to help you pick your second displacement point. Without dragging, it sometimes can be difficult to see if the selection set will fit where you want it.

When you set up a selection set handle to drag, try to pick a base point that is easy to visualize (and remember). If the base point is not in, on, or near the contents of the selection set, it will appear that you are carrying the selection set around magically without touching it. Sometimes you will osnap the points to a different but related object. Otherwise, it's a good idea to make this drag anchor (base displacement point) a reference point, like an osnap point on one of the objects.

Using DRAGMODE

When you edit very large selection sets, you may wish to control dragging. You can turn drag on or off using the DRAGMODE command. The default for DRAGMODE is Auto, which causes AutoCAD to drag everything that makes sense. If you want to be selective about what you drag, you can turn DRAGMODE on. If DRAGMODE is on and you want to drag in the middle of a command, type DRAG <RETURN> before picking the point that you wish to drag. Off turns DRAGMODE off entirely and ignores a typed DRAG <RETURN>.

Adding and Removing Modes for the Selection Set

Sometimes you put too many objects into a selection set and you need to take some out. AutoCAD has two modes for handling selection set contents: the default Add mode and a Remove mode. In Add mode, you get the default select objects prompt. Picking individual objects or using any other object selection mode, such as Window or Last, puts the objects into the selection set.

You also can type R for Remove in response to the normal Add mode prompt. You will get the remove objects prompt. Remove objects from the selection set by using any type of object selection in the Remove mode. Type A to return to Add mode.

Using a Crossing Window

There is a second type of window object selection called a *crossing window*. Crossing selects everything that either falls within your selection window or crosses the boundary of the window. You will find Crossing handy when you want to select objects in a crowded drawing. AutoCAD also knows the difference between objects within the window and objects crossing the window. Some advanced editing commands, like the STRETCH command, treat selected objects in the window differently from those crossing the window boundary.

Use the next example to combine a crossing window and the Remove mode to move the ROM chip, using a polar displacement. Select the capacitor and the ROM chip together with Crossing, then remove the capacitor from the selection set. The capacitor is the circle with a C in it.

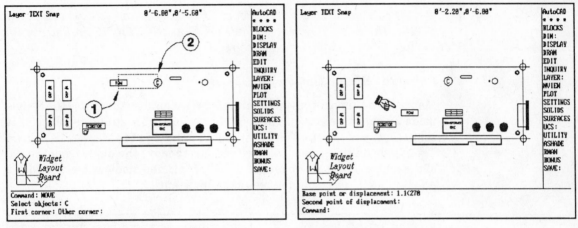

Using a Crossing Window to Move Objects   ☞ *ROM Chip Is Moved*

Using Crossing, Add, and Remove Selection Set Modes

```
Command: MOVE
Select objects: C                              Select ROM chip and capacitor.
First corner:                                  Pick first corner point at ①.
Other corner:                                  Pick second corner point at ③.
4 found.                                        Highlighting indicates they are selected.
Select objects: R                              Remove mode.
Remove objects:                                Select the circle.
1 selected, 1 found, 1 removed                 The circle is removed from the selection set.
Remove objects:                                Select the character C.
1 selected, 1 found, 1 removed                 The C is removed from the selection set.
Remove objects: <RETURN>
Base point or displacement: 1.1<270            A polar displacement.
Second point of displacement: <RETURN>         Use previous input as displacement.
```

What's in the Selection Set?

In a complex drawing, you may notice the time it takes AutoCAD to search through the drawing file for entities that qualify for the selection set. Every time you select more objects for the selection set, AutoCAD lets you know how many you selected and how many it actually found. These numbers are not always the same for two reasons. First, you can select objects that do not qualify for editing. Second, you may have already selected that entity. In the latter case, AutoCAD lets you know it found a duplicate. In all cases (except Multiple mode selections), AutoCAD uses the highlighting feature to show you what is currently in the selection set.

➡ *TIP: To speed up the selection of complex selection sets, you can turn the HIGHLIGHT system variable off. Type HIGHLIGHT (in Release 10, use SETVAR) and set it to 0 (off).*

Using the SIngle Option for Object Selection

Menu items that expect you to select exactly one object may use the SIngle mode of object selection. As soon as an object (or group of objects) is selected, object selection ends without your having to enter a <RETURN>. Try SIngle and an absolute displacement to move the diode from the top of the widget down to the left. Remember that the diode was made with a polyline, so it selects and moves as a single entity.

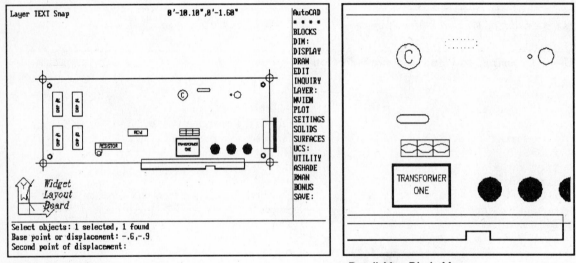

Before Diode Move   Detail After Diode Move

Using the SIngle Option for Object Selection

```
Command: MOVE
Select objects: SI                          SI for SIngle.
Select objects:                             Pick any point on diode.
1 selected, 1 found.
Base point of displacement: -.6,-.9         A negative absolute displacement.
Second point of displacement:               Use previous input as displacement.

Command: SAVE                               Save the drawing.
```

SIngle was designed for use in menu macros. You can precede any of the object selection modes with SI for SIngle.

Previous Selection Set Option

You will find the Previous selection option helpful when you cancel an editing command or use several commands on the same selection set. Previous object selection reselects the object(s) that you selected in your previous editing command.

Previous lets you edit the previous set without having to individually select its objects again. Previous is different from the Last option, which selects the last created object visible on the screen. Previous does not work with some editing commands (like STRETCH) where a window, crossing, or point selection is specifically required.

Tired of moving? Let's take a look at copying.

The COPY Command

The basic COPY command is similar to the MOVE command. The only difference between a copy and a move is that COPY leaves the original objects in place.

We'll copy the widget's transformer, using a BOX selection. BOX combines a window and a crossing window. If you make your box left to right, it acts like a window. Right to left acts like a crossing window. Try canceling the command and using Previous to reselect the selection set to copy.

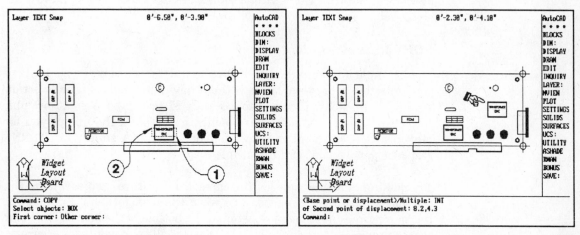

Selecting the Transformer    *Copied Transformer*

Using the COPY Command and BOX Mode

```
Command: COPY
Select objects: BOX                     Enclose transformer and text right to left for crossing.
First corner:                           Pick first corner at ①.
Other corner:                           Pick second corner at ②.
3 found.
Select objects: <RETURN>
<Base point or displacement>/Multiple: <^C>    Cancel it.

Command: COPY
Select objects: P                       Previous.
3 found.
Select objects: <RETURN>
<Base point or displacement>/Multiple: INT      Intersection.
of                                      Pick lower left corner of transformer.
Second point of displacement: 8.20,4.30
```

Remember, you can always use osnap and snap functions as modifiers to help you get an exact displacement location, or to help select objects for the selection set.

COPY Options

The COPY command options are similar to the MOVE options. They include displacement points identification, object selection options, and a new one — Multiple (for multiple copies, not to be confused with Multiple object selection).

COPY Multiple Option

The Multiple option of the COPY command lets you copy the contents of your selection set several times without having to respecify the selection set and base point. If you respond with M to the base point prompt, AutoCAD will reprompt for base point, then repeatedly prompt you for multiple <Second point of displacement> points. A simple <RETURN> response gets you out of the Multiple loop.

Try making multiple copies of the capacitor. Put three copies next to the original capacitor. Put one copy between the transformers. Finally, put two more copies next to the resistor on the bottom of the board. The polar coords shown are for your reference; they are all snap points for accuracy.

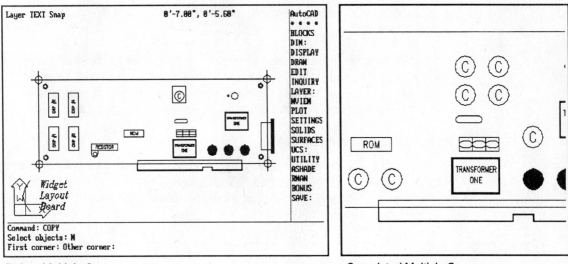

Before Multiple Copy   Completed Multiple Copy

Using COPY Multiple to Make Copies of the Capacitor

```
Command: COPY
Select objects: W                      Put a window around the capacitor.
First corner:                          Pick first corner point.
Other corner:                          Pick second corner point.
2 found.
Select objects: <RETURN>
<Base point or displacement>/Multiple: M
Base point:                            Pick center of capacitor.
Second point of displacement:          Pick polar point @0.40<270.00.
Second point of displacement:          Pick polar point @0.50<0.00.
Second point of displacement:          Pick polar point @0.64<321.34.
Second point of displacement:          Pick polar point @2.26<225.00.
Second point of displacement:          Pick polar point @1.94<235.49.
Second point of displacement:          Pick polar point @1.41<315.00.
Second point of displacement: <RETURN>
```

Let's look at another type of multiple copying — making *arrays*.

ARRAY — Making Multiple Copies in a Pattern

Often, you want to make multiple copies of an object or group of objects in a regular pattern. For example, suppose you have a rectangle that represents a table in a cafeteria. It would be useful if AutoCAD had some way of placing that table repeatedly every nine feet in the X direction and every fourteen feet in the Y direction to make five rows and eight columns of tables. Or drawing evenly spaced bolt holes around the circumference of a tank top.

The ARRAY command works like the COPY command. However, instead of making individually placed copies of the selection set, ARRAY makes a regular pattern of entities. You determine the number of copies and the repetition pattern. The two basic patterns are rectangular and polar.

Rectangular Arrays

You make a rectangular array by specifying the number of rows and columns that you want and an X,Y offset distance. You can have a single row with multiple columns, a single column with multiple rows, or multiple rows and columns.

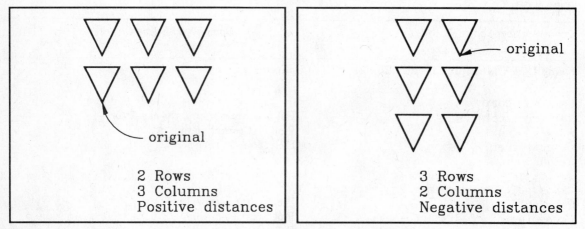

Positive Array Offsets	Negative Array Offsets

You can show the displacement between rows or columns by picking two points at the distance between rows prompt. Or you can specify the offsets by entering positive or negative offset values. The offset distance is the X and Y direction from the original selection set. Entering negative values will produce an array in the negative X and/or Y directions. A positive X value gives columns to the right. A negative X value gives columns to the left. A positive Y gives rows up. A negative Y gives rows down.

Try making a rectangular array using the ROM chip.

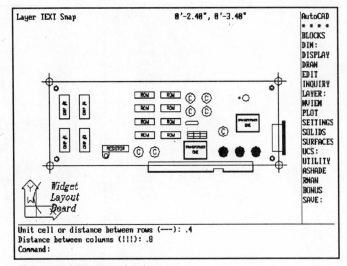

Completed Rectangular Array

Using ARRAY to Make a Rectangular Array

```
Command: ARRAY
Select objects:                              Pick the ROM chip and its text.
2 selected,  2 found.
Select objects: <RETURN>
Rectangular or Polar array  (R/P): R         Rectangular.
Number of rows (---) <1>: 4
Number of columns (|||) <1>: 2
Distance between rows (---): 0.40
Distance between columns (|||): 0.80         And the array draws.
```

If you set up a big array (many rows and columns), AutoCAD will ask if you really want to repeat the selection set so many times. If it gets out of hand, you can stop it with a <^C> and then reverse it with a U for Undo.

➡ *TIP: ARRAY is useful even if you want to make only one row or column of entities. It is quicker than COPY Multiple.*

Try making a set of logo arcs next to the widget layout text at the bottom left of your drawing. This is the single-row array of arcs shown in the detail illustration below.

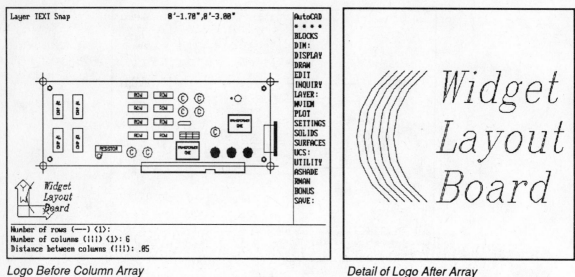

Logo Before Column Array   *Detail of Logo After Array*

Making a Single-Column Array

```
Command: ARRAY
Select objects:                               Pick the logo arc.
1 selected, 1 found.
Select objects: <RETURN>
Rectangular or Polar array  (R/P): R
Number of rows (---) <1>: <RETURN>           One row.
Number of columns (|||) <1>: 6
Distance between columns (|||): 0.05          And the array draws.
```

Polar Arrays

In polar arrays, you place the entities in the selection set around the circumference of an imaginary circle or arc. Polar arrays are useful for creating mechanical parts like gear teeth, or bolt patterns. Examples of regular and rotated circular arrays are shown in the Polar Array illustrations below.

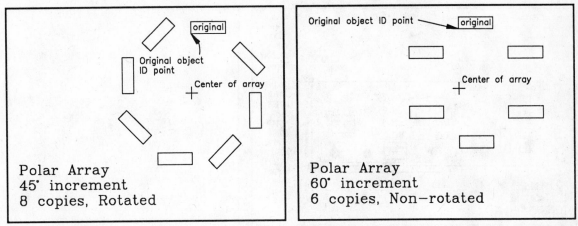

Polar Array Rotated   Polar Array Non-Rotated

When you form a polar array, you specify the number of items you want in the array, the angle you want to fill, and whether you want the items rotated. One item is one copy of the selection set to be arrayed. When you count your items, remember to include the original. You can array around a full circle or part of a circle. If you array around part of a circle, you will need one more item than the total arc angle divided by the incremental angle. For example, if you are arraying 90 degrees and you want the items at 30-degree increments, you will need 90/30 + 1 = 4 items.

The following exercise shows how to array the contact around part of a circle. The contact is the small circle to the left of the switch (large circle) on the right side of the widget.

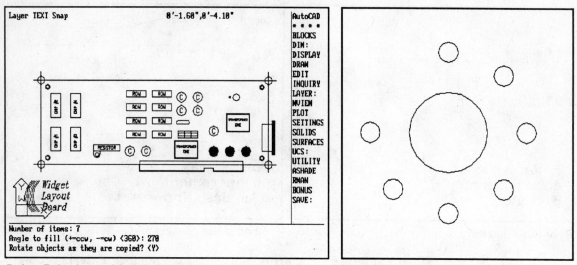

Before Polar Array of Switch Contacts

Detail View After Array

Using Polar Array on Switch Contacts

```
Command: ARRAY
Select objects:                              Select small circle to left of switch.
1 selected, 1 found.
Select objects: <RETURN>
Rectangular or Polar array (R/P): P          Polar.
Center point of array: CEN                   Osnap it.
of                                           Pick any point on large circle.
Number of items: 7                           That's 270/45 + 1.
Angle to fill (+=ccw, -=cw) <360>: 270
Rotate objects as they are copied? Y <RETURN>  It doesn't matter for circles!
```

➡ *TIP: Polar arraying a line twice around its midpoint or four times around its endpoint will create a cross. A large number of items will create a sunburst.*

If an array can rotate entities, you must be able to rotate entities individually.

The ROTATE Command

The ROTATE command lets you turn existing entities at precise angles. Like MOVE, you specify a first point as a base point. This rotation base point doesn't need to be on the object that you are rotating. You can put it anywhere and AutoCAD will turn your selected entities relative to the base point. But be careful — it's easy to become confused with rotation base points (like bad drag handles) that are not on the entities you intend to rotate. After you specify the base point, give a rotation angle. Negative angles produce clockwise rotation, positive angles produce counterclockwise rotation (with the normal direction setting in units).

As an alternative to specifying an angle, you can use a reference angle. You can change the angle of an entity by giving AutoCAD a reference angle that should be set equal to the new angle. In effect you say, "Put a handle on 237 degrees (for example) and turn it to 165." This is often easier than calculating the difference (72 degrees clockwise) and typing that number at the prompt. You need not even know the actual angles; you can pick points to indicate angles. To align with existing objects, use osnaps when picking the points of the angle(s).

Try two rotations. First, use ROTATE to reposition the jumper. The jumper is the rectangular thing with three ellipses in it, just above the transformer. Rotate the jumper into position vertically at the left of the transformer.

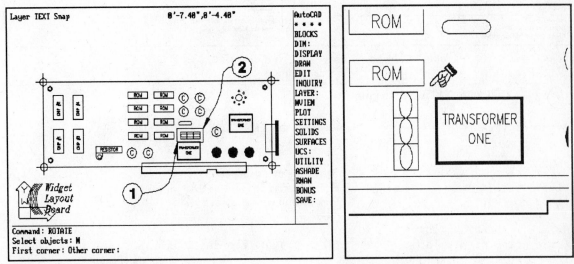

Selecting Jumper With Window   *Jumper After Rotate*

Using the ROTATE Command

```
Command: ROTATE
Select objects: W                    Place window around jumper.
First corner:                        Pick first corner point at ①.
Other corner:                        Pick second corner point at ②.
6 found.
Select objects: <RETURN>
Base point: 6.45,4.3.
<Rotation angle>/Reference: -90
```

Next, combine a COPY command and a ROTATE command to place another mounting tab nut and flange on top of the resistor. This COPY/ROTATE technique is an efficient trick.

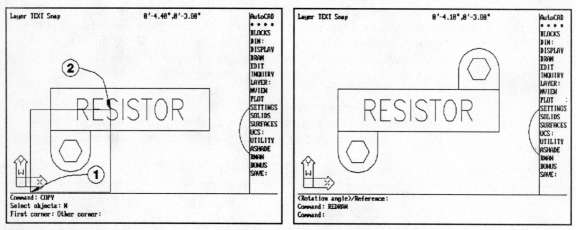

Selecting Resistor Nut With Window   *Nut After Copy and Rotate*

Using the COPY/ROTATE Technique

```
Command: VIEW                        Restore view RESISTOR.

Command: COPY
Select object: W                     Select the mounting tab.
First corner:                        Pick first corner point at ①.
Other corner:                        Pick second corner point at ②.
4 found.
Select objects: <RETURN>
<Base point or displacement>/Multiple: 0,0    Zero displacement.
Second point of displacement: <RETURN>        Copies entities on top of themselves.
```

```
Command: ROTATE                      Rotate mounting tab to opposite corner of resistor.
Select objects: P                    Previous reselects entities.
4 found.
Select objects: <RETURN>
Base point:                          Pick absolute point 4.50,3.80.
<Rotation angle>/Reference:          Drag cursor 180 degrees to left and pick.
                                     Rotation takes place again.


Command: REDRAW                      Shows the complete resistor.
```

➥ *NOTE: This exercise shows how handy COPY and ROTATE can be for avoiding redrawing entities in new positions.*

MIRROR — Copying Through the Looking Glass

The MIRROR command creates a mirrored copy of objects. You can mirror the contents of a selection set at any angle. MIRROR prompts you to identify a selection set in the usual manner. Then comes the mirror twist. AutoCAD prompts you for the beginning and endpoint of a mirror line. The line can be any direction. If you want a straight 180-degree flip, use ortho to help you get a straight mirror line. If you want mirroring at a precise angle, use relative polar coordinates, @8<60 for example, or use a rotated snap or UCS.

Finally, AutoCAD asks if you want to keep the original entities in place or to delete them. Think of this as either copying or moving the contents of the selection set through the mirror.

If you have text in your selection set (as our example does), you need to consider whether you want to pass the text through the mirror unchanged or mirrored. If you do not want text mirrored, you can set the MIRRTEXT system variable to 0, allowing mirror-inverted graphics, but letting text come out reading the way it goes in.

Mirror the resistor you have been working on. Set MIRRTEXT to 0 so text is not mirrored. Mirror the resistor by flipping it 180 degrees. Keep the original in place.

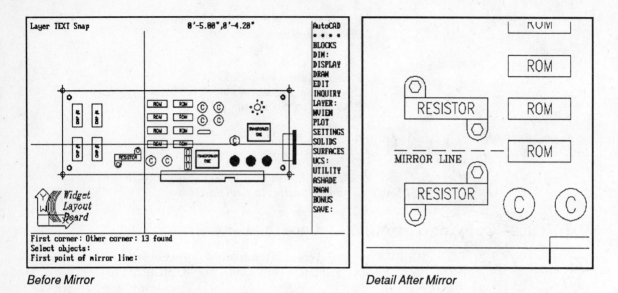

Before Mirror   *Detail After Mirror*

Using MIRROR to Mirror the Resistor

Command: **MIRRTEXT** New value for MIRRTEXT <1>: **0**	Release 10 users use SETVAR to set MIRRTEXT.
Command: **ZOOM**	Zoom Previous to see the layout board.
Command: **MIRROR** Select objects: **W** First corner: Other corner: 13 found. Select objects: **<RETURN>** First point of mirror line: Second point: <Ortho> Delete old objects? <N> **<RETURN>**	Place window around resistor. Pick first point at 4.00,3.40. Pick second point at 5.00,4.20. Pick point 5.00,4.20. Toggle ortho on with <^O> or <F6> and pick any point to left.
Command: **SAVE**	Save and continue or end and take a break.

If you need to take a break, end your drawing. So far, the editing commands that you have worked with are variations on a theme — moving or copying single entities, or making multiple copies of entities. The next group of editing commands involves deleting portions of entities, or, in the case of ERASE, deleting entire entities.

ERASE and Its Sidekick, OOPS

Like a hammer, ERASE can be a constructive tool. But, like a hammer, watch out! The ERASE command has been the scourge of many a good drawing file.

The following exercise uses ERASE, but adds a good friend, the OOPS command. You will find OOPS prominently displayed on the [ERASE] screen menu and the [Modify] pull-down menu (and also available by typing it). OOPS asks no questions — it just goes about its business of restoring whatever you just obliterated with ERASE.

Let's get rid of the original resistor and the diode with an ERASE. You can reload your WIDGEDIT drawing, or continue from the previous exercise.

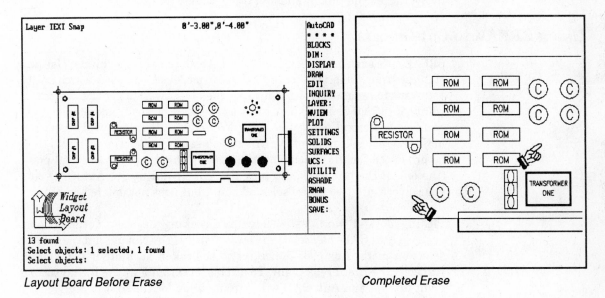

Layout Board Before Erase   Completed Erase

Using ERASE

Edit an EXISTING drawing named WIDGEDIT, or continue from previous exercise.

```
Command: ERASE
Select objects: W          Window the original resistor. (If continuing, you can use Previous
                           instead.)

13 found.
Select objects:            Pick the diode.
1 found.
Select objects: <RETURN>   The deletion takes place.
```

Every time you execute an erase, AutoCAD keeps a copy of what you erased in case you want to oops it back into the file. But only the most recent erase is kept oops-ready!

Try OOPS now to get your objects back.

Using OOPS on Your Last Erase

Command: **OOPS**   Here come the resistor and diode.

OOPS lets you recover from the unthinkable. After you have mistakenly deleted an entity from your drawing, you can recover the last deletion (under most circumstances) with OOPS. The OOPS command won't recover after you plot or end and then resume a drawing.

Using BREAK to Cut Objects

BREAK cuts existing objects into two or erases portions of objects. Use any of the standard selection set techniques to let AutoCAD know which entity you want to break. Picking is usually the safest way to get the object you want. AutoCAD uses the pick point as the start of the break and prompts you for the second point. Crossing, Window, or Previous will break the most recently selected entity. Unless you select by picking, you will then be prompted for the first point (the start of the break) and second point (the end of the break). If you pick the same point again, AutoCAD cuts your object into two at the selected point, but does not delete any of it.

Picking doesn't work as well when breaking between intersections, because AutoCAD may select the wrong entity. You can use another object selection method or pick the object to be broken at another point, then respecify the first break point. To do this, enter an F at the initial second point prompt and AutoCAD will reprompt you for the first point.

Here's the prompt sequence for breaking out the line at the port on the right side of the widget.

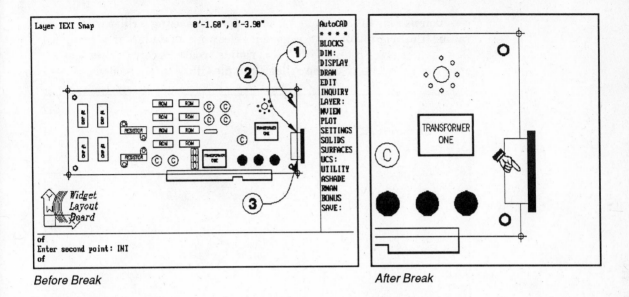

Before Break   *After Break*

Using BREAK to Break a Line

```
Command: BREAK                                      Pick line of widget board at ①.
Select object:                                      Reprompt for first point.
Enter second point (or F for first point): F        Use OSNAP INT to pick first point at ②.
Enter first point:                                  Use OSNAP INT to pick second point at ③.
Enter second point:
```

BREAK works on lines, arcs, circles, traces, and polylines (including polygons and donuts). Take care to select the first and second points in counterclockwise order when breaking circles. Closed polylines need a little experimentation. BREAK's effects will depend on the location of the polyline's first vertex. The break cannot extend across this vertex. If a point is off the entity, it acts as if you used osnap NEArest. If one point is off the end of an arc, line, trace, or open polyline, that end is cut off instead of breaking the entity into two.

The FILLET Command

A fillet is a tangent arc swung between two lines to create a round corner. The FILLET command is simple; AutoCAD asks you to identify the two lines that you would like joined. You identify the lines by picking them. AutoCAD then shortens or extends the lines and creates a new arc for the fillet corner.

You can specify the radius of the arc to create the fillet corner. The default radius is <0>. The fillet radius you set becomes the new default. The most common use for FILLET is to round corners, but using a fillet with a zero radius (the original default) is good for cleaning up under- or overlapping lines at corners. FILLET with a zero radius creates a corner, but does not create a new entity. See the Fillet Examples illustration below.

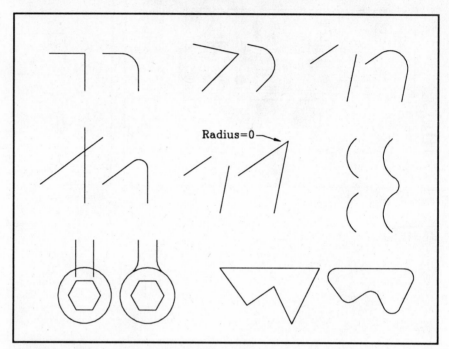

Fillet Examples

FILLET works on any combination of two arcs, circles and non-parallel lines, or on a single polyline. You can select lines or a polyline by Window, Last, or Crossing, but the results may be unpredictable. Selection by picking is safer, and is required for arcs or circles. Arcs and circles have more than one possible fillet, so they are filleted closest to the pick points.

Try filleting the four corners of the layout board.

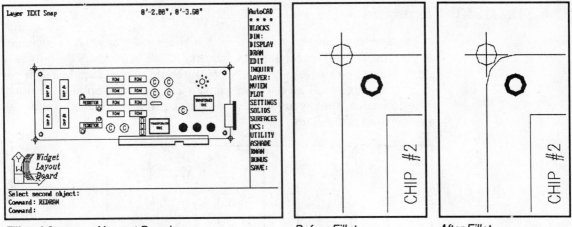

Filleted Corners of Layout Board   Before Fillet   After Fillet

---

Using FILLET to Round Corners

```
Command: FILLET
Polyline/Radius/<Select two objects>: R
Enter fillet radius <0'-0.00">: .2
Command: FILLET
Polyline/Radius/<Select two objects>:
```

Fillet a corner of the layout board.
Pick the two lines that make up the corner.

Repeat the FILLET command for the remaining corners.

```
Command: REDRAW
```

Refresh the screen.

Your screen should look like the Filleted Corners of Layout Board illustration.

➡ *TIP: When you are faced with a task where the fillets have the same radius arc (like the exercise above), you can speed up the edit by using the MULTIPLE command to make multiple fillets.*

Filleting Polylines

There are two ways to fillet polylines: one vertex or all vertexes. If you select the polyline by Window, Crossing, or Last, the most recent vertex will be filleted. If you pick two points on adjacent segments, the vertex between those segments will be filleted. If you enter a P at the first fillet prompt, you will be prompted to select a polyline and all of its vertexes will be filleted.

The CHAMFER Command

A chamfer is a beveled edge. Adding a chamfer is easy. As you might expect, the CHAMFER command works like FILLET. CHAMFER works only on two lines or a single polyline. To get the chamfer, you supply a chamfer distance along each line that you want to join, rather than an arc radius. The distance that you supply is the cut-back distance from the intersection of the lines.

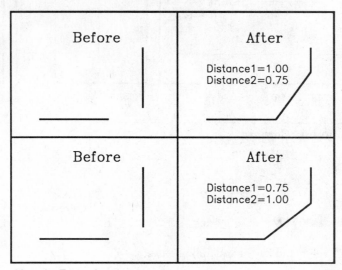

Chamfer Examples

Try two sets of chamfers. Chamfer all four corners of the second transformer polyline with 45-degree chamfers (equal distances). Then chamfer two corners on the right side port.

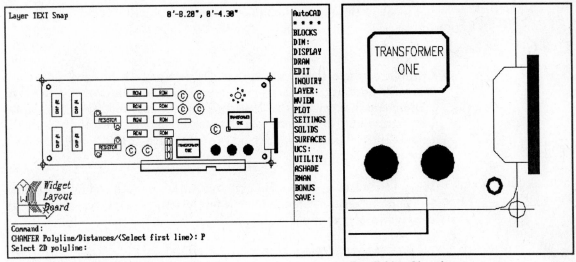

Transformer and Port Before Chamfers   *Detail After Chamfers*

Using CHAMFER on the Layout Board

```
Command: CHAMFER
Polyline/Distances/<Select first line>: D
Enter first chamfer distance <0'-0.00">: .05
Enter second chamfer distance <0'-0.05">: <RETURN>    Defaults to equal first.

Command: <RETURN>
CHAMFER Polyline/Distances/<Select first line>: P
Select 2D polyline:                                   Pick the transformer polyline
                                                      on the right.

4 lines were chamfered

Command: <RETURN>
CHAMFER Polyline/Distances/<Select first line>: D
Enter first chamfer distance <0'-0.05">: .1
Enter second chamfer distance <0'-0.10">: <RETURN>

Command: <RETURN>
CHAMFER Polyline/Distances/<Select first line>:       Pick top horizontal port line.
Select second line:                                   Pick vertical port line.

Command: <RETURN>
CHAMFER Polyline/Distances/<Select first line>:       Pick bottom horizontal port line.
Select second line:                                   Pick vertical port line.
```

As you can see from the exercise, it is easy to chamfer polylines. All four
corners were modified at the same time.

Let's look at two more commands that modify existing entities.

The CHANGE Command

CHANGE can selectively edit one or more parameters that give a drawing entity its identity, location, and appearance in the drawing file. We recommend that you use CHANGE in 2D drawings to modify entity points, text, or attribute definitions (see Chapter 13) and use a second command, called CHPROP (see below), to modify appearance. CHPROP works in both 2D and 3D.

When you select objects to change, AutoCAD prompts you for the points and parameters that are changeable for the entities that you select. These vary with the type of entity.

How CHANGE Affects Different Entities

■ Lines. CHANGE point changes the endpoint of a line. If several lines are selected, their nearest endpoints will converge at the change point picked. If ortho is on, they will be forced parallel instead of converging — a good trick to try.

■ Circles. CHANGE point changes the circumference of an existing circle, forcing it to pass through the change point, while keeping the same center point.

■ Text (and attribute definitions). Changes location, rotation angle, height, style, and/or text string. CHANGE acts as a second chance to reset your text parameters.

■ Blocks (see Chapter 9). CHANGE lets you change the insertion point or rotation angle.

If you select several different entities, even different types, CHANGE will ignore any change point you pick and instead cycle through the entities in the order selected, prompting for the appropriate changes.

Try CHANGE to change the text of the second transformer from "ONE" to "TWO." Then, change the diameter of the switch circle on the right side of the board.

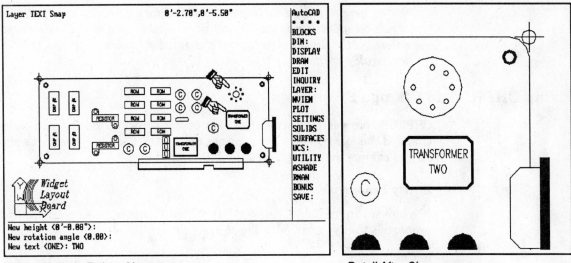

Text and Circle Before Changes   Detail After Changes

Using CHANGE to Modify the Layout Board

```
Command: CHANGE                    Change text in transformer on the right.
Select objects:                    Select text string ONE.
1 selected, 1 found.
Select objects: <RETURN>
Properties/<Change point>: <RETURN>
Enter text insertion point: <RETURN>
Text style: STANDARD
New style or RETURN for no change: <RETURN>
New height <0'-0.08">: <RETURN>
New rotation angle <0.00>: <RETURN>
New text <ONE>: TWO              Change ONE to TWO.
Command: CHANGE                  Change diameter of switch.
Select objects:                  Pick the center switch circle.
1 selected, 1 found.
Select objects: <RETURN>
Properties/<Change point>:       Pick absolute point 8.20,5.30 as the new
                                 circumference point.
```

You also can use CHANGE to modify the properties of entities. Using CHANGE to modify properties in 2D drawings works fine, but it may not always work in 3D drawings. That is why AutoCAD has the CHPROP command, which always works.

➡ *TIP: When you redefine an existing text style with STYLE, only changes to the font and vertical orientation affect existing text. But you can use the CHANGE command to force existing text to reflect modifications to* *width, height, obliquing angle, etc. Entering a style name at the new style prompt will update all text parameters, even if the style name entered is the same as the currently defined style. Pressing <RETURN> leaves all parameters unchanged.*

Using CHPROP to Change Properties

CHPROP changes properties in a 2D or 3D drawing. So far you have changed the location, size, or shape of entities already in place. Let's see how to change their properties.

Entity Properties

If you recall our earlier discussion on entities (Chapter 2), all entities have properties that you can edit. These are:

- Color

- Elevation

- Layer

- Linetype

- Thickness

When you created the lines in your widget drawing, you gave them a color and linetype. You might not have thought about it at the time. It may seem like a lot of edits ago! You created the individual widget parts on the layer PARTS with both entity color and linetype BYLAYER (PARTS has a cyan [4] default color and a continuous default linetype). When you created the parts, these entities picked up their characteristics from the layer defaults. While you were editing these lines, they retained their BYLAYER color and linetype. (At this point, the widget's entities have 0 elevation and thickness. These properties apply to 3D drawings. You will learn about them in Part Two, which covers 3D drawing and editing.)

Using CHPROP is the best way to change the properties of entities that you have already drawn. Use CHPROP to change the interior connector line's layer property to the HIDDEN layer. The object selection prompts are abbreviated in this and most of the remaining exercises, leaving you on your own for selection method. Once you select the objects, you will get a prompt for the property that you want to change.

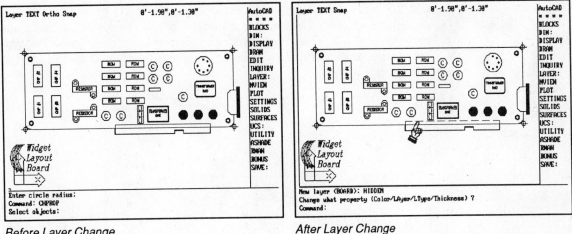

Before Layer Change   After Layer Change

Using CHPROP to Change Layers

```
Command: CHPROP
Select objects:
Change what property (Color/LAyer/LType/Thickness) ? LA
New layer <BOARD>: HIDDEN
Change what property (Color/LAyer/LType/Thickness) ? <RETURN>
```

Change lines to the HIDDEN layer.
Select the connector lines.

Your drawing should show a red hidden connector line. The linetype and color properties are still BYLAYER.

Entity color and linetype properties can be independent of layer. In fact, an entity can have any color or linetype. Try using CHPROP to change the color of the solid donuts. Then take one last look at your widget layout drawing with all its edits, and end it.

Using CHPROP to Change the Color of Donuts

```
Command: CHPROP
Select objects:
Change what property (Color/LAyer/LType/Thickness) ? C
New color <BYLAYER>: 6
Change what property (Color/LAyer/LType/Thickness) ? <RETURN>

Command: ZOOM
Command: END
```

Change the entity color of the solid donuts.
Select the three solid donuts.

Change color to magenta.

All to get a full view.

Now the donuts are magenta, overriding the cyan PARTS layer default.

CHPROP provides an easy method for changing entity properties. But for organized controlled drawings, it is usually best to deal with color and linetype by layer settings. Instead of changing color and linetype properties, try expanding and redefining the layers you set up in your drawings.

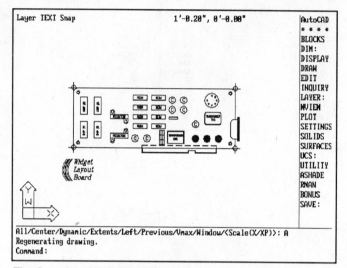

The Completed WIDGEDIT Drawing

As we promised, you now have a full four-color widget layout board. Save this drawing, you can use it later when we take up plotting in Part Two.

➡ *NOTE: You can now delete the WIDGET, PSPLOT, MVPLOT, and VPLAYER drawings; you no longer need them.*

Summing Up

Now you can see how important editing is in constructing a drawing. In the beginning of the chapter on graphic entities, we said that drawings are dynamic. With a first course in editing under your belt, you can see just *how* dynamic a drawing can be.

Are you ready for the next engineering change order? Here's an Editor's Guide to Editing to keep you prepared.

Editor's Guide to Editing

Plan ahead for editing. When you first set up a drawing, think about how you are going to use your layers. Having everything on one layer complicates editing, so plan to use multiple layers. Think about repetitive features. Draw it once, copy it forever. Think about your building blocks. Start by defining your basic components and building your drawing up from there.

You should not have a favorite edit command. Use them all. Use snap, ortho, and osnaps to set up your MOVE and COPY displacements. MIRROR and ARRAY can help you complete a repetitive drawing in a hurry. Be careful with ERASE. To avoid disasters, there's always OOPS and Undo.

Learn to use all of the object selection options including the Remove option. All the selection set options have their roles. Last and Previous are used all the time when you realize that AutoCAD did what you said, not what you meant. The object picking method is best for detail work, especially with osnap. Window is powerful, but it doesn't do it all. Remember, what you see in the window is what goes into the selection set. You can use Crossing like a knife to slice out a selection set. BOX and SIngle are best for menu macros, as we shall see when we get to customization. AUto is a good habit. You can use it like a window, a crossing, or just to select an object. Previous saves time in repetitive editing. Don't forget, a U undoes the last object selection operation.

Think ahead about individual edits. Use display control to keep your field of view small and your concentration level high. Don't get caught setting up the base point of a displacement only to find that the second point is off the screen (if that happens, cancel, zoom, and try again). Don't underestimate the power of CHANGE. It really is an effective tool. Changing an endpoint is easier than erasing and adding a new line segment. Changing text is almost always easier than retyping text. AutoCAD prompts you for every change. CHPROP allows you to change the layer, color, and linetype properties of existing entities.

Stay informed about what AutoCAD is up to. Watch the current layer name on the status line. Create entities on the layers you want them on. Watch the prompt line for edit prompts — it is easy to start creating a selection set window while the prompt line is waiting for you to enter W to initiate the window selection. Use the Flip Screen key to see what's going on.

On to More Editing

So far, you've looked at some of AutoCAD's basic editing commands. Let's move on to more advanced editing commands and see how you can combine them with some electronic drafting techniques to get more productivity out of editing your drawings.

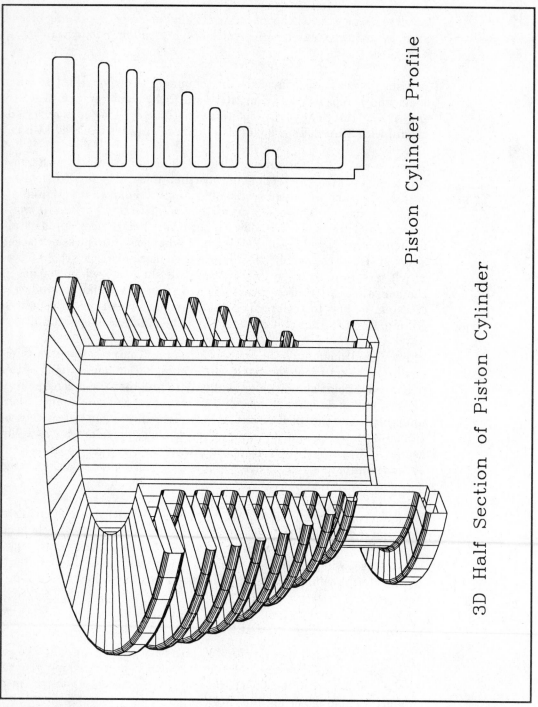

Piston Cylinder Profile

3D Half Section of Piston Cylinder

3D Piston Cylinder and Profile

CHAPTER 7

Advanced Editing

PUTTING DRAWINGS TOGETHER — CAD STYLE

To take full advantage of AutoCAD's power, you need to combine AutoCAD's editing commands with CAD drafting techniques. While the editing commands you learned in the last chapter will help you speed up your drafting, the editing commands and techniques you learn in this chapter will change the way you create your drawings. These advanced editing commands, like EXTEND, STRETCH, TRIM, and OFFSET, go beyond copying and moving entities. They build on AutoCAD's geometrical knowledge of the entities in your drawing. By combining these commands with construction techniques, setting up construction lines, parallel rules, and construction layers, you can rough out a drawing quickly, then finish it perfectly.

Besides construction techniques, we want to emphasize how to get *continuity* in your two-dimensional drawings by using polylines and by editing with PEDIT. Continuous polylines are important to AutoCAD's hatch patterns and 3D. Polylines provide continuity when you form three-dimensional faces and meshes. If your two-dimensional drawing has breaks in its line profile, you will not be able to form a complete three-dimensional surface. The facing page illustration shows the effect of taking a continuous polyline and forming a 3D mesh.

Drawing polylines and modifying them with PEDIT, or converting or joining existing entities into new polylines with PEDIT, are basic 2D skills that you want to master before working in 3D. The exercises in this chapter will show you how to use PEDIT and the other advanced editing commands to combine entity creation and CAD construction techniques into a single drawing process.

Advanced Editing Tools

The editing commands covered in this chapter's exercises are found on the [EDIT] screen menu and the [Modify] pull-down menu. These commands include EXTEND, OFFSET, SCALE, STRETCH, TRIM, and PEDIT. The PEDIT command, labeled [PolyEdit] on the pull-down menu, has an extensive set of options for global PEDITs, and options to edit individual vertexes of polylines. The trick to using these advanced editing commands is to plan ahead. The operations of commands like EXTEND, STRETCH, and TRIM can involve a number of entities. PEDIT requires continuity to join lines and arcs. These commands require more setup and more planning for how you are going to use them.

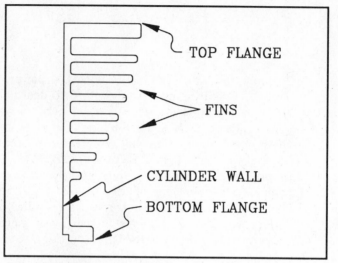

TOP FLANGE

FINS

CYLINDER WALL

BOTTOM FLANGE

Cylinder Profile Target Drawing

Setting Up the Cylinder Drawing

The drawing that you will create in this chapter's exercises is the piston cylinder profile. The full cylinder is approximately 10 inches high by 14.60 inches wide. Here are our sample calculations for estimating a drawing scale factor and setting a sheet size.

```
Finned Piston Cylinder Wall              14.60" x 10.00"
Plot sheet size                          11" x 8 1/2"
Test 1/2" = 1" scale is a scale factor of 2.
    11" x 2 = 22" and 8 1/2" x 2 = 17"    22" x 17" limits
```

Create a new drawing called CYLINDER. Use the default decimal units, each unit representing one inch. If you were to dimension this drawing, you could have AutoCAD's dimensioning automatically add inch marks. Set your limits at 22 x 17. Use the table settings below to help you complete your setup. If you are using the IA DISK, begin your CYLINDER drawing by setting it equal to IA6CYLIN.

Setup for CYLINDER Drawing

 Begin a NEW drawing named CYLINDER=IA6CYLIN.

 Begin a NEW drawing named CYLINDER and complete the setup shown in the Cylinder Drawing Settings table. Set the 2D layer current.

AXIS	COORDS	GRID	SNAP	ORTHO
Off	On	1	0.1	ON

UNITS	Default decimal units, 2 digits to right of decimal point, default all other settings.
LIMITS	0,0 to 22,17
ZOOM	Zoom All.

Layer Name	State	Color	Linetype
0	On	7 (white)	CONTINUOUS
2D	On/Current	2 (red)	CONTINUOUS
3D	On	3 (green)	CONTINUOUS

Cylinder Drawing Settings

If you want to practice individual editing commands, you can use a layer named SCRATCH. Create some entities, try out some editing variations, then freeze your SCRATCH layer and pick up again where you left off with the exercise sequences.

Using Lines and Polylines to Rough-In a Drawing

Let's start by roughing-in the section profile of the cylinder. First, use a polyline to draw the top, side, and bottom of the cylinder. Then, draw one line and array it to form the construction lines for what will later become the cylinder fins. Finally, draw an arc on the right side as a construction line to help form the ends of the fins. Your current layer is 2D.

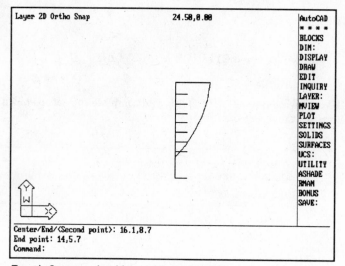

Rough Construction Lines of Cylinder Wall

Using PLINE, LINE, and ARC to Rough-In the Cylinder Wall

```
Command: PLINE                                    Draw a profile of the cylinder wall and flanges.
From point:                                       Pick absolute point 17,12.
Current line-width is 0.00
Arc/Close/Halfwidth/Length/Undo/Width/<Endpoint of line>:        Pick @3<180.
Arc/Close/Halfwidth/Length/Undo/Width/<Endpoint of line>:        Pick @8<270.
Arc/Close/Halfwidth/Length/Undo/Width/<Endpoint of line>:        Pick @1<0.
Arc/Close/Halfwidth/Length/Undo/Width/<Endpoint of line>: <RETURN>


Command: LINE                                     Draw a line from 14.00,11.00 to @1<0.


Command: ARRAY                                    Array the fin lines from the line.
Select objects: L                                 L selects the last entity.
1 found.
Select objects: <RETURN>
Rectangular or Polar array (R/P): R
Number of rows (---) <1>: 7
Number of columns (||||) <1>: <RETURN>
Unit cell or distance between rows (---): -.8


Command: ARC                                      Draw three-point arc from 17,12 to 16.1,8.7 to 14,5.7.
```

Your arc should extend down from the polyline endpoint on the top right, intersect the first line that you drew, and intersect the polyline on the left a little more than halfway between the bottom and the intersected line. This arc will act as a construction line boundary to form the cylinder fins. The fin lines will be formed by extending them to the arc.

Extending Entities

To extend the lines to the arc, the command we turn to is EXTEND. You use EXTEND to extend lines, polylines, and arcs. The command is straightforward. The boundary edge(s) can be lines, polylines, arcs, circles, and viewport entities (when in paper space). Use normal object selection to select the boundary edge(s) that you want to extend to, then pick the objects you want to extend. The main thing to remember is that you have to individually pick each object to extend. You cannot use other modes to fill a selection set full of objects that you want extended, and then extend them all at once. Objects to extend are ignored unless EXTEND can project them to intersect a boundary object.

Use EXTEND when you are faced with the problem of not knowing (or not wanting to calculate) drawing intersection points. In these cases (and in the current exercise), it is easier to use a construction line, and extend your entities. There are a few constraints on using EXTEND: you cannot extend closed polylines and you cannot use EXTEND to shorten objects. That's a job for TRIM.

Try using EXTEND to lengthen the fin lines until they meet the construction arc.

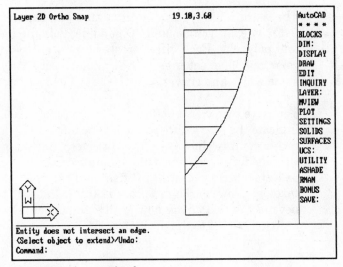

Extending Lines to the Arc

Using EXTEND to Extend Lines to an Arc

```
Command: ZOOM                          Get into a closer working area.

Command: EXTEND
Select boundary edges(s)...
Select objects:                        Pick the arc.
1 selected, 1 found.
Select objects: <RETURN>
<Select object to extend>/Undo:        Pick each of the upper six arrayed lines.
```

The seventh line already crosses the arc, so EXTEND can't adjust it. We could use TRIM, but we'll save it for a STRETCH exercise and use TRIM later for something more complicated. Now we need to add some thickness to the fins.

The OFFSET Command

Each of the cylinder fins as well as the cylinder wall itself is made up of parallel lines. The command you use to duplicate parallel drawing lines is OFFSET. You have to individually pick each entity that you want to offset and AutoCAD creates a parallel copy.

There are some types of entities that you cannot offset. The legal offset list is line, arc, circle, and 2D polyline. Polyline includes donuts, ellipses, and polygons. Each offset creates a new entity with the same linetype, color, and layer settings as the original entity. Polylines will also have the same width and curves.

You have two ways to offset. You can provide an offset distance and then indicate the side where you want the offset to go. You can input values or pick a point to show the offset distances, but you *must* use a pick to show the side for placement. Offset distances cannot be negative. Or, you can pick the entity you want to offset and then pick a point for it to be offset *through*. This Through option is the default. If the through point falls beyond the end of the new entity, the offset is calculated as if the new entity extended to the through point, but is drawn without that imaginary extension.

Use OFFSET with a through point to create a double cylinder wall and with a distance to double the lines that will form the fins. Then draw lines to close the ends of the wall and fins.

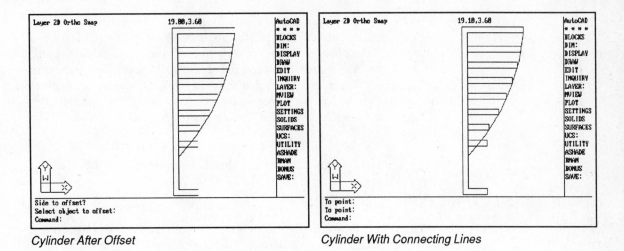

Cylinder After Offset   Cylinder With Connecting Lines

Using OFFSET to Create Wall and Fin Lines

```
Command: OFFSET
Offset distance or Through <Through>: <RETURN>        Through.
Select object to offset:              Pick polyline on left.
Through point:                        Pick any point 0.3 (3 snap units) to left of polyline.
Select object to offset: <RETURN>


Command: <RETURN>
OFFSET Offset distance or through <Through>: .3        Use a distance.
Select object to offset:              Pick one of the fin lines.
Side to offset?                       Pick any point above the line.
Select object to offset:              Continue to offset the fin lines, placing
                                      each offset line above the selected line.


Command: OSNAP                        Set running osnap to ENDPoint.
Command: LINE                         Draw vertical lines between ends of each pair of fin lines.
Command: OSNAP                        Set running osnap to NONe.
Command: SAVE                         Save the drawing.
```

While this exercise has shown how to offset lines and polylines, you can also use OFFSET to form concentric circles.

➡ *NOTE: OFFSET forms a new entity by drawing the entity parallel to the original entity. OFFSET will fail to form a new entity inside an arc or circle if the offset distance exceeds the original radius. (You can't create a negative radius.) Donuts, polygons, and arc or short segments in other polylines are treated similarly. OFFSET makes a logical attempt at small zig-zag segments and loops in polylines, but you may get confused results. Use PEDIT to clean the offset up if you don't like the results.*

Let's thicken the flanges and shorten that bottom fin with STRETCH.

Using STRETCH for Power Drawing

The STRETCH command lets you move *and* stretch entities. You can not only stretch entities in the sense of lengthening them, you can also shorten them and alter their shapes.

The key to STRETCH is to use a crossing window. After you select your objects with a crossing window, you show AutoCAD where to stretch your objects with a displacement, a base point and a new point. Then, everything inside the crossing window you selected is moved, and entities crossing the window are stretched. Inside the window means that all of an object's endpoints or vertex points are within the window. Crossing the window means one or more points are inside and one or more points are outside the window.

The STRETCH command is built around the crossing window selection set. (A window will only move, but not stretch, entities.) If there are objects within the crossing window that you want left untouched, you can use the Remove mode to remove them from the selection set. However, you can only add objects you want moved to the selection set with a window. But, because STRETCH only recognizes the last Crossing or Window selection used, using Crossing or Window to add or remove entities will generally not get the results you want.

STRETCH interacts differently with different entities. Try your hand at using STRETCH on lines and polylines, widening the top and bottom of the cylinder.

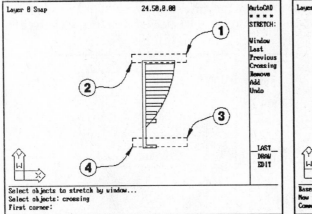

Crossing Windows to Stretch Flanges

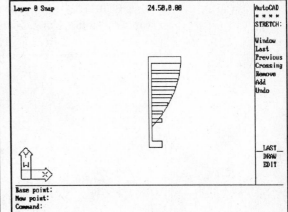

Top and Bottom Flanges After Stretch

Using STRETCH to Widen the Flanges

```
Command: STRETCH                              Stretch the top flange up.
Select objects to stretch by window
Select objects: C                             Use Crossing.
First corner:                                 Pick upper right corner at ①.
Other corner:                                 Pick lower left corner at ②.
3 found
Select objects: <RETURN>
Base point:                                   Pick any point on the screen.
New point:                                    Pick a point @.3<90 degrees.


Command: <RETURN>                             Repeat to stretch the bottom flange up.
STRETCH Select objects to stretch by window
Select objects: C                             Use Crossing.
First corner:                                 Pick upper right corner at ③.
Other corner:                                 Pick lower left corner at ④.
2 found
Select objects: <RETURN>
Base point:                                   Pick any point on the screen.
New point: @.3<90
```

➡ *NOTE: STRETCH won't accept absolute X,Y or polar displacements, like MOVE and COPY do. Recall that an X,Y or @dist<angle value at the first prompt becomes an absolute displacement if you <RETURN> at the second point prompt in MOVE and COPY. Picking any point for the base point and then typing relative coordinates, such as @0,-7.5, is STRETCH's equivalent to an absolute displacement.*

Use STRETCH again to shorten the fin lines that extend beyond the construction arc on the right, bringing the bottom fin in line with the arc.

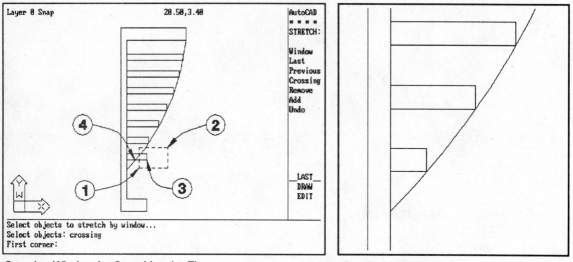

Crossing Window for Stretching the Fin   Detail of Stretched Fin

---

Using STRETCH to Shorten the Fin

```
Command: STRETCH
Select objects to stretch by window...
Select objects: C                Pick corner points between ① and ②.
4 found.
Select objects: <RETURN>
Base point:                      Pick corner of fin at ③.
New point:                       Use an INT osnap to pick intersection of arc and line at ④.
```

As you worked through this stretch, you may have noticed that the construction arc was highlighted by the crossing window but was not changed by the stretch. The arc was not moved or stretched because its endpoints were not enclosed in the window. STRETCH operates differently with different entities.

Some of the significant points for entities with STRETCH are:

- The endpoints or vertex points of lines, arcs, polyline segments, viewports, traces, and solids determine what is stretched or moved.

- The center points of arcs or polyline arcs are adjusted to keep the sagitta (altitude or distance from the chord midpoint to nearest point on the arc) constant.

■ Viewport contents remain constant in scale.

■ The location of a point, the center of a circle, or the insertion point of a block, shape, or text entity determine whether these entities are moved or not, but they are never stretched.

We encourage you to play around with STRETCH to discover some of its quirks. Once you get used to these little idiosyncrasies, STRETCH will do what you expect.

Using TRIM in Quick Construction

Frequently, you are faced with the drawing problem of trimming existing lines. When you are working with a large number of entities, going in and breaking individual entities is tiresome and cumbersome. You can get the same results faster using TRIM. Like EXTEND, TRIM makes use of boundary entities. Also like EXTEND, TRIM's boundaries may include lines, arcs, circles, polylines, and, in paper space, viewports. The entities that you select as your boundary edge become your *cutting edge*. Once you select your cutting edge, you pick the individual entities that you want to trim. You can trim lines, arcs, circles, and polylines. Other objects to trim are ignored.

Use TRIM to cut the interior lines of the cylinder fins. You'll probably have to toggle snap off to be able to pick the lines you want to trim.

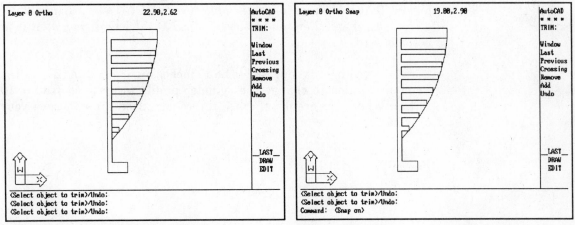

Cylinder With Three Fins Trimmed   *Cylinder After Trim*

Using TRIM to Cut Fin Lines

```
Command: TRIM
Select cutting edge(s)...
Select objects:                          Use Window to select all the entities in the drawing.
26 selected, 26 found
Select objects: <RETURN>
<Select object to trim>/Undo: <Snap off>    Toggle snap off with <F9> or <^B> and pick
                                             a point on cylinder wall between fin lines.
<Select object to trim>/Undo:               Continue picking until all cylinder wall fin
                                             lines are trimmed.
<Select object to trim>/Undo: <Snap on> <RETURN>    Toggle snap on and end command.
```

➥ *NOTE: The same entity can be in the cutting edge boundary and be cut as an object to trim.*

The SCALE Command

While we don't like to admit it, occasionally we get our drawing symbol and text scale wrong, or we have to change an object's size in mid-drawing. SCALE lets you shrink or enlarge objects that you have already placed in your drawing. When you rescale drawing objects, you use a scale factor to change the size of entities around a given base point. The base point you choose remains constant in space; everything around it grows or shrinks by your scale factor. You can enter an explicit scale factor, pick two points to show a distance as a factor, or tell SCALE you want to use a reference length. To use a reference length, you show AutoCAD a length (generally on an entity) and then tell or show AutoCAD the length you want it to become.

The piston cylinder is supposed to be 10 inches high. Use SCALE with the Reference option to change the cylinder profile to make it exactly 10 inches. When you are done, erase the construction arc and save your drawing.

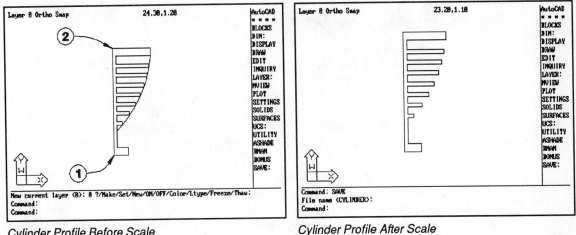

Cylinder Profile Before Scale   Cylinder Profile After Scale

Using SCALE to Enlarge the Cylinder

Command: **ZOOM**	Zoom All.
Command: **SCALE**	
Select objects:	Select every entity.
Base point:	Pick corner of wall at ①.
<Scale factor>/Reference: **R**	The Reference option.
Reference length <1>:	Pick corner of wall at ①.
Second point:	Pick corner of wall at ③.
New length: **10**	Type or drag and pick a new 10-inch length.
Command: **ERASE**	Erase the construction arc.
Command: **SAVE**	Save the drawing.

At this point, your drawing should look like the Cylinder Profile After Scale illustration and it should be exactly ten inches high.

➡ *TIP: The scale base point is also the base point of the new length in the Reference option. If you want to show the length on another object by picking, place your base point there, scale the selection, then adjust its location with MOVE Previous.*

This drawing is a mixture of polylines and lines. Let's turn our attention to polyline editing. In the next section, you will do some simple polyline edits like changing polyline width, and you will form a new polyline by joining the individual entities which make up the cylinder profile.

PEDIT Gives Ultimate Control Over Polylines

Since polylines can be a complex, continuous series of line and arc segments, AutoCAD provides a command called PEDIT just for editing polylines. As you think about polyline properties, you are probably already imagining the list of PEDIT subcommands. To manage the list, AutoCAD divides PEDIT into two groups of editing functions. The primary group of functions works on the whole polyline you are editing. The second group works on vertexes connecting segments within the polyline.

There are more restrictions on using the PEDIT command when you edit three-dimensional polylines, as you will see in Part Two on 3D. For now, we will concentrate on editing two-dimensional polylines. However, we will show you how to revolve the final cylinder drawing at the end of this chapter to demonstrate how a three-dimensional polyline mesh is formed from two-dimensional polylines.

Here are the PEDIT options.

Primary PEDIT Options

Close/Open — Close will add a segment (if needed) and join the first and last vertexes to create a continuous polyline. PEDIT toggles between open and closed. When the polyline is open, the prompt shows Close; when closed, the prompt shows Open. A polyline can be open even if the first and last points coincide and it appears closed. Unless you use the Close option when you draw it, or later use the PEDIT Close option, a polyline will be open,

Join — Lets you add arcs, lines, and other polylines to an existing polyline. Their endpoints must exactly coincide to be joined.

Width — Sets a single width for all segments of a polyline, overriding any individual widths already stored.

Edit vertex —Presents a set of options for editing vertexes and their adjoining segments.

Fit curve — Creates a smooth curve through the polyline vertexes.

Spline curve — Creates a curve controlled by, but not usually passing through, a framework of polyline vertexes. The type of spline and its resolution are controlled by system variables.

Decurve — Undoes a Fit or Spline curve back to its original definition.

Undo — Undoes the most recent editing function.

eXit — As you might imagine, the default <X> gets you out of PEDIT and returns you to the command prompt.

Using PEDIT Join to Create a Polyline

Use PEDIT to join the cylinder lines into a single closed polyline. Use a window to select all the entities that you want to join. After you have created the polyline, increase its width to .02 inch. Then, exit the PEDIT command and use FILLET to fillet all the corners in the polyline profile.

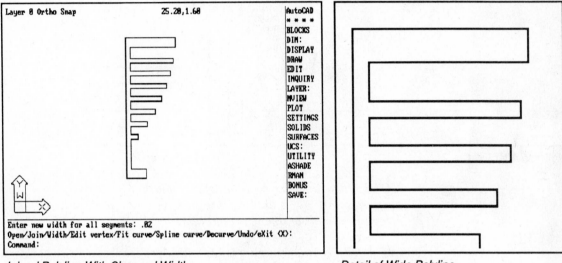

Joined Polyline With Changed Width   Detail of Wide Polyline

Using PEDIT to Join and Change a Polyline

```
Command: ZOOM                                          Zoom in closer.

Command: PEDIT
Select polyline:                                       Select the bottom line of one of the middle fins.
Entity selected is not a polyline                      If it isn't a polyline, you can make it into one.
Do you want to turn it into one? <Y> <RETURN>
Close/Join/Width/Edit vertex/Fit curve/Spline curve/Decurve/Undo/eXit <X>: J
Select objects:                                        Select all of the entities with a window.
Select objects: <RETURN>                               End selection and the polyline is created and closed.
35 segments added to polyline
Open/Join/Width/Edit vertex/Fit curve/Spline curve/Decurve/Undo/eXit <X>: W
Enter new width for all segments: .02
Open/Join/Width/Edit vertex/Fit curve/Spline curve/Decurve/Undo/eXit <X>: <RETURN>

Command: FILLET                                        Set a radius of 0.125.
Command: <RETURN>
FILLET Polyline/Radius/<Select two objects>: P
Select 2D polyline:                                    Pick polyline.
36 lines were filleted
```

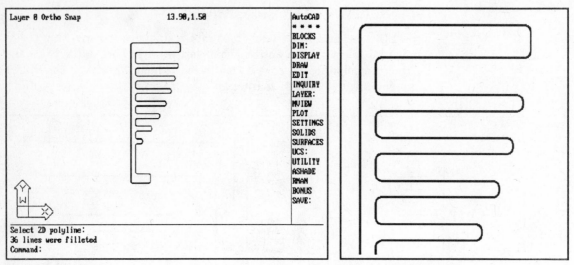

Polyline After Fillet   *Detail of Filleted Polyline*

➡ *NOTE: Like linetype scale, polyline width is set for a good plot appearance. It may look irregular on screen, or not show its width at some zoom levels or display resolutions.*

Joining polylines and changing their width properties are two common edits that you will use frequently. Later, we will show you how to use the curve fit options.

➡ *TIP: Joining becomes tricky and may fail if the endpoints of the entities do not coincide exactly. Not using snap and osnaps when drawing, and occasional round-off discrepancies can all cause problems. Edit or replace stubborn entities, osnapping to the adjacent endpoints, and pedit again. Using FILLET with a zero radius is a good way to make endpoints coincide.*

Right now, let's look at how you edit individual segments or vertexes within a polyline. Knowing that each polyline segment belongs to and is controlled by the preceding vertex helps you understand how PEDIT works. The Edit vertex option gets you into a separate set of Edit vertex subcommands where the first vertex of the polyline is marked with an X. This X shows you what vertex you are editing. Move the X until you get the vertex you want to edit.

Here are the options.

PEDIT Edit Vertex Options

Next/Previous — Next/Previous gets you from one vertex to another by moving the X marker to a new current vertex. Next is the initial default.

Break — Splits the polyline into two or removes segments of a polyline at existing vertexes. The first break point is the vertex where you invoke the Break option. Use Next/Previous to get to another vertex for the second break point. Go performs the break. (Using the BREAK command is usually more efficient than using a PEDIT Break unless curve or spline fitting is involved.)

Insert — Adds a vertex at a point you specify following the vertex currently marked with an X. This can be combined with Break to break between existing vertexes.

Move —Changes the location of the current (X-marked) vertex to a point you specify.

Regen —Forces a regeneration of the polyline so you can see the effects (like width changes) of your vertex editing.

Straighten — Removes all intervening vertexes from between the two you select, replacing them with one straight segment. It also uses the Next/Previous and Go options.

Tangent — Lets you specify a tangent direction at each vertex to control curve fitting. The tangent is shown at the vertex with an arrow, and can be dragged or entered from the keyboard.

Width — Controls the starting and ending width of an individual polyline segment.

eXit — Gets you out of vertex editing and back to the main PEDIT command.

Using PEDIT Edit Vertex Options

Once you have formed a polyline, you often need to move a vertex or straighten a line segment. Try exercising these two editing functions by removing two of the fillets. Remove one at the top left of the cylinder profile and another on the bottom flange. After you get into the PEDIT Edit Vertex option, you need to move the X to get the right segment. Then, use the Move option to move the top left vertex to the corner. This will create a bump at the corner from the existing fillet arc segment. You can use a transparent 'ZOOM if you want to see the bump. Use the Straighten option to make a 90-degree corner and eliminate the bump.

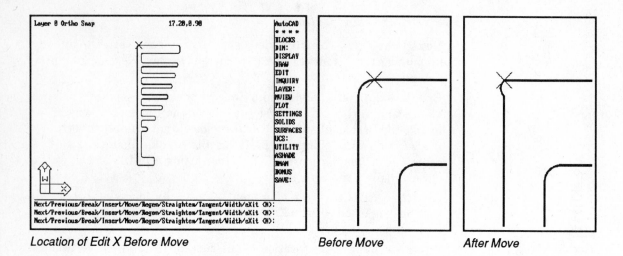

Location of Edit X Before Move   Before Move   After Move

Using PEDIT Vertex Editing to Remove Fillets

```
Command: PEDIT
Select polyline:                          Select the polyline.
Open/Join/Width/Edit vertex/Fit curve/Spline curve/Decurve/Undo/eXit <X>: E
Next/Previous/Break/Insert/Move/Regen/Straighten/Tangent/Width/eXit <N>: <RETURN>
```

An X appears on the polyline. Repeat <RETURN> until Next moves the X to match the Location of Edit X Before Move illustration.

```
Next/Previous/Break/Insert/Move/Regen/Straighten/Tangent/Width/eXit <N>: M
Enter new location:                       Pick polar point @0.125<180.
```

Now straighten the bump. Use 'ZOOM if you want to see it, then zoom back out.

```
Next/Previous/Break/Insert/Move/Regen/Straighten/Tangent/Width/eXit <N>: S

Next/Previous/Go/eXit <N>: <RETURN>       Next moves the X below the bump.

Next/Previous/Go/eXit <N>: <RETURN>       Moves X to match Location of X Before Straightening
                                          illustration.

Next/Previous/Go/eXit <P>: G              Go straightens the line.
Next/Previous/Break/Insert/Move/Regen/Straighten/Tangent/Width/eXit <N>:
```

Stay in the command for the next exercise.

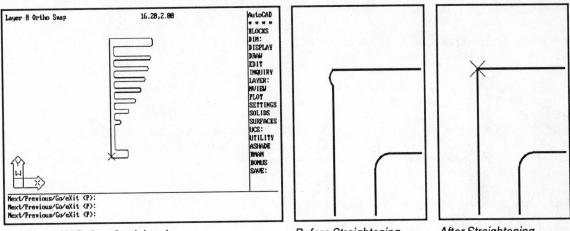

Location of X Before Straightening   Before Straightening   After Straightening

➡ *TIP: If you make a mistake, exit the Edit vertex mode to the primary PEDIT mode and use the Undo option. Then re-enter Edit vertex mode and redo your work. Undo will undo all operations of the Edit vertex session. When doing a long sequence, occasionally exiting and re-entering Edit Vertex mode will protect the work you've done so far from subsequent mistakes.*

You can repeat the above Move and Straighten options to clean up the lower right corner.

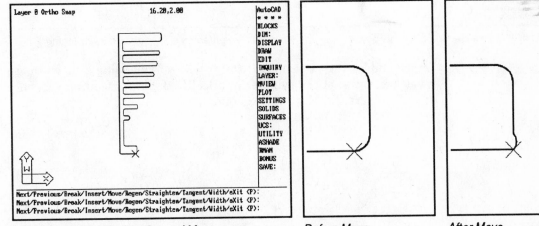

Location of Edit X Before Second Move   Before Move   After Move

Straightening the Lower Right Corner

Press <RETURN> three times and Next moves the X to match Location of Edit X Before Second Move illustration.

```
Next/Previous/Break/Insert/Move/Regen/Straighten/Tangent/Width/eXit <N>: M
Enter new location: @0.125<0        Type in polar coordinate.
Next/Previous/Break/Insert/Move/Regen/Straighten/Tangent/Width/eXit <N>: S
Next/Previous/Go/eXit <N>:          <RETURN> twice to move X to match Location of X
                                    Before Second Straightening illustration.
Next/Previous/Go/eXit <N>: G        Go straightens the line.
Next/Previous/Break/Insert/Move/Regen/Straighten/Tangent/Width/eXit <N>:
```

Stay in the command for the next exercise.

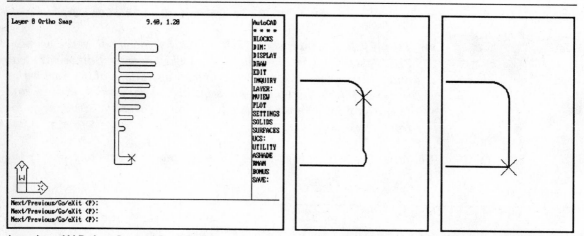

Location of X Before Second Straightening   Before Straightening   After Straightening

You can add a vertex to an existing polyline. Try adding a notch to the lower left corner of the cylinder profile. The following editing sequence uses the Insert and Move vertex options.

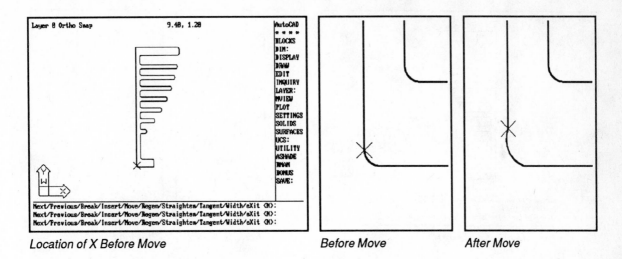

Location of X Before Move   Before Move   After Move

Using PEDIT to Add a Notch

```
Next/Previous/Break/Insert/Move/Regen/Straighten/Tangent/Width/eXit <N>: P
```

Press <RETURN> again to move the X to match the Location of X Before Move illustration.

```
Next/Previous/Break/Insert/Move/Regen/Straighten/Tangent/Width/eXit <P>: M
Enter new location: @0.175<90                   Move up to make .3" notch.

Next/Previous/Break/Insert/Move/Regen/Straighten/Tangent/Width/eXit <P>: I
Enter location of new vertex:                   Pick polar point @0.30<0
Next/Previous/Break/Insert/Move/Regen/Straighten/Tangent/Width/eXit <P>: N
Next/Previous/Break/Insert/Move/Regen/Straighten/Tangent/Width/eXit <N>: <RETURN>
Next/Previous/Break/Insert/Move/Regen/Straighten/Tangent/Width/eXit <N>: M
Enter new location: @0.175<0
Next/Previous/Break/Insert/Move/Regen/Straighten/Tangent/Width/eXit <N>: X
Open/Join/Width/Edit vertex/Fit curve/Spline curve/Decurve/Undo/eXit <X>: <RETURN>

Command: SAVE
```

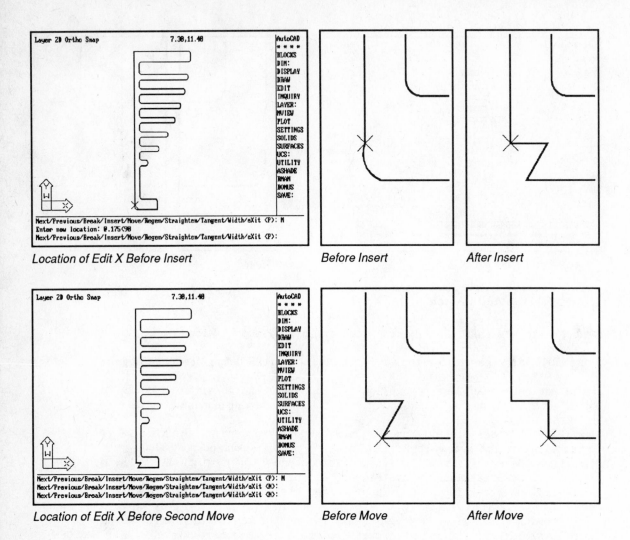

Location of Edit X Before Insert   Before Insert   After Insert

Location of Edit X Before Second Move   Before Move   After Move

Using EXPLODE on Polylines

If you are faced with extensive edits on polylines, it's hard to know whether it's easier to edit the vertexes or to explode the polyline into individual segments, do your edits, then re-join the segments. EXPLODE is the command you use to break a polyline into its individual segments. There are drawbacks to exploding polylines. They lose their width and tangent information. EXPLODE locks in curves and splines by converting the polyline to many arcs or small straight lines. Wide polylines come out of an explosion looking like shaved poodles, with only their center lines showing. If you were to explode the cylinder's polyline, you would get 72 entities.

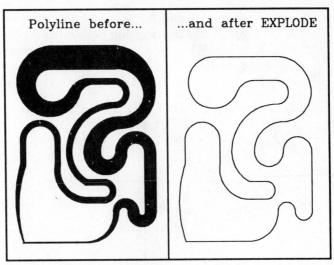

Polyline Before and After Explosion

PEDIT Fit and Spline Curves

The PEDIT command provides two options for making polyline curves through control points: a fit curve and a spline curve. One reason we chose the cylinder profile to demonstrate pedits is that this profile dramatically shows the different results between fit curves and spline curves. A fit curve passes through your vertex control points. Fit curves consist of two arc segments between each pair of vertexes. A spline curve interpolates between your control points but doesn't usually pass through the vertexes. The framework of vertexes is called the *spline frame*.

PEDIT spline curves create either arcs or short line segments approximating the curve of the arc. To help you visualize your spline curve, AutoCAD provides a system variable called SPLFRAME. You can set SPLFRAME on 1 to show you the reference frame and vertex points for a spline curve. The fineness of the approximation and type of segment is controlled by the SPLINESEGS system variable. The numeric value controls the number of segments. A positive value generates line segments while a negative value creates arc segments. Arcs are more precise, but slower. The default is 8.

You can generate two kinds of spline curves, controlled by the SPLINETYPE system variable. The types are a quadratic b-spline (type 5) or a cubic b-spline (the default, type 6).

Try both fit and spline curves using the cylinder fins as your control points. After you have generated the spline curve, turn SPLFRAME on to see the reference frame for the curve. The exercise sequence will show you how to regenerate the drawing within the PEDIT command to make the frame visible. When you are done, use the Undo option to restore the original cylinder profile. Be careful with the Decurve option; it will remove the fillets in the drawing. If you try it, undo to recover.

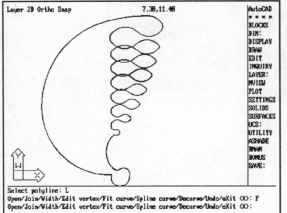

Piston Cylinder After Fit Curve

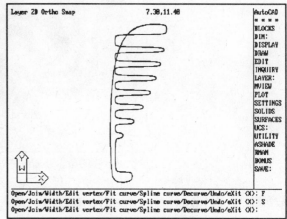

Piston Cylinder After Spline Curve

Using PEDIT to Make a Fit and a Spline Curve

```
Command: PEDIT                          Try a fit curve, then a spline curve.
Select polyline: L                      Last.
Open/Join/Width/Edit vertex/Fit curve/Spline curve/Decurve/Undo/eXit <X>: F
Open/Join/Width/Edit vertex/Fit curve/Spline curve/Decurve/Undo/eXit <X>: S
Open/Join/Width/Edit vertex/Fit curve/Spline curve/Decurve/Undo/eXit <X>: 'SPLFRAME
                                        (Release 10, use 'SETVAR to set SPLFRAME.)
>New value for SPLFRAME <0>: 1          Turns on frame.
Resuming PEDIT command.                 The frame won't show until you use Edit vertex to regenerate.
Open/Join/Width/Edit vertex/Fit curve/Spline curve/Decurve/Undo/eXit <X>: E
Next/Previous/Break/Insert/Move/Regen/Straighten/Tangent/Width/eXit <N>: R
Next/Previous/Break/Insert/Move/Regen/Straighten/Tangent/Width/eXit <N>: X
Open/Join/Width/Edit vertex/Fit curve/Spline curve/Decurve/Undo/eXit <X>: U
Open/Join/Width/Edit vertex/Fit curve/Spline curve/Decurve/Undo/eXit <X>: X
Command: U                              Undo the PEDIT, restoring the cylinder profile.
```

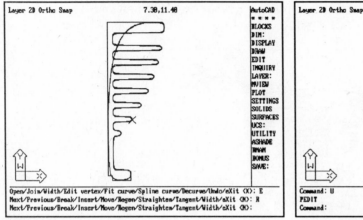

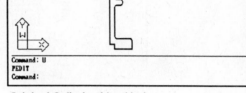

Spline Curve With Frame   Original Cylinder After Undo

When you displayed the reference frame for spline curves, it showed the original cylinder profile and points. If you are editing a spline curve and you need to know where your control points are located, use the SPLFRAME system variable to get your frame of reference back.

After undoing your curve fitting, your screen should look like the Original Cylinder After Undo illustration. Although you have moved, stretched, curved, and pummeled the poor polyline, it is still a *continuous* polyline.

➡ *NOTE: The BREAK and TRIM commands make curve- and spline-fitting permanent. The PEDIT Break option and EXTEND command allow subsequent PEDITs to decurve and refit curves or splines. Curve- and spline-fit polylines get complex. See the AutoCAD Reference Manual for quirks and interactions with other editing commands.*

Using REVSURF to Create a 3D Surface Mesh

Use your cylinder profile to get a 3D surface mesh. The following exercise sequence will guide you through a quick 3D setup, giving you a 3D viewpoint that looks down at the cylinder so that you can see the surface mesh as it is formed. You will use a 3D entity command called REVSURF to form the surface mesh. REVSURF forms a polyline surface mesh from the two-dimensional polyline making up the cylinder profile.

Don't worry about the commands or the sequence used to create the 3D cylinder. Just try the exercise to see how easily a complex 3D part is created. If the results whet your appetite, you will be pleased to know that

there is much more to come in Part Two on 3D. When you are done, save
your drawing as 3DCYLIND.

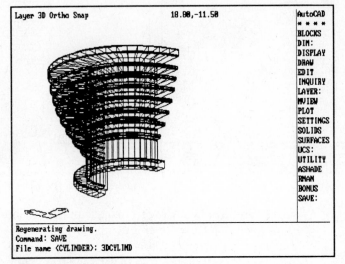

3D Half Section of Cylinder

Using REVSURF to Make a Quick 3D Mesh

Continue from the previous exercise.

Command: **<Grid off>**	Turn grid off with <F7> or <^G>.
Command: **ZOOM**	Zoom All.
Command: **LINE**	Draw from absolute point 10,15 to polar point @13<270. This is a rotation line.
Command: **LAYER**	Set layer 3D current.

With Release 10, use SETVAR to set the following three settings.

Command: **SURFTAB1**	Set vertical mesh value to 24.
Command: **SURFTAB2**	Set horizontal mesh value to 4.
Command: **WORLDVIEW**	Set to 0 for viewpoint change.
Command: **REVSURF**	Create 3D half section of piston cylinder.
Select path curve:	Pick the polyline.
Select axis of revolution:	Pick the rotation line near the bottom.
Start angle <0>: **<RETURN>**	
Included angle (+=ccw, -=cw) <Full circle>: **180**	
Command: **LAYER**	Freeze layer 2D.
Command: **UCS**	Rotate the X axis -90 degrees.

```
Origin/ZAxis/3point/Entity/View/X/Y/Z/Prev/Restore/Save/Del/?/<World>: X
Rotation angle about X axis <0>: -90
```

```
Command: VPOINT                      Move to a better viewpoint.
Rotate/<View point> <0.00,1.00,0.00>: R
Enter angle in X-Y plane from X axis <270>: 215
Enter angle from X-Y plane <0>: 17

Command: SAVE                        Save as 3DCYLIND.
```

To cut down on computing time, the exercise only created a half section of the cylinder. You could revolve the polyline 360 degrees to get the full cylinder. If you have six minutes to an hour to kill (depending on your machine's speed), you can do a HIDE to let AutoCAD sort through all those lines and generate a more realistic image by getting rid of the hidden lines.

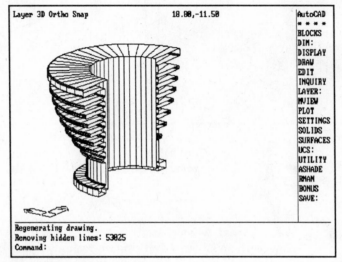

Piston Cylinder After HIDE

Using HIDE to View Cylinder

```
Command: HIDE                Start your timer!

Command: QUIT                When you're done, quit. You already saved the drawing in 2D and 3D.
```

You can get some sense of how powerful 3D editing commands are by how easy it is to create the complex cylinder surface mesh from the two-dimensional polyline of your cylinder profile. We mentioned how important continuity becomes in 3D. To show the effect of discontinuity, we have gone back and *nicked* the cylinder polyline in two places. Then, we revolved the cylinder again with REVSURF to get a 3D surface mesh.

The nicked profile is shown in the Broken 2D Polyline illustration. The two Xs mark the places where we broke the polyline. The resulting 3D image is shown in the accompanying illustration. As you can see, the 3D mesh formation halts at the break points. The nicked 2D profile looks the same as your original profile, but it gives vastly different results when you form a 3D surface image.

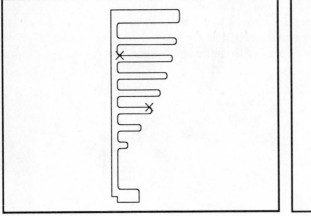

Broken 2D Polyline

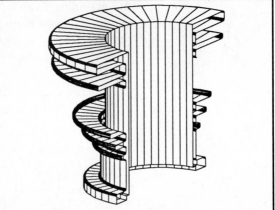

3D Half Cylinder With Nicked Polyline

➡ *NOTE: You can erase the CYLINDER drawing; you won't need it again.*

Summing Up

We said that when you start editing, your drawings become dynamic. Now, with an advanced editing course under your belt, you may sense that the drawing process itself can give you added power and control. The editing commands, EXTEND, OFFSET, STRETCH, TRIM, SCALE, and PEDIT, are *new* tools. They don't have exact counterparts in the manual world. All of these editing commands operate on multiple entities. When you combine these advanced editing tools with the electronic equivalent of construction lines, you can create fast, accurate drawings.

The trick to using these commands is to plan ahead. Don't get trapped into traditional thinking. It would have been a laborious process to draw the cylinder profile line by line and point by point. Plan on using EXTEND, OFFSET, STRETCH, and TRIM to rough-in your drawing. Then, get the details that you want using PEDIT.

A second trick to using these new editing commands is to think about *how* the drawing is constructed. As you work with the more complex commands, the behind-the-scenes construction is almost as important as the appearance of the final drawing. You saw how two little nicks in a 2D polyline can have a drastic effect on a 3D object.

There are two more editing techniques that we want to show you in the next chapter. These are using XYZ point filters as super fast invisible construction lines, and undo marks, a way to mark your drawing file so that you can backtrack and try different editing paths as you draw.

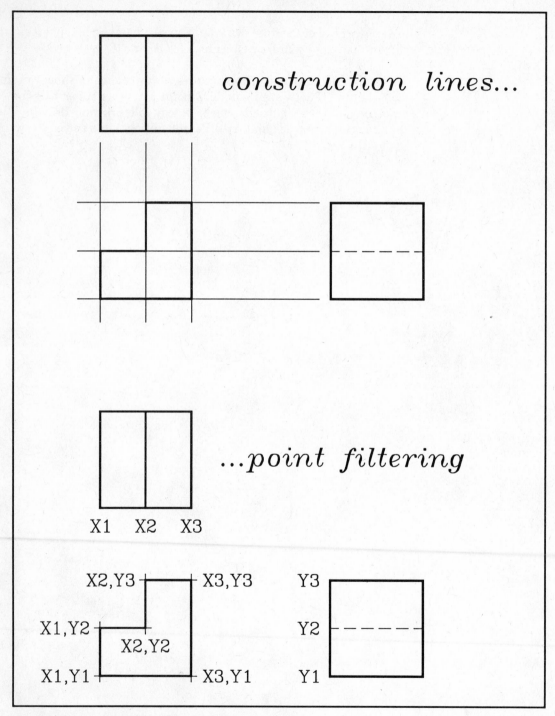

Construction Lines and Point Filter Techniques

CHAPTER 8

Drawing Construction Techniques

QUICK WAYS TO BUILD WHOLE DRAWINGS

Advanced Construction Methods

This is a methodology chapter. It will show you how to combine the drawing and editing commands that you learned in the previous chapters with construction lines, point filters, and undo marks. You will learn how to use these powerful tools to rapidly construct drawings.

Point Filters and Construction Lines

Point filters are construction tools. The best way to visualize point filters is to think of them as invisible construction lines. The facing page illustration compares construction lines and point filters. Construction lines are as important in CAD as they are in manual drafting. When you use a construction line to help draw an entity, you are really looking for the coordinate values of an intersection point, say an X value and a Y value. Point filters give you the advantages of construction lines without any extra work ahead of time. When you use point filters, you indicate the coordinate values that will give you the intersection point, eliminating the need to actually draw a construction line. Once you get the hang of using point filters, they will increase your drawing productivity. They are a fast on-the-fly tool.

To get a handle on drawing construction techniques, we will build a new drawing called MOCKUP. If you are using the IA DISK, you have the MOCKUP drawing setup stored as the IA6MOCK drawing. A second drawing on the disk, IA6MOCK2, has the completed left view of the flange. Point filters are used to help construct the section view on the right. If you want to jump directly to the section on point filters, turn to *Using XYZ Point Filters for Section Construction* in the last third of the chapter and use the IA6MOCK2 drawing as your starting drawing.

Undo Marks

You have seen the simple use of U or UNDO to reverse the effects of a command that botches up your drawing file. As you design and draft, you often try alternatives that may or may not work out. These often involve a long series of commands. You can always undo repeatedly to back up and try again. But it would be easier if you could place a *mark* in your drawing session at the beginning of the alternative branch, so that you could backtrack to that editing point in a single step. Well, you can. Undo marks are like editing checkpoints in your drawing. After placing a mark, you can try an editing sequence, then go back to your mark if it doesn't work and try an alternate sequence.

You place a mark with the UNDO command. Each time you start an editing session, AutoCAD keeps track of every command you execute by writing it to a temporary file on disk. This temporary file records all your moves whenever you are in the drawing editor. You won't find this file on disk when you're done with an editing session because it is a hidden file. At the end of a session, AutoCAD wipes it out and cleans up the disk. However, while you are in an editing session, you can play this sequence in reverse, undoing each command, or if you undo too much, you can redo parts of your past command sequence.

➡ *TIP: If you have a printer hooked up to your system, you can get a hard copy of all your command prompt lines by pressing <^Q> to start your printer printing, or select the PRINTER TOGL on the tablet menu. It will print everything that scrolls by on the text screen. Another <^Q> turns off printing.*

After you master this chapter, don't expect AutoCAD to do all your work for you. However, you can look forward to a better division of drafting labor — you can do the thinking and setting up, and AutoCAD can do the bulk of the carrying out.

Advanced Editing Tools

The editing commands that you will use are on the [EDIT] screen menus and the [Modify] pull-down menu. Selecting [FILTERS >] from the [Assist] pull-down menu replaces the [Assist] pull-down menu with a [Filters] pull-down. You can also find the filters on the [POINTS] screen menu, via the [DRAW] menu, but you can probably type them faster. [UNDO:], on the second [EDIT] screen menu page, leads to an [UNDO] menu. Several undo items are also on the [Utility] pull-down menu.

```
Assist  Draw  Modify  Display  Settings  Options  Utility  File  Solids
        Line                                                     * * * *
        Point                                                    ATTDEF:
        Circle      >                                            BASE:
        Arc         >                                            BLOCK:
        3D Face                                                  INSERT:
        ──────                                                   MINSERT:
        Polyline                                                 WBLOCK:
        3D Poly
        Donut                                                    XBIND:
        Ellipse                                                  XREF:
        Polygon
        ──────
        Insert
        Xref
        ──────
        Surfaces...                                              LAST
        Objects...                                               DRAW
        ──────                                                   EDIT
        Dtext
        Hatch
        Dim...
Command:
Command:
Command:
```

Editing and Construction Tools Menus

This chapter's exercises also use the OFFSET, ARRAY, TRIM, FILLET, CHAMFER, CHANGE, CHPROP, and PEDIT editing commands. If you need to review these commands, refer to the two previous editing chapters.

Setup for the Mockup Drawing

The mockup is actually a plan and section drawing of a flange. Like the now-familiar widget drawing, you don't have to know or care about flanges to learn the basic concepts of undo marks, construction lines, and point filters. The dimensions needed to create the drawing are shown in the Dimensioned Mockup Target Drawing illustration.

Although in reality this would probably be drawn in decimal units, we'll set up the MOCKUP drawing with fractional units for variety. Set your drawing limits to 34 inches by 22 inches. The scale factor is 1:2 for a 17" x 11" final drawing.

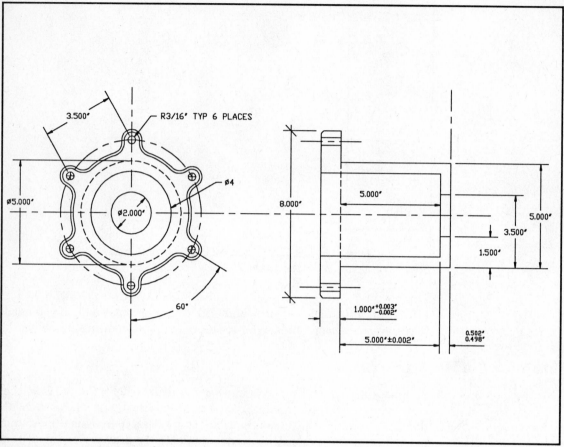

Dimensioned Mockup Target Drawing

Setting Up the Mockup Drawing

  Begin a NEW drawing named MOCKUP=IA6MOCK.

  Begin a NEW drawing named MOCKUP and set up your drawing to match the Mockup Drawing Settings table.

COORDS	GRID	LTSCALE	ORTHO	SNAP
On	1	1	ON	.5

UNITS	Set UNITS to 5. Fractional, 64ths denominator. Default the other Units settings.
LIMITS	Set LIMITS from 0,0 to 34,22.
ZOOM	Zoom All.
VIEW	Save view as A.

Layer Name	State	Color	Linetype
0	On	7 (white)	CONTINUOUS
CENTER	On/Current	1 (red)	CENTER
DIMS	On	2 (yellow)	CONTINUOUS
HIDDEN	On	4 (cyan)	HIDDEN
PARTS	On	3 (green)	CONTINUOUS

Mockup Drawing Settings

Using Construction Lines

The first step in making the mockup is to rough-in some construction lines. Notice that there are two center lines and a circle center line in the illustration. Create these lines, using your CENTER layer as a background layer to help you lay in the two major sections of the drawing. Then, you can use the PARTS layer to draw the flange and its section view.

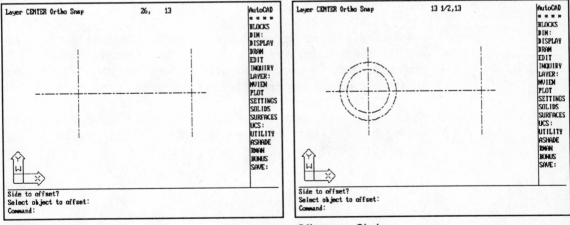

Offset on a Line   *Offset on a Circle*

Using OFFSET to Create Construction Lines

```
Command: LINE                                  From absolute point 4,13 to polar point @24<0.
Command: LINE                                  From absolute point 10,7 to polar point @12<90.

Command: CIRCLE                                Draw a 3" radius circle at absolute point 10,13.

Command: OFFSET
Offset distance or Through <Through>: 16
Select object to offset:                       Pick vertical line.
Side to offset?                                Pick any point to the right of line.
Select object to offset: <RETURN>

Command: <RETURN>
OFFSET Offset distance or Through <Through>:   Offset circle to outside with distance 1
                                               to create a 4" radius circle.
```

The two circles on your screen are temporary construction lines to help you form the complex entity that makes up the perimeter of the flange.

Placing an Undo Mark

Look at the Dimensioned Mockup Target Drawing again. The perimeter of the top flange is a polyline with six lugs sticking out. It would be difficult to draw this entire perimeter as a single polyline. The next three exercises will show you how to create one-sixth of the perimeter, array this sixth to get the basic perimeter, then form a polyline by joining the arrayed entities.

Since you will be creating several entities to represent the top flange and you will also be using several different editing commands, this is a good place to put an undo mark in your drawing file. If you botch the next three sequences, you can easily come back to this point.

Use UNDO to place a mark in your drawing, then resume construction of the lug that sticks out from the top of the flange perimeter. Construct the lug on your PARTS layer.

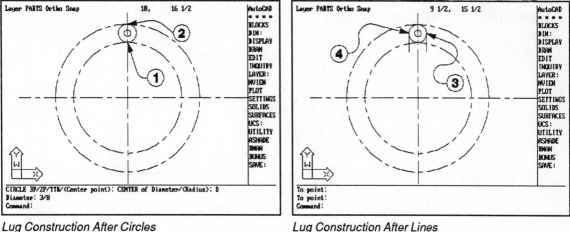

Lug Construction After Circles   *Lug Construction After Lines*

Using Construction Entities to Draw a Lug

```
Command: UNDO
Auto/Back/Control/End/Group/Mark/<number>: M    Set a mark.
```

`Command: ZOOM`	Position window around circles for a better view.
`Command: LAYER`	Set layer PARTS current.

```
Command: CIRCLE                        Use 2P to draw a 1" diameter circle.
3P/2P/TTR/<Center point>: 2P
First point on diameter:               Pick first point at ①.
Second point on diameter:              Pick second point at ②.
```

```
Command: <RETURN>
CIRCLE 3P/2P/TTR/<Center point>:  Pick center of last circle.
Diameter/<Radius>: D              Draw a 3/8" diameter circle.
Diameter: 3/8
```

```
Command: LINE                          Use osnap QUAdrant to add the lines of the flange cut.
From point: QUA
of                                     Pick a point on the circle at ③.
To point:                              Pick any point below the circle at 270 degrees.
To point: <RETURN>
```

```
Command: <RETURN>
LINE From point:                       Repeat for line at ④.
Command: SAVE                          Save the drawing.
```

Let's pause for a moment and look at undoing and redoing command sequences.

Controlling AutoCAD's UNDO

There are three basic commands that control undos in your draw and edit sequences. These are U, UNDO, and REDO.

You may be thinking, "I already know how to use the ERASE Last command to delete the last entity that I drew. If I make an erase mistake, I can even use OOPS to restore the last item erased. And I already know how to use U."

However, erasing the last item you drew is only part of going back through your drawing file. When you decide to go back, it is often to undo a whole sequence of draw and edit commands. Here is where the Undo set of commands comes in handy.

The U Command

The U command is a mini-undo which backs up by one step or command. Whatever you did immediately before issuing the U command will be undone when you type U. But, unlike the OOPS command, U works any number of times, stepping back through each previous *last* command, one by one. In this sense, U is similar to the Undo option within LINE or PLINE which gets rid of line or polyline segments by going back one segment at a time. You can even undo an OOPS or an ERASE with a U.

The UNDO Command

The UNDO command offers more control than U. You can UNDO <number>, where <number> equals the number of steps you want to return. Or you can set marks or group a series of commands together so if what you are working on doesn't work out, you can undo the whole series at once.

REDO Gives an Extra Measure of Safety

Say you undid more than you planned. If you issue REDO immediately after any undo, REDO will undo the undo. This means you can be daring if you are not sure how far back you want to go. You can do something drastic like UNDO 20, then recover with a REDO. You can even *play back* your drawing sequences with UNDO, and then use REDO to show or teach someone else what you have done.

Use the following illustrations and exercise sequence to test the U, UNDO, and REDO commands. When the test is complete, your drawing should look the same as it does now. Type the commands; if you use a menu, your results will differ because UNDO groups menu items.

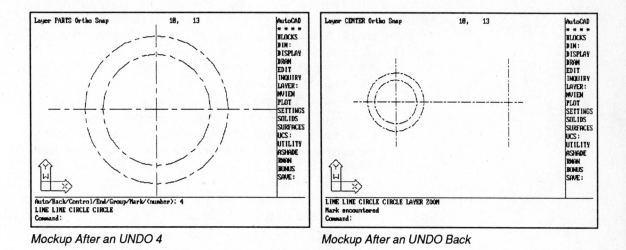

Mockup After an UNDO 4   Mockup After an UNDO Back

Using U, UNDO, and REDO on an Editing Sequence

```
Command: U                              A simple U undoes the last command.
SAVE                                    AutoCAD shows the last command it undid.


Command: REDO                           Reverses the U command.


Command: UNDO                           Undo the last four commands.
Auto/Back/Control/End/Group/Mark/<number>: 4
SAVE LINE LINE CIRCLE


Command: REDO                           Reverse the UNDO command.


Command: UNDO                           Undo back to the mark set at the beginning of the exercise.
Auto/Back/Control/End/Group/Mark/<number>: B
SAVE LINE LINE CIRCLE CIRCLE LAYER ZOOM
Mark encountered


Command: REDO                           Reverse the UNDO command.
```

If you accidentally undo too much and can't recover, just reload your saved drawing. Although UNDO showed SAVE as an undone command, commands that write to the disk are never actually undone. The UNDO Back that you used is only one of six options that control UNDO. Here is the complete list.

UNDO Options

<number> — If you enter a number, AutoCAD steps back by that many steps.

Auto — is an on/off setting. Auto affects menu items only. Sometimes a single menu item creates or edits many entities. Normally, everything done by one command is one step back in UNDO. Setting Auto ON (the default) causes an entire menu item to be treated as a single step by making it an undo *group*.

Back and **Mark** — An UNDO Back will undo all the way back until it comes to the beginning of the editing session, an undo mark, or a PLOT or PRPLOT command (because they re-initialize the undo file as if beginning the editing session at that point). If no mark has been placed, you get a warning, "This will undo everything. OK <Y>." You respond Yes or No. You set an undo mark simply by executing the UNDO command with the Mark option. You may mark as many times as you like, each time setting a stop for the next UNDO Back.

Control — Creating the temporary undo file can take a lot of disk space. Control lets you specify how active the temporary file will be with three options — All/None/One. All is the default. None turns UNDO off. One limits UNDO to just one step back. When set to One, none of the other UNDO options are available. All restores UNDO to its full function.

Group and **End** — Like Back and Mark, Group and End put boundaries on series of commands in the temporary file so that you can undo the series in one step. You begin a group with the Group option, end the group with the End option, and continue doing work. Later you step back with U or UNDO <number>. When the backstep gets to an End, the next UNDO step will wipe out everything between the End and Group markers as a single step.

Watch out for undoing more than you want. Any settings during a command, including toggles (such as snap) or transparent commands, will be undone along with the main command. UNDO has the power to wipe out your entire drawing in one step, but if you catch it *immediately* with REDO, you can save it.

In the rest of the book, and in your own work, try placing your own undo marks to give yourself additional checkpoints in the editing session. Then, if you need to retry a sequence, you can easily step back and do it.

Using Array Techniques to Construct the Flange Perimeter

Let's resume drawing the flange. First, finish the lug using the TRIM command. This is easier than trying to calculate the exact arc and line lengths that make up the lug. It also insures that all the endpoints match.

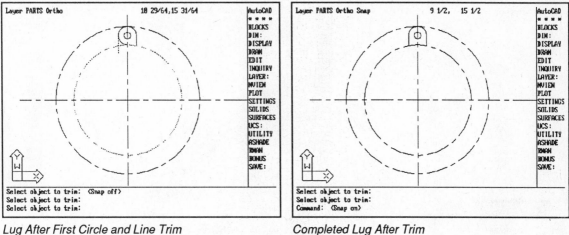

Lug After First Circle and Line Trim   Completed Lug After Trim

Using TRIM to Draw First Lug of Flange

```
Command: <Snap off>                    Toggle snap off with <^B> or <F9>.
Command: TRIM
Select cutting edge(s)...
Select objects:                        Pick the 3" diameter circle on the CENTER layer.
1 selected, 1 found.
Select objects:                        Pick the first lug line.
1 selected, 1 found.
Select objects:                        Pick the second lug line.
1 selected, 1 found.
Select objects: <RETURN>
<Select object to trim>/Undo:          Pick the bottom right half of 1" diameter circle.
<Select object to trim>/Undo:          Pick bottom end of right lug line.
<Select object to trim>/Undo:          Pick the bottom half of 1" diameter circle again.
<Select object to trim>/Undo:          Pick bottom end of left lug line.
<Select object to trim>/Undo: <Snap on><RETURN>          Toggle snap back on, exit TRIM.
```

The first lug is complete. The perimeter in the target drawing showed the lug in six places. You could array the lug now and draw the remaining entities between the arrayed lugs, but it is more efficient to create one-sixth of the perimeter and then do the array.

Completing a One-Sixth Portion to Array

Here we will rely on AutoCAD's editing commands to do the calculation and construction. Use the ROTATE command to set up a one-sixth segment of the circle. Then use the ARC and FILLET commands to complete the segment.

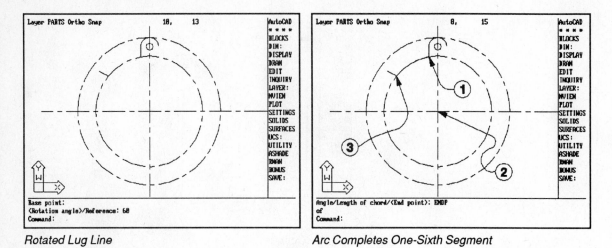

Rotated Lug Line   Arc Completes One-Sixth Segment

Using ROTATE and ARC to Construct a Perimeter Segment

```
Command: ROTATE
Select objects:                     Select short lug line on the right.
1 selected, 1 found.
Select objects: <RETURN>
Base point:                         Pick center of circles at absolute point 10,13.
<Rotation angle>/Reference: 60

Command: ARC
Center/<Start point>: ENDP
of                                  Pick endpoint of left lug line ①.
Center/End/<Second point>: C
Center: INT
of                                  Pick intersection of center lines ②.
Angle/Length of chord/<End point>: ENDP
of                                  Pick endpoint of rotated lug line ③.
```

Now, fillet the perimeter segment.

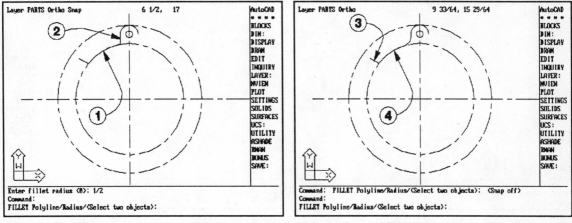

Picks for First Fillet   *Picks for Second Fillet*

Using FILLET to Complete the Perimeter Segment

```
Command: <Snap off>              Toggle snap off with <^B> or <F9>.

Command: FILLET                  Set fillet radius to 1/2 inch.
Command: FILLET                  Pick arc at ① and line at ③.
Command: FILLET                  Pick line at ③ and arc at ④.

Command: <Snap on>               Toggle snap back on.
```

Now you are ready to create the perimeter by arraying the one-sixth segment. If you followed the construction sequence, all the entity points will line up. Notice that you have made only one trivial calculation: dividing the circle into sixths (60 degrees). By using osnaps and editing commands, you have let AutoCAD do all the hard calculations and locations.

Using ARRAY and PEDIT to Create the Perimeter

Use a polar array to replicate the one-sixth segment to complete the perimeter of the flange. Then, use PEDIT Join to group the entity segments into a single polyline. After you have joined the segments, create two circles in the interior of the flange.

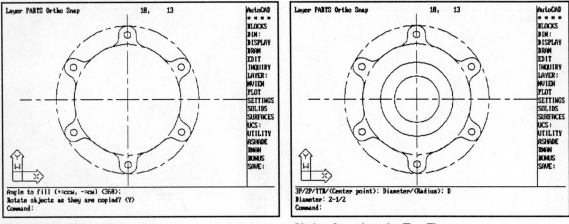

Top Flange After Array   Circles Complete the Top Flange

Using ARRAY and PEDIT to Complete the Flange

```
Command: ARRAY
Select objects: W
First corner:
Other corner:                 Put window around all flange entities on the PARTS layer.
7 found.
Select objects: <RETURN>
Rectangular or Polar array (R/P): P
Center point of array: INT
of                            Pick intersection of center lines at absolute point 10,13.
Number of items: 6
Angle to fill (+=ccw, -=cw) <360>: <RETURN>
Rotate objects as they are copied? <Y> <RETURN>

Command: PEDIT
Select polyline:              Pick first arc created on top flange.
Entity selected is not a polyline
Do you want to turn it into one? <Y> <RETURN>
Close/Join/Width/Edit vertex/Fit curve/Spline curve/Decurve/Undo/eXit <X>: J
Select objects: W
First corner:                 Make the window as large as you like.
Other corner:                 As long as it includes all the top flange entities,
44 found.                     Join will ignore extra entities.
Select objects: <RETURN>
35 segments added to polyline
Open/Join/Width/Edit vertex/Fit curve/Spline curve/Decurve/Undo/eXit <X>: <RETURN>

Command: CIRCLE               Draw 4" diameter circle for inside wall of flange.

Command: CIRCLE               Draw 2-1/2" diameter circle for center hole in bottom of part.
```

The PEDIT Join requires that each entity endpoint matches the adjacent endpoint exactly. If you did not get a join, undo, and try again.

➡ *TIP: You can use a far-off drawing corner or a scratch UCS for background construction, putting together pieces of a drawing that you can later move, copy, or array into place.*

Editing by Recycling Entities

Frequently, you can save a little drawing time by recycling the now-surplus construction circles rather than creating new ones. Change the inner construction circle's layer (linetype) and radius to make a hidden line for the outer wall, and change the outer circle's radius to make a bolt ring center line.

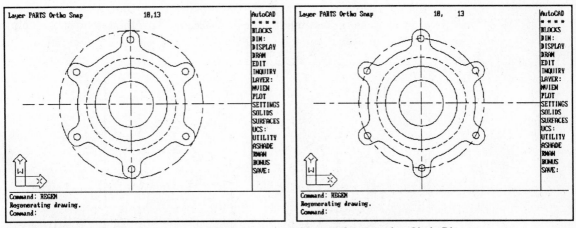

Change Construction Circle Layer and Diameter   Change Construction Circle Diameter

Using CHPROP and CHANGE to Complete Top View

```
Command: CHPROP
Select objects:                Select inner center line construction circle.
Change what property (Color/LAyer/LType/Thickness) ? LA
New layer <CENTER>: HIDDEN
Change what property (Color/LAyer/LType/Thickness) ? <RETURN>

Command: CHANGE
Select objects: P              Previous reselects the circle.
Properties/<Change point>: <RETURN>
Enter circle radius: 2.5       Remember you can type decimal entry even in fractional units.
```

Command: **CHANGE**	Change the radius of the outside circle to 3-1/2".
Command: **REGEN**	Regenerate drawing to verify changes.
Command: **END**	Save as default drawing.

The plan view of the flange is finished. This is a good point to take a break. The next section uses XYZ point filters to construct the section view of the flange.

Using XYZ Point Filters for Section Construction

If you look at the Mockup Target Drawing below, you will see that most of the geometry you need to draw the section view on the right already exists in the plan view. You can draw an accurate section quickly by aligning the new section lines with intersections of the lines and entities making up the plan view. However, you cannot draw the lines by simply aligning your cursor crosshairs because some of the intersection points are not on snap increments (for practice, we'll pretend none of the points are snappable).

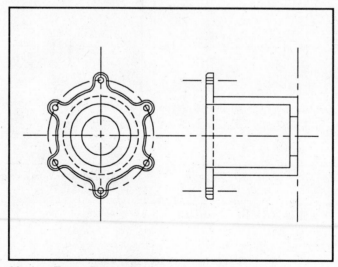

Mockup Target Drawing

Using XYZ point filters makes this alignment easy. Point filters let you pick X, Y, and Z coordinates independently. Because we are drawing in two dimensions, we are only concerned with X and Y coordinates. Don't worry about Z filtering for now.

If you are resuming your MOCKUP drawing, re-check your setup with the table at the front of the chapter. If you are using the IA DISK and jumping in at this point, use the IA6MOCK2 drawing. This drawing contains the completed plan view of the flange. Your current layer should be PARTS. Restore View A to start the drawing.

Setting Up for XYZ Point Filters

Begin a NEW drawing named MOCKSECT=IA6MOCK2.

Begin a NEW drawing named MOCKSECT=MOCKUP and use VIEW to restore view A.

To use point filters, precede a point that you pick (or type) with a .X or .Y (pronounced dot-X or dot-Y). The dot (period) distinguishes the point filter from some command options that begin with an X or Y. AutoCAD will then take only the specified coordinate from the following point, and reprompt you for the other coordinate values. For example, when you specify a .X value, you pick a point or osnap to an entity that has the X value that you want, then AutoCAD will tell you that you need a Y value. You can pick, type or use an osnap to get your Y value, giving you the X,Y intersection point.

Since the flange is symmetrical, you only need to draw half of the section view, then mirror the other half. Use the next exercise sequence with X and Y filters to create the lower half of the section.

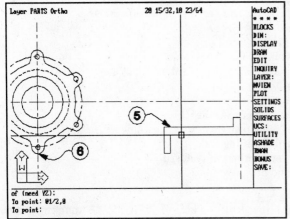

First and Second Lines of Section

Third Line of Section

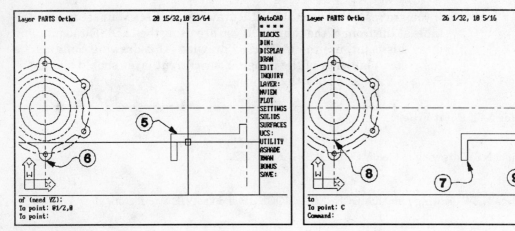

Fourth and Fifth Lines of Section   *Completed Section*

Using XYZ Point Filters to Draw a Section View

Command: **ZOOM**	Zoom into area shown.
Command: **OSNAP**	Set a running osnap to INT,END.
Command: <Snap off>	Toggle snap off.
Command: **APERTURE**	Set to 6.
Command: **LINE**	
From point: **.X**	Build the first line.
of	Pick anywhere on vertical base line at ①.
(need YZ):	Pick intersection of hole and vertical center line at ②.
To point: **@-.5,0**	
To point: **.X**	Build the second line.
of	Pick left side of last line drawn at ③.
(need YZ):	Pick inside of flange circle and vertical center line at ④.
To point: **@-5.5,0**	Draw the third line.
To point: **.X**	Build the fourth line.
of	Pick left side of last line drawn at ⑤.
(need YZ):	Pick intersection of arc and vertical center line at ⑥.
To point: **@1/2,0**	Draw the fifth line.
To point: **.X**	Build the sixth line.
of	Pick right side of last line drawn at ⑦.
(need YZ):	Pick intersection of hidden circle and vertical line at ⑧.
To point: **PERP**	Use PERP to override running osnap.
to	Pick anywhere on vertical base line at ⑨.
To point: **C**	Close to beginning point.

Your screen should now show half a section view of the mockup part.
Complete the section half by using XYZ filters to add the lines for the hole
in the top flange.

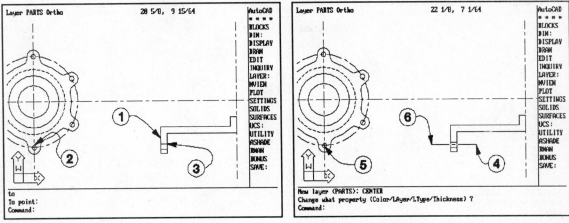

Section View With Hole Lines   *Center Line Through Hole*

Using XYZ Filter to Draw a Hole in the Section View

```
Command: LINE
From point: .X
of
(need YZ):
To point: PERP
to
To point: <RETURN>
Command: LINE
```
Build first line of hole.
Pick line of top flange in the section view at ①.
Pick where the drilled hole and center line intersect at ②.

Pick line in the section view at ③.

Repeat the process for second hole botttom line.

```
Command: LINE
To point: .X
of
(need YZ):
To point:
To point: <RETURN>
```
Build center line for hole.
Pick a point 1" to the right of the bottom flange at ④.
Pick center of lug hole at ⑤.
Pick a point 1" to the left of the top flange at ⑥.

```
Command: CHPROP
```
Change last line to the CENTER layer.

Mirroring the Section View

All you need to do to get the rest of the section view is to mirror the lower half, and add four more lines. Here is the exercise sequence.

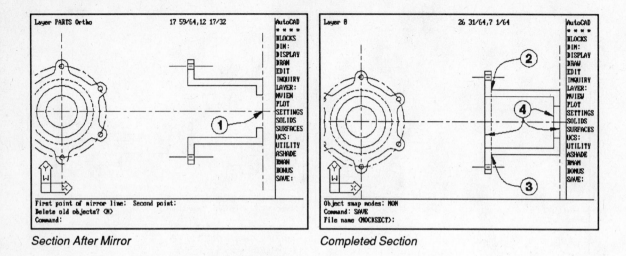

Section After Mirror   Completed Section

Using **MIRROR** to Complete the Section View

```
Command: MIRROR
Select objects: W                 Enclose the entire section image.
First corner:                     Pick first corner point.
Other corner:                     Pick second corner point.
11 found.
Select objects: <RETURN>
First point of mirror line:       Pick intersection of center lines at ①.
Second point:                     Select any point 180 degrees to the left.
Delete old objects? <N> <RETURN>

Command: LAYER                    Set HIDDEN layer current.
Command: LINE                     Draw hidden line from ② to ③.
Command: LAYER                    Set PARTS layer current.
Command: LINE                     Draw the three lines at ④ to complete the section.
Command: OSNAP                    Set to NONe.
Command: SAVE                     Save to the default drawing.
```

The target flange has a chamfer. Take one more moment to chamfer the section view, then add the chamfer to the plan view by offsetting the perimeter. Here are two illustrations and a sequence to help you.

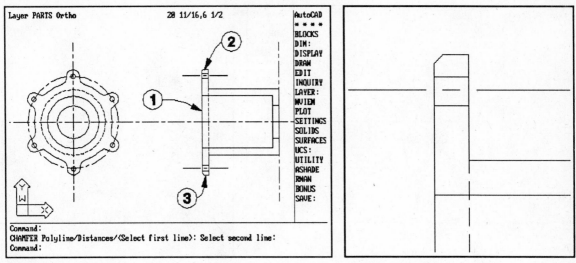

Section After Chamfer   Detail of Chamfer

Chamfer Edge of Flange

Zoom to view shown.

```
Command: CHAMFER
Polyline/Distances/<Select first line>: D
Enter first chamfer distance <0>: 1/8
Enter second chamfer distance <1/8">: <RETURN>
```

```
Command: <RETURN>
CHAMFER Polyline/Distances/<Select first line>:          Pick top flange line at ①.
Select second line:                                      Pick end flange line at ②.
```

```
Command: <RETURN>
CHAMFER Polyline/Distances/<Select first line>:          Pick top flange line at ③.
Select second line:                                      Pick end flange line at ④.
```

```
Command: OFFSET
Offset distance or Through <Through>: 1/8
Select object to offset:          Pick any perimeter point on the top flange in the plan view.
Side to offset?                   Pick a point inside the perimeter.
Select object to offset: <RETURN>
```

```
Command: END                      Save your work and exit.
```

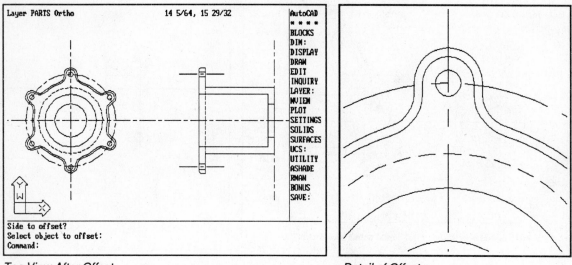

| Layer PARTS Ortho | 14 5/64, 15 29/32 | AutoCAD |

Side to offset?
Select object to offset:
Command:

Top View After Offset   *Detail of Offset*

You will use this MOCKSECT drawing later when we practice dimensioning.

➥ *NOTE: You can delete the MOCKUP drawing, which is no longer needed.*

Summing Up

AutoCAD's drawing construction tools are as much a frame of mind as a framework of commands and options. In the course of constructing the mockup, you have learned how to drop construction lines, use a construction underlayer, and trace over construction lines. You also have learned how to use point filters, combining them with osnaps to create a section view.

There is never just one way to build an AutoCAD drawing. In fact the opposite is true — there are always many ways to build the same drawing. The trick is to find the methods that work most intuitively and efficiently for you. Planning ahead can save you many unnecessary steps. Recycling entities can save erasing and drawing anew. Try to envision the commands you will use well in advance. If you can visualize the construction technique ahead of time, your drawing productivity will increase dramatically.

Use point filters and construction lines to line up entities. Use construction lines for center lines, base lines and lines to align large numbers of points. Use point filters for everyday on-the-fly alignments.

Use osnaps to help you pick filtered points. Set up one or more layers for your construction lines. Construction lines don't need to be linear — use arcs and circles for angular or curved tracing. A few extra construction lines never hurt and can make your drawing life easier.

Use UNDO to protect your work sequences. Use REDO for a rescue — but only immediately after an undo. Marks and Groups help control undos and make going back easier. Watch out for PLOT and PRPLOT when you plan to undo! Going back to a mark is no substitute for saving regularly. Saving is still the best way to protect your drawing file.

On to Blocks

Talk about saving — wouldn't it be useful if you could save the contents of the selection set and use it as a rubber stamp whenever you need it? You can — with blocks. We'll show you how in the next chapter.

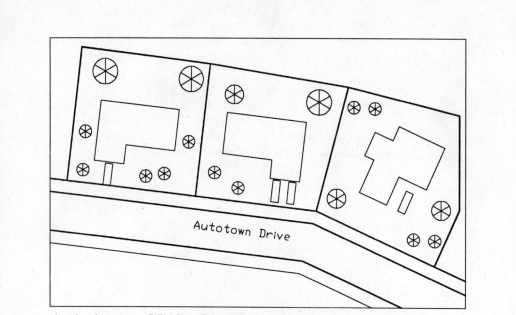

Autotown With Simple Blocks

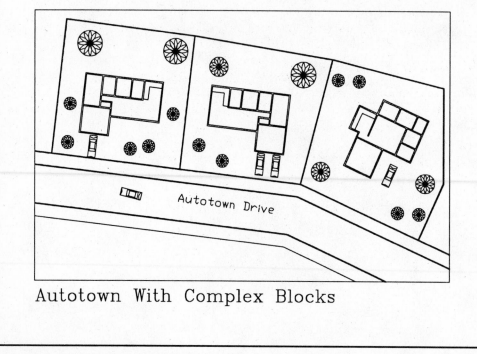

Autotown With Complex Blocks

Autotown Drawing With Simple and Complex Blocks

CHAPTER 9

Grouping Entities Into Blocks

DRAWING WITH PARTS AND SYMBOLS

The Benefits of Using Blocks and Xrefs

In this chapter, you will learn how to create, store, and use blocks. Blocking entities into groups allows them to be repeated easily and efficiently within one or more drawing files, or made into permanent symbols in a symbol library.

You will also learn how to work with xrefs (not available in Release 10), which are similar to blocks. Xrefs make workgroup drafting (in which several people work on different parts of the same drawing) simple and error-free. They are the key to effective distributed design. Xrefs are more efficient than blocks, and automatically update drawings when changes are made. We'll cover xrefs as a separate topic after we explore blocks.

Blocks: Parts and Symbols

Blocks group individual entities together and treat them as one object. Symbols and drawing parts are typical candidates for such groupings. We consider *parts*, such as a car or a desk, to represent real objects, drawn full size or at one-unit scale. *Symbols*, such as section bubbles, electrical receptacles and weld symbols, are symbolic objects, scaled appropriately for plot size.

To move or copy symbol objects as individual drawing entities, you collect the individual entities into a selection set. However, as drawings become crowded, it becomes more difficult to select the entities that you want. It is much easier if the entities are grouped together as a block. A block is saved with a name and can be later reused in the same drawing or in other drawings.

AutoCAD blocks let you operate on the group as a whole. Entities in blocks stick together; move one part of the block and the whole block moves. You can, of course, break up a block by *exploding* it if you need to edit it.

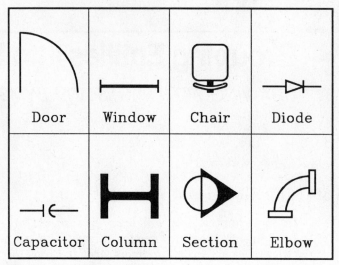

Common Symbols and Parts

Block Speed and Versatility

Building up libraries of frequently used blocks will speed up drawing creation. A library can consist of: many individual drawing files, each used as a single block; a few files, each containing many blocks; or a combination of both. Building such a library takes time, but it dramatically reduces your design time later on.

Besides their convenience, blocks provide additional drawing and editing benefits. It's a lot faster to insert a block than to redraw the same objects 20 times in 20 different drawings, or copy them 20 times in the same drawing. When you insert blocks into your drawing file, you can change their scale and rotation. Instead of using multiple instances of the block, you can use one block, such as a window or bolt head, to represent many different sizes of the same object. This allows you to build your drawing quickly and easily by modifying simple blocks. You can also globally replace one block with another, revising an entire drawing with a single command.

Block Efficiency and Storage

One of the biggest advantages to using blocks is that they help keep your drawing file sizes to a minimum. A smaller file takes up less disk space and uses less memory when it loads. For example, when you draw 100 lines, you add 100 entities to your drawing. When you make a block containing 100 lines, AutoCAD creates a block definition containing 100 entities. Block definitions are stored in the drawing file. When you insert a block in your drawing, you only add one new entity — a reference to the block definition. So if you insert a block containing 100 lines into your drawing in 12 places, you only have 112 entities for AutoCAD to store: 100 lines in the block definition and 12 block references for the visible inserts. Without blocks, if you draw and copy 12 groups of 100 lines, you add 1200 entities to your drawing file. It's easy to see that blocks can save huge amounts of disk space.

How the Block Exercises Are Organized

You can use this chapter's exercises in several ways. First, the exercises in the early part of the chapter guide you through the basic block commands, including writing blocks to disk files and redefining blocks in a drawing. If you don't have the IA DISK, you'll need these blocks for the final Autotown exercise.

Second, the section on xrefs guides you through creating, attaching, detaching, controlling, and converting xrefs. This section can be done independently from the rest of the chapter, if you like.

This chapter's last section, the final Autotown block exercises, creates the AUTOTOWN drawing. This section uses blocks created in the first section. This will give you more extensive practice working with blocks and xrefs in a simple but realistic drawing. It also shows other drawing techniques, such as using a UCS to locate drawing objects within each building lot and inputting distance<angle measurements in surveyor's units for the site plan.

Block Editing Tools

Grouping entities into blocks is really very simple. You use BLOCK to create a block definition, INSERT to place a block reference in a drawing, and WBLOCK to store a block's entities permanently as a separate drawing file on disk. These commands are on the [BLOCKS] screen menu, along with two other block commands, BASE and MINSERT. You will also find an [Insert] menu item on the [Draw] pull-down menu.

```
 Assist  Draw  Modify  Display  Settings  Options  Utility  File  Solids
         Line                                                        * * * *
         Point                                                       ATTDEF:
         Circle    >                                                 BASE:
         Arc       >                                                 BLOCK:
         3D Face                                                     INSERT:
                                                                     MINSERT:
         Polyline                                                    MBLOCK:
         3D Poly
         Donut                                                       XBIND:
         Ellipse                                                     XREF:
         Polygon

         Insert
         Xref

         Surfaces...
         Objects...                                                  LAST
                                                                     DRAW
         Dtext                                                       EDIT
         Hatch
         Dim...
Command:
Command:
Command:
```

Blocks Screen Menu and Draw Pull-Down Menu

Besides these block commands, we will introduce three additional commands that you use with blocks. These are the EXPLODE, DIVIDE, and MEASURE commands. You will find these commands on the [EDIT] screen menus. The [Modify] pull-down menu also includes [Divide] and [Measure] items, for which you can preset options with the [Options] pull-down menu.

➤ *NOTE: AutoCAD has another type of symbol entity called a SHAPE. Text is a special form of the shape feature. To learn more about shapes, see CUSTOMIZING AutoCAD from New Riders Publishing.*

Setup for Blocks

Let's set up a drawing to create some blocks that you'll use later in Autotown. Autotown is our version of a site plan. It encompasses three building lots along an elegant street, "Autotown Drive." The drawing uses feet and decimal inches. Set your drawing limits at 360 feet by 240 feet — a 36" x 24" D-size sheet plotted at 1" = 10'.

Setting Up Blocks Exercises

Begin a NEW drawing named IABLOCKS and set up the layers and settings shown in the Blocks Drawing Settings table.

AXIS	COORDS	GRID	SNAP	UCSICON
Off	ON	10'	6"	OR
UNITS	Engineering, 2 decimal places, decimal degrees, default all other settings.			
LIMITS	0,0 to 360',240'			

Blocks Drawing Settings

Your current layer should be layer 0. Before you can do anything, you need to draw some objects on layer 0 to make into blocks.

Making Some Objects

Trees and cars can be found in most subdivisions. Draw a car and a tree using the dimensions in the following drawings. (Don't worry if the tree looks a little sparse. We'll spruce it up later.)

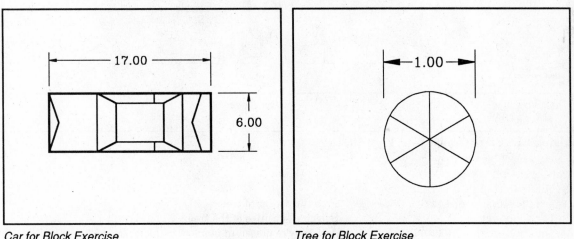

Car for Block Exercise   *Tree for Block Exercise*

Making a Car and Tree Symbol

Command: **ZOOM**   Zoom in to center of screen with height 15'.

Draw the car using the dimensions shown in the illustration.

Command: **ZOOM**   Zoom in below the car with a height of 8".

Set snap to .25 and draw a 1" (yes, one inch) diameter tree.

The car is drawn and inserted full size, but the tree is drawn tiny (one unit in diameter) so it can be easily scaled to make different sized trees when inserted.

The BLOCK Command

Now, turn the car and tree into blocks. When you execute the BLOCK command, AutoCAD will first ask you for the block name that you want to use. Name the blocks TREE1 and CAR2. Then, AutoCAD will ask you for an insertion base point. This is the reference point that you will later use to put the block in a new location. After you identify a base point, select the entities that will form the blocks.

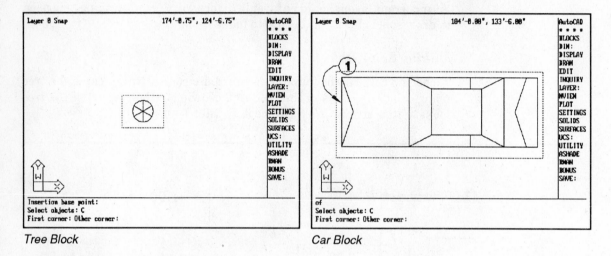

Tree Block   *Car Block*

Using BLOCK to Create Your First Blocks

```
Command: BLOCK
Block name (or ?): TREE1
Insertion base point:               Pick the center of tree.
Select objects:                     Select all entities of the tree.
Select objects: <RETURN>            And they're placed in memory as a block.

Command: ZOOM                       Previous.
Command: SNAP                        Set back to 6".

Command: BLOCK
Block name (or ?): CAR2
Insertion base point: MID           Use MIDpoint osnap.
of                                  Pick the front of the car at ①.
Select object                       Select all entities of the car.
Select objects: <RETURN>
```

You should now have a blank screen. After being selected, your entities disappeared. They are not lost. The entities are safely stored away in memory as two blocks named CAR2 and TREE1.

Where are they? AutoCAD keeps track of all blocks in an invisible part of the drawing file called the block table. When you used the BLOCK command, it created a definition of the car and the tree and stored the definitions in the block table. Each block definition defines the entities associated with the block name. When you save the drawing, they will be stored as part of the drawing file.

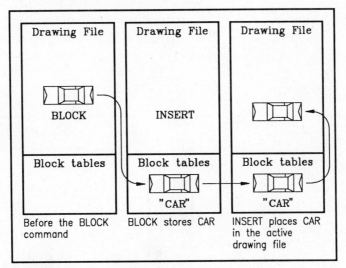

BLOCK and INSERT With Block Table Area

The INSERT Command

We will leave the tree in storage for now (in memory). To get the car back, you INSERT it from the block table into the active part of the drawing file. First, AutoCAD wants to know which block you want to insert. If you respond with a question mark, AutoCAD lists the names for all blocks that are currently defined in the table area of your drawing. Take a look at the names.

Using INSERT ? to Get Block Names

```
Command: INSERT
Block name (or ?): ?                    Show the defined blocks.
Block(s) to list <*>: <RETURN>          Screen flips to text mode and displays:
Defined blocks.
  CAR2
  TREE1

User     Unnamed
Blocks   Blocks
  2        0
```
When you've seen the list, press <F1> to do a flip screen.

Now, insert your car. After you supply the block name, CAR2, you can drag
the block to insert it, or you can give coordinates for the insertion point.
AutoCAD will also ask for scale and rotation factors. Default these factors.
After you insert the car, copy it.

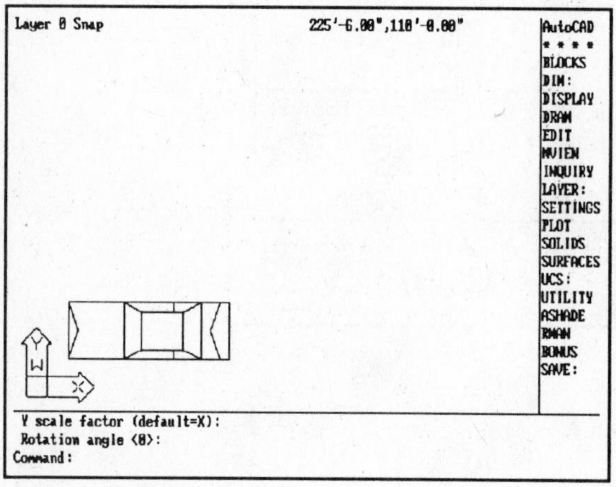

Inserted Car

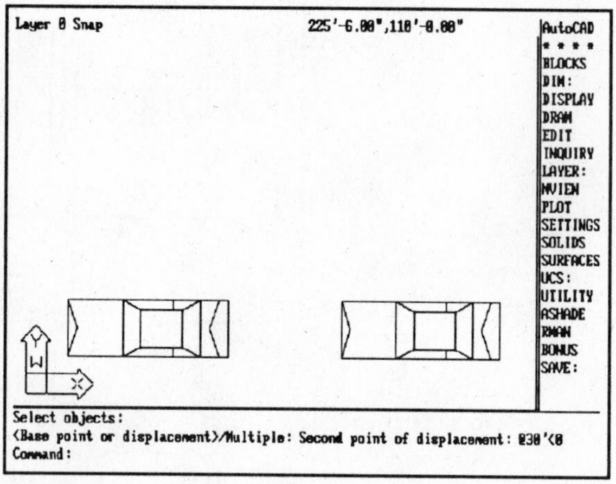

Copied Car

Using INSERT to Insert the Car Block

```
Command: ZOOM                           Zoom left corner 168',110' with height 40'.

Command: INSERT
Block name (or ?): CAR2
Insertion point:                        Drag car and pick point 174',118'.
X scale factor <1>/Corner/XYZ: <RETURN> Defaults to 1:1.
Y scale factor <default=X>: <RETURN>    Defaults to 1:1.
Rotation angle <0.00>: <RETURN>         Car is inserted with 0 rotation.

Command: COPY              Select by picking car and copy with polar displacement @30'<0.
```

Your car came back on the screen with the insertion. But this car is not the same individual entities as your original car. When you copied the car, you selected it with a single object pick. Once you have inserted a block in your drawing, you can move and copy it as a single entity.

What took place behind the drawing insertion? INSERT did three things: it created a block reference to the block definition; it left the original block definition in the block table area; it drew an image representing the entities which make up the block definition.

➡ *NOTE: Not only can you insert blocks that you have created in the current drawing, but you can also insert any drawing file that you have saved on disk. A previously saved drawing inserts as a block in the current drawing. The saved drawing's origin becomes the insertion base point unless you have set another base point with the BASE command (discussed later in this chapter). Inserting a drawing creates a new block definition containing all of that drawing's entities. If AutoCAD cannot find a block that you know you have on disk, check its location against the list of directories AutoCAD searches in Appendix B.*

Scaling and Rotating Block Insertions

When you insert a block reference in the active drawing area, you can enter different values for its scale and rotation. You scale by inputting X and Y scale factors. The default scale prompt for the Y factor uses the X factor you enter to make it easy to scale your drawing symbol to a 1:1 ratio. Or, you can use different X and Y scales by entering different responses (the XYZ option is for 3D control). You can also give an angle of rotation by entering an angle or by dragging the rotation and picking.

Try two modified car block insertions. First, insert your car using different X and Y scales. Use the values given in the sequence below to elongate the car like a stretch limousine. Second, insert another car at an angle. If you make a mistake, use UNDO or ERASE Last to remove the block insertion.

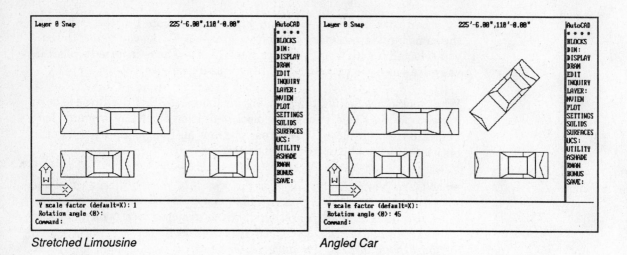

Stretched Limousine   Angled Car

Using INSERT With Scale and Rotation Changes

```
Command: INSERT
Block name (or ?) <CAR2>: <RETURN>
Insertion point:                              Pick point 174',128'.
X scale factor <1>/Corner/XYZ: 1.5
Y scale factor <default=X>: 1
Rotation angle <0.00>: <RETURN>

Command: INSERT
Block name (or ?) <CAR2>: <RETURN>
Insertion point:                              Pick point 205',128'.
X scale factor <1>/Corner/XYZ: <RETURN>
Y scale factor <default=X>: <RETURN>
Rotation angle <0.00>: 45
```

What happened behind the insertion scenes this time? Again, INSERT made references to the block table, this time modified by the scale and rotation values, that it applied to the image of the car in the active drawing.

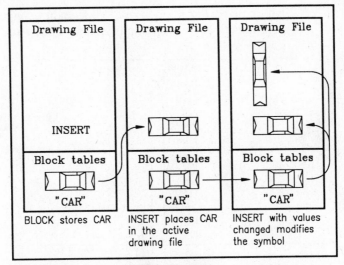

Car Drawing — Inserted With Changes

➡ *TIP: A handy trick for inserting objects that are normally horizontal or vertical is to use your pointer to pick a rotation angle with ortho <^O> turned on. This limits the rotation angle to 0, 90, 180, or 270 degrees.*

While you were inputting your scale values, you may also have noticed a second option, called Corner, to input scale factors. When you use the Corner option to input your scale values, you can scale the block by indicating the X and Y size of a rectangle. The insertion point is the first corner of the rectangle. Drag and pick the other corner to determine scale. AutoCAD uses the width as the X scale and the height as the Y scale. The width and height are measured in current drawing units.

You do not need to type a C to use corner point scaling. Just pick a point at the X scale prompt and then pick another point. The Corner option is used in menus because it limits scale input to corner point picking and issues an Other corner: prompt.

➡ *NOTE: Whether you use keyboard scale entry or the Corner option, you can specify negative scale factors to mirror the block's insertion, turn it upside-down, or both.*

Be careful with corner point scaling! The dragged scale is relative to *one unit* (1") square. It works great if your block definition is about one unit in size. But if your block definition is many drawing units in size, like CAR2, even a small rectangle will give a large scale factor.

When using corner scale input, use snap or osnap to control accuracy. It is most useful when inserting unit scale blocks such as parts.

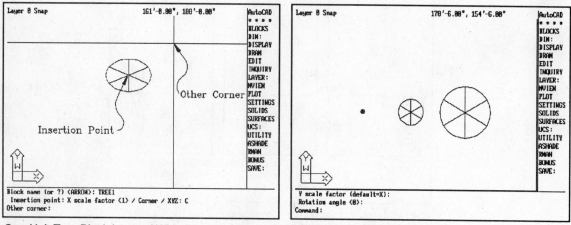

One-Unit Tree Block Inserted With Corner Scaling   One-Unit Tree Inserted at 12", 6' and 12'

Using Unit Scale to Make Flexible Blocks

At first you may think that you will use insertion scale and rotation only occasionally. Nothing could be further from the truth! Being able to scale and rotate blocks during insertion is a valuable feature.

The trick is to create your parts in a *1 x 1 unit cell*. Then, when you insert a block, you can stretch or shrink it to fit. The block is good at any scale with any insertion scale factor. For example, you can store a door or window part so that the endpoints are on the left and right edges of the unit cell. Then insert the symbol with appropriate scale factors to fill the area you need. Remember, you draw a unit block at 1 inch, so to insert it scaled to 3 feet, you use a scale factor of 36, not 3.

To show how versatile one-unit blocks are, let's insert the tree and scale it down to a bush.

Inserting a One-Unit Block With Corner Point Scaling

```
Command: INSERT
Block name (or ?) <CAR2>: TREE1
Insertion point:                          Pick any clear point.
X scale factor <1> / Corner / XYZ:        Drag it to a good bush shape and size, then
                                          pick a corner.

Rotation angle <0>: <RETURN>
```

```
Command: BLOCK
Block name (or ?): BUSH
Insertion base point:
Select objects:
```

Block as BUSH to use again later.

Pick the center.
Pick the bush.

One-unit blocks are very useful. You can create libraries full of one-unit parts, then insert them at different sizes depending on the situation. Don't create whole libraries full of different sizes of windows or bolts — just create a single one-unit part, then insert it to whatever scale you need.

Using Preset Scales

So far, you have inserted blocks by giving an insertion point first, then specifying scale and angle. This is quick and easy, but you can't see the angle or how big the block is until after you have placed it. This makes it hard to visually drag scaled or rotated blocks into place. Fortunately, you can preset the scale and rotation. When you preset the block's scale and angle, insertion point dragging is suspended until you have completed your preset options. Then, you can see the block's scale and angle as you drag it to pick the insertion point.

Try making one more stretch limousine using preset values.

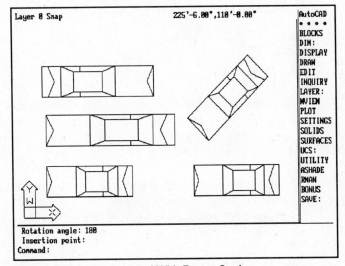

Stretch Limousine Inserted With Preset Scale

Using INSERT With Preset Scales

```
Command: INSERT                          Insert a stretched car rotated 180 degrees.
Block name (or ?) <TREE1>: CAR2
Insertion point: X                       Preset the X scale.
X scale factor: 1.3
Insertion point: Y                       Preset the Y scale.
Y scale factor: 1
Insertion point: R                       Preset the rotation angle.
Rotation angle: 180
Insertion point:                         Drag it around, then pick point 196',138'.
```

Presets offer several options, but they are not shown in the insert prompt. Here is a complete list.

Preset Scale and Rotation Options

Scale and **PScale** will prompt for scale factor which will be preset to X, Y, and Z axes.

Xscale and **PXscale** only preset an X scale factor.

Yscale and **PYscale** only preset a Y scale factor.

Zscale and **PZscale** only preset a Z scale factor.

Rotate and **PRotate** preset rotation angle. Enter from the keyboard or by picking two points.

Just type the first one or two characters of the preset option to tell AutoCAD what you want to preset.

P stands for preliminary, not preset. Options prefixed with a P establish a preliminary scale and rotation value to aid in insertion. After the insertion point is selected, the normal prompts are displayed to let you change the preset values.

Preset scale factors have limitations. You cannot mix fixed presets, like Xscale, with preliminary presets, like PYscale. If you try to mix them, the preliminary presets become fixed, and you will not be reprompted for their values.

➥ *NOTE: Preset options work best when you use them in menu macros. These macros can transparently apply preset options, making dragging while in the INSERT command natural and easy to do.*

When Is a Block Not a Block?

You use the BLOCK command to collect entities into a single group. When you insert the block in a drawing file, the insertion is a single entity. When you erase a block, the whole block (but not its stored definition) is erased. The same holds true for moving and copying blocks.

When is a block not a block? A block is not a block when it is *inserted or exploded.

Using *INSERT

Sometimes you want to be able to individually edit the different entities that make up a block after you insert them. But, individual entities lose their identities when they are stored as a block.

What if you want to edit a block after you insert it? To edit individual pieces of a block after insertion, AutoCAD provides an option for the INSERT command. Placing an asterisk (*) in front of a block name at insertion time tells AutoCAD to break the block back into its individual entities. This is commonly called an *insert-star* or *star-insertion*. A *insertion does not insert a block reference; it duplicates the original entities of the block definition. However, unlike duplicating entities with COPY, a *insertion allows you to modify the scale and rotation of the copy.

Inserting a separate drawing file into the current drawing creates a block in the current drawing unless you *insert it. *Insertion inserts only individual entities, without creating a block.

Let's zoom in and insert the car in the clear area of the screen. Then to prove the new car is really a collection of separate entities, we'll change it into a sports car. Use some editing commands on the *inserted car and create a car as complex as you like, making sure it looks different from the original. It will be used in a later exercise.

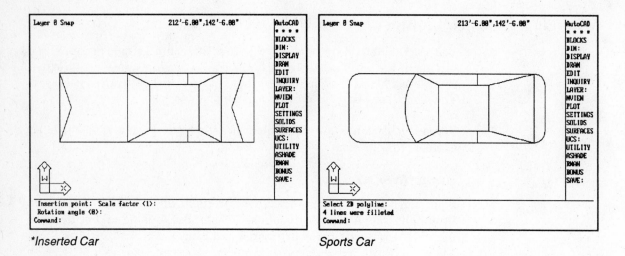

*Inserted Car

Sports Car

Using *INSERT to Break Blocks Into Components

Command: **ZOOM**   Zoom in to a height of 15' in a clear area.

Command: **INSERT**
Block name (or ?) <CAR2>: ***CAR2**
Insertion point: Pick a point, and default scale and rotation.

Command: **ERASE**   Erase the windshield line and two lines on the trunk and hood.
Command: **STRETCH**   Stretch the rear glass towards the back.
Command: **STRETCH**   Make the roof smaller.
Command: **ARC**   Draw a new windshield.
Command: **FILLET**   Round the corners of the car.

Command: **ZOOM**   Previous.
Command: **SAVE**

When you use the star option to insert a block, AutoCAD restricts your flexibility in rescaling the objects as they are placed. You can only specify a single, positive scale factor in the * mode. Negative and unequal X and Y scales are not allowed. But you can rescale your *inserted blocks with STRETCH, SCALE, EXTEND, and other editing commands after insertion.

➤ *TIP: If you place a complex *inserted block in the wrong place, use Undo to get rid of all the pieces.*

What if you want to modify a block after it has already been inserted? Explode it.

The EXPLODE Command

You can achieve the same effect on an existing block that you get with a *insertion. AutoCAD gives you the EXPLODE command to separate a block back into its original entities. Try exploding the first car you inserted on the far bottom left of your drawing.

Using EXPLODE to Explode a Block

```
Command: EXPLODE
Select block reference, polyline, dimension, or mesh:    Pick first car in the lower left corner.
                                                         The block is redrawn as it explodes.
```

The exploded car pieces look identical to the image before the explosion. There may be exceptions where byblock, color, linetype, and layer assignments can come undone when you explode a block. If an exploded block includes nested blocks, only the outer level of nesting is broken up by the explosion. (We will cover nesting and byblock properties a little later in this section's discussion of block properties.)

There are some things that you cannot explode. You can't explode an *inserted block because it already is exploded. You can't explode a *minserted* block. And, you can't explode mirrored blocks or a block with differing X and Y (and Z) scale factors.

The MINSERT Command

A block is more than a block when it is minserted. Suppose you wanted to put a whole bunch of cars (or desks, or printed circuit board drill locations, or any other symbol you might have blocked away) in your drawing. You could insert one copy of the block and then use ARRAY to make several columns and rows.

MINSERT provides another option. Think of MINSERT (Multiple INSERTion) as a single command that combines insertion and rectangular arrays (no polar arrays with MINSERT). However, there is a difference. Each entity that the ARRAY command generates is an individual entity in the drawing file — it can be edited, deleted, copied, or even arrayed individually. Each component of the block that MINSERT generates is part of a single minserted block. You cannot edit the individual component blocks. (You also cannot *minsert blocks.)

Use MINSERT to fill your screen with cars. Pan to the right side of your drawing to get a clear space. After you have minserted the cars, use an ERASE Last to get rid of them.

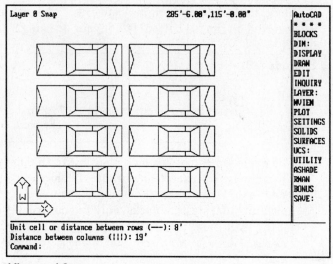

Minserted Cars

Using MINSERT to Insert a Block

Command: **PAN**   Pick a point and pan by a displacement of @60'<180.

Command: **MINSERT**
Block name (or ?) <*CAR2>: **CAR2**
Insertion point: Pick a point in the lower left.
X Scale factor <1>/Corner/XYZ: **<RETURN>**
Y Scale factor <default=X>: **<RETURN>**
Rotation angle <0.00>: **<RETURN>**
Number of rows (---) <1>: **4**
Number of columns (||||) <1>: **2**
Unit cell or distance between rows (---): **8'**
Distance between columns (||||): **19'**

Command: **ERASE**   Use Last to prove that all are tied to one another.

➥ *NOTE: When you specify a rotation in MINSERT, the array is rotated, along with the individual blocks within it.*

MINSERT is an efficient way to place multiple copies of a block in a drawing file. In an array, every entity occurrence takes up disk space. In a minsert, the block reference occurs only once and includes information about the number of rows, columns, and spacing of elements.

There are two additional commands that you can use to insert multiple copies of a block. These are the DIVIDE and MEASURE commands.

The DIVIDE Command

Frequently, you are faced with the problem of placing blocks in a drawing at a set interval. You can use the DIVIDE command to divide an entity, say a polyline, into equal length parts, and insert a block at the division points. DIVIDE does not actually break the polyline (or other entity), it only marks the divisions. You can divide lines, arcs, circles, and polylines.

Create a new car block from CAR2 in the space where you erased your minserted cars. Call this new car block CAR3 and change its insertion point so that the cars will set back from the polyline when they are inserted. Next, create a polyline. The direction in which you drew the polyline determines which side the cars insert on. Then use DIVIDE to divide the polyline into seven segments and insert the new car blocks.

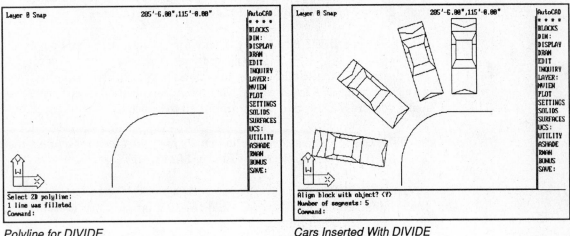

Polyline for DIVIDE   Cars Inserted With DIVIDE

Using DIVIDE to Insert a Car Block

```
Command: INSERT
Block name (or ?) <CAR2>: <RETURN>
Insertion point:                    Pick a point in the center and default the scale.
Rotation angle <0.00>: -90          We want it at right angles to the polyline.

Command: BLOCK
Block name (or ?): CAR3
Insertion base point: @0,3'          Makes insert point 3' in front of car.
```

```
Select objects: L
1 found.
Select objects: <RETURN>              CAR3 is now a nested block containing CAR2.

Command: PLINE                        Draw a polyline from 275',133' to @22'<180 to @ 17'<-90.
Command: FILLET                       Fillet corner with a 12' radius.

Command: DIVIDE
Select object to divide:              Pick the polyline.
<Number of segments>/Block: B
Block name to insert: CAR3
Align block with object? <Y> <RETURN>
Number of segments: 5
```

After you are done, your screen should have four cars, one between each of the five segments. Each inserted block is a separate entity.

You can divide a line or polyline even if you do not use blocks. DIVIDE will insert point entities to which you can osnap with NODe. You can make them display more visibly with PDMODE and PDSIZE.

When you use DIVIDE to insert blocks (or points), AutoCAD saves the inserted entities as a Previous selection set. You can get the group again for editing by using the Previous selection set option. For example, if you want to change the layer of the cars, you can select them all simply by using the Previous option when prompted to select objects in CHPROP.

➥ *TIP: You can use a construction entity for your block insertions, then erase it after you do your DIVIDE (or MEASURE) insert.*

DIVIDE (and MEASURE) don't let you scale a block. If you wanted to insert the original one-unit size trees, you'd create a larger block and insert it, or rescale each block after insertion.

The MEASURE Command

MEASURE works much like DIVIDE. However, instead of dividing an entity into equal parts, MEASURE lets you specify the segment length. Once you specify a block name to insert and a segment length, either by inputting a value or by picking two points, AutoCAD inserts them at segment length intervals.

Are you getting tired of seeing just cars? For good measure, try adding some bushes to the parking area, using the BUSH block that you made in the one-unit block exercise.

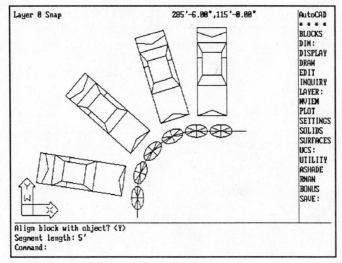

Bushes Inserted With MEASURE

Using MEASURE to Insert Bush Blocks

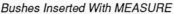

```
Command: MEASURE
Select object to measure:              Pick the polyline.
<Segment length>/Block: B
Block name to insert: BUSH
Align block with object? <Y> <RETURN>
Segment length: 5'                     Place a bush every five feet.
```

Like DIVIDE, MEASURE works with blocks or points, and forms a Previous selection set that you can use for subsequent editing.

WBLOCK — The Write BLOCK Command

So far, the blocks you have created and stored in the block table have been self-contained in the current drawing file. They will be stored in this drawing when you save or end it. Whenever you work in this drawing file, these block definitions will be there. However, sooner or later you will want to use them in another drawing.

Sending Blocks to Disk as Drawing Files

WBLOCK lets you save any block in your current drawing as a separate drawing file on disk. Or you can select a set of entities and write them to a separate drawing file without making them into a block in the current drawing. Any block or selection set can be stored as a separate drawing file, and any drawing file can be inserted as a block.

The drawing file created by WBLOCK is a normal drawing containing the current drawing settings and the entities that make up the block definition. The entities are normal drawing entities and are not defined as a block in the new file.

Try storing CAR2 as a separate file called CAR2.DWG, and TREE1 as TREE1.DWG.

Using WBLOCK to Write a Block to Disk

```
Command: WBLOCK
File name: CAR2                  AutoCAD automatically adds the .DWG.
Block name: =                    Responding to Block name with = tells AutoCAD the block
                                 name equals the filename.

Command: WBLOCK
File name: TREE1
Block name: =
```

➡ *TIP: If a block is really useful, wblock it to a disk file. Periodically group your wblocked symbols into library files.*

To later insert (or *insert) CAR2.DWG into another drawing file, use the INSERT command and call the file using its disk filename, CAR2.

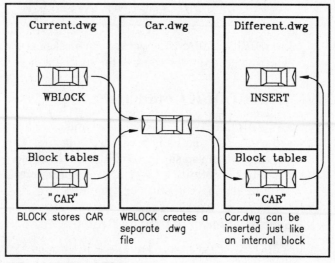

WBLOCK and INSERT

Using Entity Selection to Wblock a File

You can wblock a file without creating a block first. If you enter a <RETURN> instead of giving an existing block name in response to a block name prompt, you will be prompted for an insertion base point and object selection. You can use any of the standard object selection techniques to select items for wblocking. When you finish selecting with a final <RETURN>, the entities are copied to the disk file you specified.

The entities are not defined as a block in the current drawing unless you also insert them. The drawing file created by WBLOCK is a normal drawing containing the selected entities and current drawing settings. The entities are not defined as a block in the new file.

Wblock the sports car to the filename MY-CAR. When you use BLOCK or WBLOCK, the selected entities are erased. OOPS will restore them, just like it restores entities deleted by the ERASE command. After you create the drawing file, undo or oops the entities back.

Creating a Block Drawing File With Entity Selection

```
Command: ZOOM                        Zoom Previous, Dynamic, or pan to the sports car.

Command: WBLOCK
File name: MY-CAR
Blockname: <RETURN>
Insertion base point:                Pick front midpoint of car.
Select objects:                      Select all entities of sports car.
Select objects: <RETURN>

Command: OOPS                         Return the car to the drawing.
```

Just as you can insert an entire drawing file as a block, you can wblock an entire current drawing to disk as a new file.

Remember, the drawing file created by WBLOCK is just like any other drawing file. WBLOCK doesn't create *any* blocks. It creates a drawing file that contains the entities that you select or that make up an existing block.

WBLOCK * Writes the Entire Drawing — Almost

If you respond to the WBLOCK block name prompt with an asterisk, then it writes almost the entire current drawing to a disk file. We say almost because it does not write any *unused* named things that are referenced by entities, such as blocks, text styles, layers, or linetypes. Drawing environment settings for UCSs, views, and viewport configurations are written, however.

Using WBLOCK* to Write it All

```
Command: WBLOCK          Wblock your entire drawing.
File name: AUTOCITY
Block name: *            It writes the drawing to a new file on disk.
```

➡ *TIP: WBLOCK * is often used as an alternative method to purge unused blocks. (You can also purge them with the PURGE command.) If you wblock * to the same filename as the current drawing, it will ask if you want to replace it. If you answer yes, then quit the current drawing, you will have saved the current drawing, but without any unused blocks. This trick is commonly called a wblock star. But use it with caution because it will also delete unused layers, linetypes, and text styles.*

The PURGE Command

As you work with blocks, you can build up extraneous blocks in the block table by inserting them, then later deleting them. Use the PURGE command to remove unused block definitions from the block table of the current drawing file.

PURGE only works in an editing session *before* you modify your drawing database either by creating a new entity or by editing an existing entity. PURGE is selective and prompts you extensively, giving you information about what blocks are stored in the block table area and asking you explicitly if you want to clean them out. You can also use PURGE to clean out unused layers, views, or styles — anything that you named during a drawing editor session. Using PURGE is a good habit before backing up a drawing on diskettes. To use PURGE, load your drawing and issue PURGE as the first command.

When you create other drawing files that you may later use as blocks, you need an easy way to control their insertion base points.

The BASE Command

The BASE command creates an insertion base point in a drawing file so you can control where it inserts into another file. The base point is an insertion handle just like the insertion base point on a regular block. (The base point is not an entity or visible point.) If you make a drawing, store it on disk, and later insert it in another drawing, it defaults to 0,0 as the insertion base point unless you specify the base point.

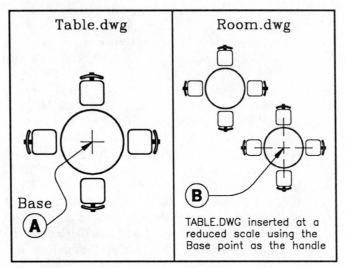

Inserting a Drawing Into Another Drawing

Naming Conventions for Blocks

As your list of blocks and wblocked drawing files grows, you will find that you need some organization and structure in naming your blocks. We recommend that you give your blocks useful names. CAR1 and CAR2 are better than C1 and C, but not as descriptive as VWBUG and PORSCHE.

Try to make your block names the same number of characters or fewer than your operating system allows for filenames. You may want to wblock them later, and having a block name that is an allowable filename lets you specify = for the filename instead of typing it. You may also want to use common prefixes for similar classes of blocks (and drawings) to make it easy to use wildcards. Keep an alphabetical log of block names in a disk text file and print it out as it changes. This way you won't accidentally call the wrong block or duplicate block names.

Block Structure

Blocks are powerful tools. Their use can make your drawing life easier. There are two additional block properties that you should be aware of when you use blocks: blocks can include other blocks, and blocks can include entities on different layers.

Nesting Blocks

A block can be made up of other blocks. This is called nesting. You can place a block inside a block inside a block. AutoCAD does not place a limit on the number of block nesting levels, although editing nested blocks can get confusing if you go more than a few levels deep. When you created the BUSH block it contained the TREE1 block as a nested block.

To include a block in another block, you simply select the first block when you block the second. You can use standard editing commands, like ARRAY, COPY, and MOVE, on nested blocks just as on normal blocks.

Nested blocks further increase the efficiency and control of blocks. The BUSH block contains only one entity (the TREE1 block) instead of one circle and three lines. In our Nested Block Example illustration, we've made the chair a nested block so that the outer TABLE block need only contain four block references instead of all of the entities that make up each chair. It also allows the CHAIR block to be redefined (changed) easily and independently of the TABLE block definition.

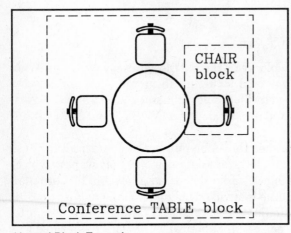

Nested Block Example

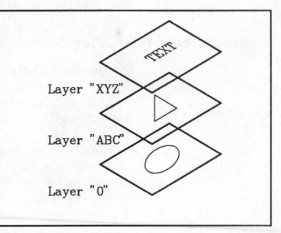

A Block Can Have Entities on Many Layers

Blocks and Layers

When dealing with blocks and layers, we are primarily concerned with what layers the entities in the block definition are on. So far, entities of all the blocks you have used have been entities drawn on layer 0. You can, however, create a block with entities on different drawing layers. For example, you can create a block with graphic entities on layer ABC, and text on layer XYZ. When you create the block, AutoCAD will store the entities inside the block on their appropriate layers.

When you insert multiple-layer blocks, each entity in the block will display according to its rules of color and linetype as they were at the time of the entity's creation. Entities included in the block at the time of block creation can have color or linetype specification set BYLAYER (the default), BYBLOCK, or by explicit color or linetype settings. If the current drawing file does not contain all of the needed block's layers, insertion will create the layers in the current drawing. The Color Layer Insertion Example illustration shows a normal block insertion where the entity retains its original explicit color when inserted on a different active layer.

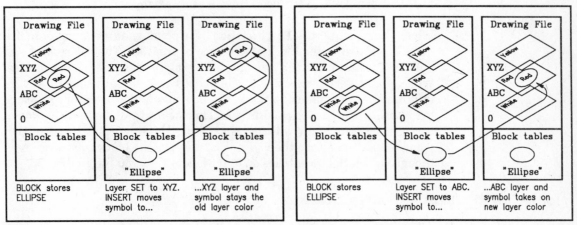

Color Layer Insertion Example   *Layer Insertion Example*

Layer 0's Special Block Insertion Properties

If you create entities on layer 0, store them in a block, and then insert the block on a different active layer, the entities will move to the layer of insertion. If they had explicit color or linetype, they will retain them. However, if they had color and/or linetype set BYLAYER, they will adopt the default layer settings of their layer of insertion. Blocks made from layer 0 BYLAYER entities act like chameleons.

➤ *NOTE: Any entities that were on layer 0 at the time of block creation will go back to layer 0 and return to their original color and linetype when you use a *insertion or explode them.*

Using BYBLOCK Colors and Linetypes

You can get a similar effect to layer 0 entities by creating them with the BYBLOCK property (or by changing existing entities to BYBLOCK with CHPROP). These BYBLOCK entities will take on the current color and linetype settings of the layer upon which the block is inserted. Unlike blocked layer 0 BYLAYER entities, which are predestined to assume the default layer color and/or linetypes of the layer upon which the entities were drawn, BYBLOCK entities in blocks are completely flexible. They assume the settings of the insertion layer at the time of insertion, whether explicit (like red), BYLAYER, or even BYBLOCK (for nesting).

Blocks and Frozen Layers

Sooner or later, we all have the experience of inserting a block with multiple-layer entities on a layer, freezing the layer, and suddenly having the block disappear from view. How does this happen?

When you give AutoCAD an insertion base point, that invisible reference point is defined in the block at the time of creation. The reference point anchors the block into the drawing file by its insertion point coordinates. When you insert a block, AutoCAD does not actually insert all the information that makes up the block, but only a block reference back to the invisibly stored block definitions. This means that whatever layer you use to insert the block will contain the block reference at the insertion point. When you freeze the layer, you suppress the block reference, even though the block has entities on other layers that you haven't frozen.

Block Substitution and Redefinition

All of these properties sound good in theory, but what about some practical techniques? We would like to wrap up this first section on blocks by showing you two useful block techniques: using substitute blocks, and redefining blocks. The Autotown block exercises will show you how to substitute working blocks and do block redefinitions.

Substituting Working Blocks

As you insert a block, you can assign a different block name by using an equal sign. You use an assignment such as IA-TREE=TREE1 to tell AutoCAD to use the graphic information stored in the TREE1.DWG file on disk. The TREE1 symbol will then be inserted in your drawing as the working block IA-TREE. Substituting the IA-TREE name within your current drawing provides you with a safety step that makes it difficult to overwrite blocks in your drawing.

Redefining Blocks

If the block name already exists in your drawing, then reinserting it with an equal sign will redefine all existing insertions of the block.

To see how block redefinition works, try replacing all your CAR2 blocks with MY-CAR blocks (the sports car you saved to disk). You can use the INSERT command to replace blocks as well as to insert them. You do not have to actually complete the INSERT command to redefine existing blocks. Just cut it short with a <^C>, and the redefinition will occur.

Using INSERT to Redefine Blocks

Zoom or pan as needed to view all cars.

```
Command: INSERT
Block name (or ?) <CAR3>: CAR2=MY-CAR
Block CAR2 redefined
Regenerating drawing.
Insertion point: *Cancel*          Type <^C> to cancel command.

Command: END
```

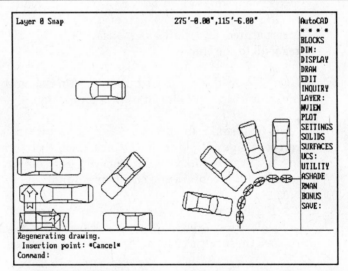

Redefined Car Blocks

You should have sports cars all over the place. Replacing a few cars with a few different cars may seem like a trivial exercise. But, if you have a minor revision to make on a block that occurs several hundred times in a drawing, it is no trivial matter! You can globally replace all your blocks with a revised block in a single insertion redefinition.

➡ *TIP: If you are satisfied with a part of a drawing (or a part on a layer) and you won't be working on that part for a while, block it and replace it with a simple block to improve redraw speed and reduce screen clutter. When you are ready, put the drawing back together again by inserting the block with an equal sign.*

External References (Xrefs) Give You Distributed Design

Let's say your building design team consists of four people — one is working on the building's structure and floor plan, one on the electrical system, one on the plumbing and other facilities, and the last is working on the interior design.

Everyone needs to know what the basic outline of the building is and where walls, doors, windows, and other features are. They can't wait for the floor plan to be finalized and completely drawn — they have to get to work right away to stay on top of the project. If a change is made to the floor plan, the rest of the team needs to know it right away.

The perfect solution is for each person on the team to insert the floor plan into his drawings as an xref. Every time he loads his drawing to work on it, the very latest revision of the floor plan will automatically be incorporated. If a wall has moved, he will know it right away and can respond to the change.

Even if you don't design buildings, this should give you an idea for incorporating xrefs into your own application.

Xrefs (external references) are collective entities similar to blocks. They can contain multiple entities (lines, arcs, and so on); you can insert them in your drawing like blocks; and you can select them as a single entity whether they contain one entity or a hundred.

The big difference between a block and an xref is that while blocks reduce multiple drawing entities in your drawing file down to a single case, xrefs remove those entities from the drawing file altogether.

When you create a block that contains 100 lines, your drawing database contains an entry for each of those lines, including each line's layer setting, color setting, linetype, and so on. You can't see a listing of that data, even if you list the drawing database's contents. The data is buried in the block definition table, but it's still there — for all 100 lines. When you insert more copies of your block onto your drawing, you duplicate only the block reference, not the original data. But the original lines always have to be in the block definition table for the block to exist.

Xrefs for Efficiency

Xrefs remove the need to store block data in the drawing at all. Xrefs do exactly what their name implies — they reference external drawings. When you insert an xref, you are inserting only its name and a few other bits of information that AutoCAD needs to be able to display the image of the xref on the screen. The entities that make up the image are still located on disk in the drawing file referenced by the xref. The drawing file saves only a reference to the external reference file.

Xrefs are like ghost images of other files. You can use them to insert images of parts and symbols into your drawing without actually inserting the data that makes up the part or symbol. And, like blocks, you can osnap to objects within the xref. If your blocks are complex, containing hundreds of drawing entities, using an xref instead of a block could remove those hundreds of entities from each drawing file that uses them, making file sizes much smaller.

Xrefs for Control

Another, and perhaps even more significant, reason to use xrefs is the control they offer. When several people work on parts of the same drawing, assembling them into one master drawing as xrefs insures that every time that master drawing is loaded or plotted, the latest revisions to the referenced drawings automatically get used. The TABLET.DWG and its three referenced drawings (TABLET-A B and S) on the Release 11 sample disk are an example of this.

Using xrefs assures that parts get automatically updated throughout an entire library of drawings. If you have parts that change from time to time, and they need to be updated to the latest revision in a number of existing drawings, you could use block redefinition, one block and one drawing at a time. But if you instead inserted them as xrefs, they would automatically update whenever a drawing was loaded or plotted.

Using Xrefs

Xrefs best lend themselves to cases where you are inserting common parts that could still be revised during your project. Because they always reflect the most current revision of the data they reference, xrefs can significantly reduce the errors normally associated with copying data from one drawing to another. If you make a change to the xref's source file, that xref will be updated in every drawing in which it is referenced.

Let's briefly examine the command options available with XREF, then run through several exercises using these options. Here is a list of the options:

XREF Options

? — Allows you to list the names of xrefs that have already been attached to your drawing. AutoCAD will prompt you for a name to list, and you can specify an individual name, enter multiple names separated by commas, or use wildcard characters to list multiple names. If you press <RETURN> in response to the prompt, AutoCAD will list all of the xrefs currently attached to the drawing.

Bind — Converts the xrefs you specify by name into standard blocks, binding them to the drawing as permanent entities.

Detach — Removes an xref from your drawing. If the xref is currently being displayed as part of the drawing, it will disappear when you detach it.

Path — Allows you to change the path to the xref's source file. Because an xref references an external file, AutoCAD needs to keep track of what disk and directory the xref's source file is on. Using the Path option, you can change the directory path associated with the xref.

Reload — Causes AutoCAD to reload the xref from disk. If a change has been made to the xref's source file, the change will become apparent after a reload. You can specify a single xref or multiple xrefs to reload.

Attach — This option attaches a new xref to your drawing. If the xref has already been attached, AutoCAD will inform you and remind you that you can reload it to update its definition.

The commands for using xrefs are found as [XREF:] and [XBIND:] on the [BLOCKS] screen menu, and [Xref] on the [Draw] pull-down menu.

Let's attach an xref to a drawing. We'll begin a new drawing named XSYMBOL. Then we'll draw a new symbol on a layer called SYMLAYER. After we save the drawing and return to the main menu, we'll attach it as an xref in a new drawing.

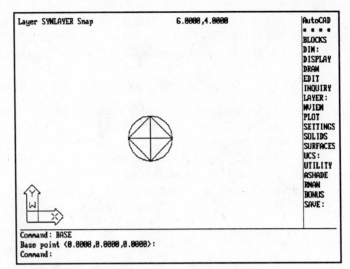

Layer SYMLAYER Snap   6.0000,4.0000   AutoCAD
                                                              * * * *
                                                              BLOCKS
                                                              DIM:
                                                              DISPLAY
                                                              DRAW
                                                              EDIT
                                                              INQUIRY
                                                              LAYER:
                                                              MVIEW
                                                              PLOT
                                                              SETTINGS
                                                              SOLIDS
                                                              SURFACES
                                                              UCS:
                                                              UTILITY
                                                              ASHADE
                                                              RMAN
                                                              BONUS
                                                              SAVE:

Command: BASE
Base point <0.0000,0.0000,0.0000>:
Command:

Symbol on Layer SYMLAYER in XSYMBOL Drawing

Attaching an Xref to Your Drawing

Begin a NEW drawing named XSYMBOL.

Command: **LAYER**   Make a red layer named SYMLAYER and set it current.

Turn snap on and draw the symbol shown with 1" radius.

Command: **BASE**   Set insertion base point at center.
Command: **END**

Begin a NEW drawing named XTEST and turn snap and coords on.

Command: **XREF**   Attach the XSYMBOL drawing as an xref.
?/Bind/Detach/Path/Reload/<Attach>: **<RETURN>**
Xref to Attach: **XSYMBOL**
Attach Xref XSYMBOL: XSYMBOL
XSYMBOL loaded.   The rest of the prompts are identical to INSERT.
Insertion point: **5,5**
 X scale factor <1> / Corner / XYZ: **<RETURN>**
 Y scale factor (default=X): **<RETURN>**
 Rotation angle <0>: **<RETURN>**
Command: **END**   End the drawing to save it.

You can see that attaching an xref is a lot like inserting a block. Xrefs act a lot like blocks. If you select any part of the xref with the ERASE command, the entire xref is deleted, just as if it were a block. You can't explode an xref to edit its entities, but you can edit the external source file. This is one way in which xrefs are very different from blocks. When you update an xref's source drawing file, you will affect every drawing in which that file is referenced. Usually, that's a good thing.

Using Xrefs for Distributed Workgroup Design

One of the main reasons xrefs were designed was to facilitate workgroup design. You can allocate different parts of a large project to members of your design team and have all the pieces come together at the end to make up the final project. Let's use the XSYMBOL drawing you just created as an example of xref's ability to provide automatic updates. Load it, then add two more circles to it and save the drawing. Then, load XTEST again to see XSYMBOL automatically update.

Updating an Xref

Edit an EXISTING drawing named XSYMBOL.

Command: **CIRCLE**	Add two concentric circles around the symbol.
Command: **END**	End the drawing to save it.

Edit an EXISTING drawing named XTEST.

Resolve Xref XSYMBOL: XSYMBOL	The current revision is loaded when you load the drawing.
XSYMBOL loaded.	

When you load a drawing that contains xrefs, AutoCAD automatically reloads any external references. You loaded XSYMBOL, changed it, then ended it. When you loaded the drawing that contained XSYMBOL as an xref, the updated version of XSYMBOL appeared in the file automatically.

But if you are part of a design team, you are probably on a network with the rest of the designers. What happens to your xrefs if someone edits the source file you have referenced in your drawing while you are still working on the drawing? Nothing happens, unless you reload the xref.

Reloading Xrefs

There are two ways to reload xrefs. The first way, which you just used, is to load the drawing again. The other way is to use the XREF Reload option. When AutoCAD asks you which xrefs you want to reload, you can specify one or more xrefs by name, or simply type * to reload them all.

We'll change the original XSYMBOL external file by drawing and wblocking a new square symbol to its filename. Then reload XSYMBOL in your XTEST drawing to update it. XTEST should still be loaded.

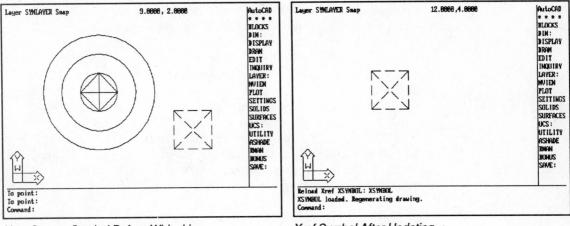

New Square Symbol Before Wblocking   *Xref Symbol After Updating*

Reloading an Xref After its Source File Has Changed

Command: **LAYER**   Make layer named SYMLAYER, color yellow and linetype
                            dashed. Set it current.

Draw a 2" square symbol with an X through it, as illustrated.

Command: **WBLOCK**   Wblock square symbol to filename XSYMBOL, overwriting existing
                             file. Use the center of the square as the insertion point.

```
Command: XREF
?/Bind/Detach/Path/Reload/<Attach>: R
Xref(s) to reload: *          Asterisk updates all xrefs.
     Scanning...
Reload Xref XSYMBOL: XSYMBOL
XSYMBOL loaded.    Regenerating drawing.
```

When you reload xrefs, AutoCAD scans your drawing for xrefs and
rereads the XSYMBOL drawing file from disk. Then it updates the symbol
in the current drawing.

We created a new SYMLAYER layer before wblocking the symbol to make
its layer name match the original xrefs. Let's examine how xrefs handle
layers.

Xrefs and Their Layers

When you insert a block into a drawing, any layers in the block's definition
are added to the drawing. (If a layer in a block already exists in the

drawing, and the entities are set BYLAYER, the block's entities take on the characteristics of the existing drawing layer.)

Xrefs work a little differently. When you attach an xref that contains layers other than layer 0, AutoCAD modifies the xref layer names to avoid duplication. It prefixes the layer names with the name of the xref using a *pipe*, a vertical bar (|), to separate the prefix from the layer name. You created the XSYMBOL data on layer SYMLAYER. When you attach XSYMBOL as an xref, AutoCAD renames SYMLAYER to XSYMBOL|SYMLAYER in the drawing in which the xref is attached. Renaming the layers prevents the xref's entities from taking on the characteristics of existing layers in the drawing.

Let's check the layers in XTEST to see that the layer has been renamed.

Listing Xref Layers

```
Command: LAYER
?/Make/Set/New/ON/OFF/Color/Ltype/Freeze/Thaw: ?
Layer name(s) to list <*>: <RETURN>
    Layer name        State         Color          Linetype
------------------   ---------    -------------   -----------
0                     On          7 (white)      CONTINUOUS
SYMLAYER              On          2 (yellow)     CONTINUOUS
XSYMBOL|SYMLAYER      On          2 (yellow)     XSYMBOL|DASHED    Xdep: XSYMBOL
Current layer: SYMLAYER

?/Make/Set/New/ON/OFF/Color/Ltype/Freeze/Thaw:            Set layer 0 current.

Command: SAVE
```

Layer 0 is the exception to layer renaming by xrefs. As with block insertions, any data in the xrefs source file that resides on layer 0 comes in on layer 0 in the current drawing, and assumes any layer settings you have assigned to layer 0.

Now you know how to attach an xref to your drawing, and you also know what happens to the xref's layers when it is attached. But what if you no longer need the xref and want to remove it completely?

Removing Xrefs From Your Drawing

If you erase an xref, the reference to the external file is still in your drawing, just as a block's definition remains in memory even after all visible insertions are erased. When the drawing is reloaded, AutoCAD will still look for the external file, even though it won't visibly appear.

Use XREF's Detach option to get the xref out of your drawing. To see how that works, use Detach to remove XSYMBOL from your XTEST drawing.

Detaching an Xref from a Drawing

```
Command: XREF
?/Bind/Detach/Path/Reload/<Attach>: D
Xref(s) to Detach: XSYMBOL
    Scanning...                    The xref disappears; it's no longer part of your drawing.
```

Bind Makes Xrefs Into Permanent Blocks

There may be times when you want to make your xref data a permanent part of your drawing instead of a reference to another external file. Otherwise, when you finish a project and want to archive it, you have to archive all of the xref source drawings along with the main drawings. If the xref source drawings are not available when you try to load your drawing, AutoCAD will give you an error message saying it can't find the xrefs. If it can't find them, it can't load and display them as part of the drawing. Binding the xrefs converts the xrefs into permanent blocks in the drawing file.

Any time you are removing a drawing from its original environment (including copying it onto diskette for distribution to a client or contractor), you must either bind the xrefs, or include the xref source drawings. Binding the xrefs is usually the safest method. However, if you are sending drawings to a consultant as work in progress, you may need to leave them as xrefs until the project is complete.

Let's go back into the XTEST drawing and use the Bind option to make the xref XSYMBOL a permanent part of the drawing.

Using Bind to Make an Xref Permanent

```
Command: XREF
?/Bind/Detach/Path/Reload/<Attach>: <RETURN>
Xref to Attach: <XSYMBOL>
Attach Xref XSYMBOL: XSYMBOL
XSYMBOL loaded.
Insertion point: 5,5
 X scale factor <1> / Corner / XYZ: <RETURN>
 Y scale factor (default=X): <RETURN>
 Rotation angle <0>: <RETURN>

Command: XREF
```

```
?/Bind/Detach/Path/Reload/<Attach>: B
Xref(s) to bind: XSYMBOL
     Scanning...
```

The Bind option attaches the xrefs to the drawing file in which they are contained. The xref becomes a standard block within the drawing. After it's attached, you can explode it and manipulate it just as you can any other block created or inserted directly in the drawing. To prove the XSYMBOL is now an ordinary block, you can explode and edit it, or list it with the BLOCK or INSERT command ? option.

Bind also makes a change to the layers that belong to xrefs. It replaces the vertical bar (|) in the layer name with n, where n is a number. If you list your layers again, you'll see that the layer XSYMBOL|SYMLAYER has been renamed to XSYMBOL0SYMLAYER. When AutoCAD renames the layers in this way, it tries to use 0 for the number. If a layer name by that name already exists, it tries a 1. It continues trying higher numbers until it comes up with a unique layer name. You can use the RENAME command to change these strange layer names to whatever you like.

➤ *TIP: If you want to insert a drawing as a block into your current drawing but you know they have conflicting layer names, attach it as an xref first, then bind it as a block. This will preserve the incoming block's unique layers.*

In addition to insuring unique layer names, AutoCAD prevents xrefs and blocks from having the same names.

Controlling Xref Names and Block Conflicts

If you try to attach XSYMBOL again, you will get an error message:

```
** Error: XSYMBOL is already a standard block in the current
drawing. *Invalid*
```

If you need to attach the xref again, you can substitute a working name in the current drawing like you do for blocks. (Or you can use RENAME to rename the XSYMBOL block to remove the conflict.) To see what filename is referenced by an xref already loaded under a substitute name, use the ? option of XREF. You can also use the ? option of the BLOCK command to get information on blocks and xrefs.

Let's re-attach XSYMBOL using the name XSYM2=XSYMBOL. Then, list it with the ? option of XREF, with the ? option of BLOCK, and with the ? option of LAYER.

Attaching an Xref With a Substitute Name

```
Command: XREF
?/Bind/Detach/Path/Reload/<Attach>: A
Xref to Attach <XSYMBOL>: XSYM2=XSYMBOL
Attach Xref XSYM2: XSYMBOL
```
XSYM2 is the xref name and XSYMBOL is the external filename.

```
XSYM2 loaded.
Insertion point:
Command: XREF
```
Pick 9,5 and default the scale and rotation.
List all xrefs with ? and *.

```
    Xref Name                        Path
--------------------          -------------
  XSYM2                       XSYMBOL


Total Xref(s): 1
```

```
Command: BLOCK
Defined blocks.
  XSYM2
  XSYMBOL
```
List all blocks and xrefs with ? and *.

Xref: resolved

```
User       External     Dependent    Unnamed
Blocks     References   Blocks       Blocks
  1            1           0             0
```

```
Command: LAYER
```
List all layers with ? and *.

```
    Layer name          State        Color        Linetype
------------------    ---------    -------------    ------------
0                     On           7 (white)    CONTINUOUS
SYMLAYER              On           2 (yellow)   DASHED
XSYM2|SYMLAYER        On           2 (yellow)   XSYM2|DASHED   Xdep: XSYM2
XSYMBOL$0$SYMLAYER On              2 (yellow)   XSYMBOL$0$DASHED
```

When you listed the xrefs with XREF and BLOCK, they showed XSYM2 as the xref name in the current drawing and XSYMBOL2 as its path, the externally referenced filename.

Although you can attach an xref with an equal sign, you can't redefine an existing xref as you can for blocks. You *can* rename an xref using the Block option of the RENAME command. If you do so, RENAME will warn you:

```
Caution! XSYM2 is an externally referenced block.
Renaming it will also rename its dependent symbols.
```

What are dependent symbols anyway? And what do XSYM2│DASHED linetype and Xdep: XSYM2 mean in the layer listing above?

Xref's Dependent Symbols

Layers, linetypes, text styles, blocks, and dimstyles are symbols in the sense that they have arbitrary names representing things like layers or styles (not to be confused with graphic symbols like your TREE1). The symbols which are carried into a drawing by an xref are called dependent symbols because they depend on the external file, not the current drawing, for their characteristics. Dependent symbols are prefixed in the same manner as XSYM2│SYMLAYER and XSYM2│DASHED to avoid conflicts. The only exceptions are unambiguous defaults like layer 0, and linetype CONTINUOUS. But, text style STANDARD can be varied, so it gets prefixed.

This prefixing is carried to nested xrefs; if the external file XSYMBOL included an xref named TITLEBLK, it would get the symbol name XSYMBOL│TITLEBLK if XSYMBOL was attached to another drawing. If TITLEBLK included the layer LEGEND, it would get the symbol XSYMBOL│TITLEBLK│LEGEND.

➡ *NOTE: If xrefs are nested deeply (one xref contains another, which contains another, and so on) or a drawing contains a lot of xrefs, things can get complex. So AutoCAD maintains a log file in ASCII text format that you can refer to. It's stored in the same directory as your drawing and its name matches your drawing name, with an .XLG filename extension. It continues to grow as the drawing is edited over many sessions, so you may want to delete all or part of it to save disk space.*

What you can do to these dependent symbols in your current drawing is limited to protect the integrity of the xref. For example, you cannot make one of an xref's layers current and draw on it like you can with a standard drawing layer. However, you can modify an xref's appearance by changing the color, linetype, and visibility of an xref's layer. Any changes you make are only temporary; they will revert to their original states when the xref is reloaded. That's true even if you save the drawing after making changes to an xref's layer settings.

However, you can selectively import these dependent symbols into your current drawing.

Finally,
more blo
setting t

Setting

You are
drawing
drawing
36" x 24

AXIS
Off
UNITS
LIMIT!
ZOOM
VIEW
Layer
0
SITE
PLAN

ATLAYC

Setting Up ATLAYOUT and Sa

Begin a NEW drawing named A'
Make sure layer SITE is current.

Command: **SAVE**

Next a

XBIND — Binding Dependent Symbols of an Xref

When you used the Bind option of XREF to convert XSYMBOL from an xref
to a block, AutoCAD converted the entire xref. All layers and data in the
xref's source file became part of the new block.

You can also use the XBIND command to bind only portions of the xref to
the drawing. If you only want to bring in text style, a block, or a layer
defined in the xref without binding the entire xref, you can do so.

To see how XBIND works, bind only the SYMLAYER layer in XSYMBOL,
not the entire xref. The data drawn on that layer will not be bound, only
the layer itself.

Binding Only Parts of an Xref With XBIND

```
Command: XBIND
Block/Dimstyle/LAyer/LType/Style: LA
Dependent Layer name(s): XSYM2|SYMLAYER
     Scanning...
Also bound linetype XSYM2$0$DASHED;
it is referenced by layer XSYM2$0$SYMLAYER.
1 Layer(s) bound.
```

Use DDLMODES or LAYER to check to see that the layer and linetype have been bound and
renamed with (0) instead of (|).

```
Command: END
```

Linetypes and other symbols that are dependent upon being bound, such
as blocks or layers, are automatically bound. The entities (lines, etc.)
contained in the xref are not bound to the drawing. But, if you bind a
block, you can then use INSERT to insert it in the current drawing.

➡ *TIP: You can extract blocks and other symbols from one drawing and
use them in your current drawing. Just attach the drawing on disk as
an xref, bind what you need, and detach the xref.*

Use BIND if you want to bind the entire xref, making it a block. Use XBIND
if you only want to bind layer, linetype, dimension styles, nested blocks,
or text styles without binding any actual entities in the xref.

The following Autotown exercise makes use of the BLOCK, INSERT,
WBLOCK, and XREF commands that you learned in this chapter's first two
sections. The exercise uses a set of simple blocks to place houses and trees

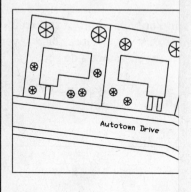

Autotown With Simple Symbols

Autotown Block Exerc

Becaus
additic
option
whole

First,
AUTOT

The ex
Lots l
survey
alread

Do the
the IA
and at
you're

The *C*
comple
blocks
create

```
Layer SITE Snap            359'-6.00",0'-6.00"        AutoCAD
                                                      * * * *
                                                      BLOCKS
                                                      DIM:
                                                      DISPLAY
                                                      DRAW
                                                      EDIT
                                                      INQUIRY
                                                      LAYER:
                                                      MVIEW
                                                      PLOT
                                                      SETTINGS
                                                      SOLIDS
                                                      SURFACES
                                                      UCS:
                                                      UTILITY
                                                      ASHADE
                                                      RMAN
                                                      BONUS
                                                      SAVE:

<Select object to trim>/Undo: U
<Select object to trim>/Undo:
Command:
```

Autotown Border and Drive

Laying Out Autotown Drive and Lots

Command: **PLINE**	Draw the border from 12'6,15' (with width 1') to 347'6,15' to 347'6,225' to 12'6,225' and close it.
Command: **PLINE**	Draw one side of Autotown drive from 12'6,115' (with width 0) to 227'9.5,90'2.5 to 359'1,30'5
Command: **OFFSET**	Create other side of drive.
Offset distance or Through <Through>: **50'**	
Select object to offset:	Pick the last polyline.
Side to offset?	Pick point below last polyline.
Select object to offset: **<RETURN>**	Trim the extended line later.
Command: **OFFSET**	Create curb lines using an offset distance of 10' and offset both drive polylines toward center of drive.
Command: **TRIM**	Trim all lines extending beyond the border.
Command: **SAVE**	

In manual drafting, converting and using surveyor's units is always a nuisance. Let AutoCAD do it for you.

Using Surveyor's Angles

Autotown's setup contains surveyor's angles. AutoCAD will still accept normal decimal angle input for surveyor's angles, and let you enter a simple N, S, E, or W for 90-, 270-, 0-, and 180-degree angles. You can specify angles in survey nomenclature, like N14d52'00"E for North 14